VICTORY

Being Mentally Tough On and Off the Mat

By Steve Fraser

Published by the
International Wrestling Institute and Museum
Newton, Iowa

VICTORY: Being Mentally Tough On and Off the Mat

An International Wrestling Institute & Museum publication

All rights reserved.
Copyright 2005 by Steve Fraser
No part of this book may be reproduced or transmitted in any form or by any means, electronic or mechanical, including photocopying, recording, or by any information storage and retrieval system, without permission in writing from Steve Fraser.

For information address: International Wrestling Institute & Museum
                           PO Box 794
                           Newton, IA 50208

Library of Congress Cataloging-in-Publication Data
1. Fraser, Steve; 2. Wrestling; 3. Olympics; 4. Greco-Roman
   VICTORY / Steve Fraser

ISBN   0-9772276-0-X

PRINTED IN THE UNITED STATES OF AMERICA

First edition

Cover photo by Steve Brown.

Dedicated with sincere appreciation
and affection to Dean Rockwell
(1912 - 2005)

Introduction

In his long and amazing wrestling odyssey, Steve Fraser has run down many paths, leaped over numerous hurdles and climbed huge mountains. I was privileged to be in press row at the Anaheim Convention Center in 1984 when he won an Olympic gold medal for the United States in the 198-pound class of the Greco-Roman competition; I was overwhelmed by Steve's drive, desire and determination. His victory path was strewn with foreign wrestlers who were simply overrun by the indefatigable American, who was on a mission.

When I created W.I.N. (Wrestling International Newsmagazine) in 1994, I was determined to bring some of wrestling's brightest thinkers to the pages. I sought out Steve to be a columnist for W.I.N., and I must say it was one of the best moves I ever made with W.I.N. Steve has proven to be as good with the pen as he was with the sword. His columns are fresh, powerful and inspirational, mainly because he writes with the same enthusiasm and clarity of mission that he took into his wrestling career.

Victory: Being Mentally Tough On and Off the Mat, is a remarkable piece of work in that an Olympic champion invites all wrestling enthusiasts to share his journey with him. By holding nothing back, Steve Fraser is able to show the reader how he overcame many obstacles and was able to climb to the pinnacle of the sports world.

Being an All-American athlete, national champion and Olympic champion has taught Steve how to work very hard for what he has earned, both on and off the mat. As Greco-Roman National Teams Coach for USA Wrestling, he has traveled the world and seen many of the world's best wrestlers in action. He has wrestled them, coached them and coached against them.

This book offers an overview of Steve's upbringing, some of the highlights of his great career and insights into the nature of wrestling. The main portion of the book consists of the many columns that he has written through the years for W.I.N. magazine. The observations and examples will be of great educational value to coaches, athletes and parents, and I believe will be immensely entertaining to fans who love the sport.

The book was a joint venture by Steve Fraser, Dean Rockwell (a man who has helped Steve Fraser tremendously in his development as a world-class athlete) and the International Wrestling Institute and Museum in Newton, Iowa. I know you will enjoy reading it.

Mike Chapman
Executive Director
International Wrestling Institute and Museum
Newton, Iowa

Contents

Introduction by Mike Chapman

Foreword by Rulon Gardner

Part One: The Steve Fraser Story

Part Two: Columns by Steve Fraser

Chapter 1 – The Fundamentals

Attitude Makes the Difference

Desire: The Biggest Key To Success

Do You Know – WHY?

Chapter 2 – Mental Toughness and Psychological Training

Learning What Toughness Is All About

Vering: Tough As They Come – 2003 World Championships

Men of Courage Do Great Things

Expose Your Weaknesses To Stress

Keeping Cool When The Pressure Is On

The Most Powerful Computer On The Planet!

Staying Cool, Calm and Collected

Creating Positive Images, At Night

Chapter 3 – Preparation

What Does It Take To Be The Best?

The Grind Match

Expect The Unexpected

Build A Team Of Mentors And Coaches

Be Ready For The Main Event

Periodization: The Art Of Peaking

Expect To Win!

How Jet Lag Can Be A Big Negative

National Greco-Roman Creed

Chapter 4 – Coaches Corner

Become An Effective Corner Coach

Coaches Do Change Lives

Why Greco-Roman Is Important Too

Coaches Influence Careers

Building The U.S. Greco-Roman Program: A Call To Coaches

Coaches Take Time To Learn Greco, by Dan Chandler

Chapter 5 – How To Train

Training Tips

Iron Sharpens Iron

Cutting Weight – Is It Worth It?

12 Ways To Break Your Opponent

Going Through Phases – The Yearly Training Cycle

Recovery, Key Element In Training

Hard Work Requires Hard Recovery

How To Become A Fearless Warrior

Money In The Bank

No Pain, No Gain: Good or Bad?

Chapter 6 – Competition

    The Art of Securing Victory

    Why Wrestle In The Spring and Summer?

    Are You Strong Enough To Handle Critics?

    Finding Your Ideal Competitive State

Chapter 7 – Overcoming Adversity

    From The Brink of Failure

    How To Refocus In Bad Situations

    Attaining Success is Difficult…That's What Makes It Great!

    Don't Be Afraid Of Adversity

Part Three: Reflections

    Advice From Champions

    Olympic Memories From 2000

    America's "Fighting Spirit" Is Key

    2001 Greco-Roman World Championships

    2002 Greco-Roman World Championships

    Gruenwald Defines Courage at 2003 Worlds

    U.S. Must Get Better at Parterre

    The Road To Athens

    Rulon Gardner: The Making of an American Hero

    Surround Yourself With Good People

    Fraser's Ten Basics of Successful Wrestling

    Anatoly Petrosyan Shows True Courage

    Momir Petkovic Leads by Example

About The Author

Olympic champions Steve Fraser (left) and Rulon Gardner, coach and pupil, shake hands prior to a clinic led by the two wrestling legends.

Foreword

When an athlete walks into the heat of competition at any level, he wants to make certain that he has had the best coaching available to prepare himself. Coaching is one of the key elements to success, and coaching doesn't just come on a mat. There are many other ways to be a coach — showing an athlete how to win in life as well as sports. It's all part of the attitude one has to develop in order to succeed at every level.

Steve Fraser is the kind of coach that understands what an athlete needs to do to get to the very top, because he was there himself. In 1984, Steve became the first American to win any kind of a medal in Greco-Roman competition in the Olympic Games. And he won gold! Steve has shown that he has the mental toughness, the desire and the perspective to be a top athlete, and he has carried that right into his coaching. He is a leader and he knows how to show others what it takes to be the very best in not only the nation, but the entire world.

In addition, he has the persona to motivate athletes to do their very best. He leads by example; he's in the practice room every day pulling on his shoes and working out himself. Though he is often outweighed by larger and younger guys, he doesn't back off one bit.

In 2000, I had to work very hard just to make the United States Greco-Roman Olympic team. Steve told me that he knew I could do it, and also that I could beat Alexander Karelin in Sydney at the Olympic Games of 2000. That was a huge asset, knowing that my coach had that much faith in me. His efforts at preparing me, both mentally and physically, and his confidence helped me pull off what some people call the biggest upset in wrestling history!

If he sees athletes are trying to take a short cut and back off, he doesn't hesitate to get in their face and let them know it's time to change. He got in my face at the 2004 Olympics, making sure that I was focused enough to get the job done.

Steve Fraser is an honest, hard-working and caring man, and that comes through in his coaching. I feel honored to have worked so closely with him for almost a decade. Steve has found success in everything he does and he has shared that formula with me and hundreds of other wrestlers, through his position as National Greco-Roman Coach at USA Wrestling, through hundreds of camps and clinics, and through his writings.

I have read Steve's columns in W.I.N. magazine through the years and know that he is a skilled writer and communicator. He has a wealth of information in this book and I highly recommend it to anyone with even an ounce of interest in this great sport.

        RULON GARDNER
        2000 Olympic Gold Medalist
        2001 World Gold Medalist
        2004 Olympic Bronze Medalist

Part One:
The Steve Fraser Story

Being "Only Average"

Ever since 1984, I have been known as an Olympic champion. It is an incredible thrill to hear myself introduced that way at clinics, at speaking engagements or when meeting people in common, day-to-day situations. The very word "Olympian" has come to mean so much in life and I am honored to be among the elite group of men and women who have earned that label. And then to have won the gold medal is almost beyond belief sometimes.

But believe me, it wasn't an easy path for Steve Fraser to become an Olympian, much less an Olympic champion. The fact is, I was an average child from an average home. I was not gifted, by any stretch of the imagination. I could claim no special athletic ability, no special smarts. I had a lot of doubts about myself as a kid, and I never thought of myself as someone who would achieve great things in life. When I went to the movies I often left the theater fantasizing about being a particular character, usually the star. It was impossible for me to conceive that one day I, too, would be a star.

I grew up in a typical suburban Detroit house, a small, two-story, tract house with white asbestos siding and one tree on the lawn. All the houses on the street looked exactly the same. We didn't even have an awning over the porch. There were two bedrooms downstairs, and the upstairs consisted of one big bedroom. I shared a bedroom with my younger brother, Ken. My two older sisters, Linda and Barbara, shared the upstairs room. The house was situated in Ferndale, Michigan, about three blocks from Hazel Park. But I have always considered myself to be from Hazel Park, since my siblings and I came up through the Hazel Park school system.

We were a lower middle-class family, probably lower-lower middle, so we didn't have everything we wanted. I can't remember much about the possessions we had, but I do remember that I had a picture of me and Willie Horton, a popular outfielder for the Detroit Tigers. I went to an auto show one day, and I walked up onto a platform and had my picture taken with him. He was there signing autographs. I was lucky because the first picture they took didn't come out, and I got to go up onto the platform with Willie Horton again.

My parents were divorced when I was five years old, and I felt I was disadvantaged not having a father. When I was in elementary school I remember thinking that I was different from the other boys and girls because I didn't have a father around. My father left, my mother always told me, because he couldn't handle the pressures of family life. He was an only child, and as an adult he had a wife and four children to deal with.

My mother is a very sweet, caring lady, whom I often refer to as a saint. She raised four kids for 11 years, and sometimes she had to break her neck to do it. After she got divorced, she went out and got a job as a bookkeeper, and she kept the same job her whole

VICTORY

life. She made about $15,000 a year.

My mother was very strong-willed in her approach to bringing us up. I wouldn't say she was very strict, but if she saw us getting into trouble, she came down on us. She didn't allow us to fight with the neighbors. If we got into a conflict, she always suggested that maybe it was our fault. "Just stay away from those kids if you can't get along," she'd say.

I remember her being gone during the day and then coming home at night and fixing dinner and taking care of us. On weekends, she cleaned the house. She was always busy, but never too busy for me. I had a paper route when I was in the fifth, sixth, and seventh grades, and I had to get up at 5 a.m. to deliver those papers, 365 days a year. Every once in a great while, if it was pouring rain or snowing heavily or if I had overslept, I would ask my mother to drive me. I asked her maybe five times a year. In those times of need I would tiptoe into her bedroom and nudge her on the shoulder. "Mom!" I'd whisper, and she'd say, "All right." She must have hated to lose that last precious hour of sleep, but she never said no to me.

My mother is also a wonderful cook. She stands about 5-feet-5-inches tall and weighs 160 pounds. Of all the wonderful dishes she made for me, my favorite was beef fricassee and mashed potatoes, a scrumptious concoction made up of hamburger, celery, onions and gravy. She'd make a big bowl of mashed potatoes, and I'd eat half of it, pouring the beef fricassee over the potatoes. I also thought my mother made the best chocolate chip cookies in Hazel Park. You can see why cutting weight was going to be murderous for me.

My father wasn't around much when I was growing up. As a young boy, I suppose I saw him about once every other month. I don't remember much about him from those days, but I do remember that I was afraid of him at times. I had seen my mother and him fight a lot, and I knew he had a temper.

My father was often late in making the alimony payments to my mother. I remember how angry she used to get, especially if she didn't have enough money to pay the bills. But even though he must have hurt her deeply, leaving her after 15 years of marriage, my mother never downgraded him in front of us. She wanted her children to make their own decisions about their father.

When I got older, my father was more interested in seeing me, and we did spend some enjoyable times together. He used to take my brother Ken and me into his home for a couple of weeks each summer. He lived about 35 minutes from Hazel Park, in an apartment complex that was next to a park area. The park had tennis courts and softball diamonds, and I spent many happy hours over there playing tennis, riding my mini-bike, and sledding in the winter. My dad also took Ken and me shooting. He had a .22-caliber pistol, and we'd go down in the parks and creeks and shoot cans.

I didn't ask my father for advice very often, but I do have fond memories of how he helped me once when I was in the eighth grade. I remember telling him that the star of our football team had pushed me around and that I was afraid of him. So my dad told me to go ahead and defend myself. Then he gave me a lesson in boxing. He took my brother and me down into the storage area of his apartment building and put these big 16-ounce boxing gloves on us.

"Okay, son," he said, "put your hands down at your sides."

I did what he said, and then he hauled off and blasted me in the face.

"That's the first thing you never do," my father said. "Never put your hands down. Always guard your face."

I think I still have a headache from that boxing lesson, but I never forgot it. I enjoyed spending time with my dad, and I wish I had been able to see more of him. I especially wish I could have shared my wrestling experiences with him. During my high school and college years, he saw me wrestle only a handful of times.

I don't know whether my father had ever been diagnosed as an alcoholic, but he had a drinking problem for a long time. I could tell when he had been drinking because he became belligerent and repeated himself. I never noticed it when I was young, but as time went on it got worse and worse. When I was in high school and college it really started to hit home.

Sometimes he would criticize me for majoring in physical education at the University of Michigan. "You've got that full scholarship," he'd say. "Why don't you take advantage of it and be a doctor or a lawyer or something?"

That used to infuriate me. He hadn't been around when I needed him as an adolescent, when I was making decisions about my future, and now he was trying to tell me what to do. Then, in the midst of my anger, it would dawn on me. He had been drinking. I would tell him that I knew. "You've been drinking, haven't you?" I confronted him, which my sisters and brother were less apt to do. I told him I was going to live my life the way I wanted, and that would just make him angrier. Many times I just hung up on him.

I have to think that our being in a one-parent family hurt all of us. We're not as close as we might have been because of the stresses we had to deal with. My siblings and I always fought a lot, although it's possible that we didn't fight any more than children in most two-parent families. My brother had a foul temper. Linda had the toughest road of all. She married a guy named Steve when she was 16. Three years later, just a little while before she had her second baby, she got divorced. Steve just couldn't take the responsibilities of a family.

It's amazing, looking back, but Steve was one of my first role models. There was no man around, and I yearned for a masculine image. So I looked up to Steve. He was a big, strong, muscular guy. He had been an athlete in his early days, but when I knew him he was what they called a "greaser," leather jacket and all. He was tough.

I would taunt Steve, and he responded by beating me up in a fun way. He'd twist my arm and punch me on the triceps muscle, physically hurting me sometimes. But I always egged him on because I wanted that. I wanted the attention and I looked up to him.

I remember that Steve had well-defined muscles, and the veins stood out on his forearms. He explained to me that when you have a lot of muscle, the veins have to stick out because they can't sit in the fat. So I used to come home from school and work out during television commercials, lifting 25-pound barbells to build up my arms. I was in the fifth or sixth grade, and my whole intent was just to have muscles like Steve's. I must have lifted those weights for 30 minutes every day.

My other early role model was the boyfriend of my other sister, Barbara. His name was Tom, and he was in the same mold as Steve, tough and muscular, but not as aggressive. I admired him, too, but my real idol was Steve. I thought Steve was cool.

VICTORY

After Steve and Linda got married, I occasionally looked after their baby when they went out at night. Then when they came home at three o'clock in the morning, Steve would take me on my paper route in his car, a souped-up '58 Chevy. After we had delivered the papers — I was about 12 or 13 years old — he'd take me down a back road and let me drive. He even taught me how to pull a "whole shot," where you push in the clutch, rev the motor, and then pop the clutch out so the wheels squeal.

When I was in the ninth grade, my mother got remarried to a man named Fred Patenaude, and I inherited a stepfather. Fred and my mother met on a blind date, and two or three months later they married and he moved into our house. Fred's son, Craig, who was a year older than I, also moved in, so I went from being the man of the house to No. 3.

Craig was a swimmer, and Fred made a habit of coming to most of Craig's swimming meets and my wrestling meets. Fred saw me wrestle quite a bit. I think that helped me to a degree, but I never saw his support as necessary. My father hadn't supported me, so I certainly wasn't going to get upset if my stepfather didn't. By that time I was wrestling for myself.

I was eight or nine years old when I got my first introduction to organized sports. I was the 10th guy on the midget baseball team. Another guy and I alternated playing right field. They always put the scrubs in right field. I hadn't had too much experience with ball games. When I came up to the plate, I was afraid I was going to get hit by the ball. I was also afraid to swing and miss. I always hoped the pitcher would walk me.

I did get a little more coordinated in baseball as I got older. A man my mother dated before she remarried taught me how to catch a one-hop grounder, the kind that bounces right in front of you and shoots up in your face. But my first faint glimmer of athletic talent became apparent in gym class, when I was in the eighth grade.

Wrestling was one of our required activities, and I kind of enjoyed it. I was strong because I had lifted those weights in order to have muscular arms like those of Linda's boyfriend. While wrestling in gym class, I'd get kids in headlocks. They were actually illegal headlocks that I was using, but I didn't know any better at the time. I squeezed and squeezed because I was so strong, and when my opponent quit I figured I was the winner. The gym teacher, Frank Stagg, saw that I liked to wrestle, and he encouraged me several times to come out for the junior high school team. "Yeah, I'd like to," I told him. But I didn't follow through. I was too shy.

One day I was standing at my locker between classes when Mr. Stagg came up behind me and grabbed me, right in the middle of the hallway, in a sleeper hold, a kind of chokehold around the neck. Lifting me off the ground, he was careful not to hurt me. But a chokehold isn't exactly like shaking hands.

"Steve," he said in my ear, still choking me a little bit, "I want to see you at practice tonight!" Of course, I didn't have any choice but to say, "Okay!"

I wasn't really surprised that Frank had grabbed me like that. He had a special way of relating to kids. He was a teacher who cared, and he represented everything that was right in the school system. In those few moments, as he was simultaneously choking me and caring about me, he changed the direction of my life. If he had not given me that extra little push, I might never have gone out for wrestling.

I wasn't nearly as good as the other wrestlers at Webb Junior High. I wasn't even the

No. 2 man in my weight division, and I didn't make the team. I wrestled only one match for the varsity that year at 126 pounds. But I loved the sport immediately. I liked the training, and I liked the combat. The physical aspect of it was exhilarating to me.

Frank Stagg was a great teacher and motivator, and he knew how to get you in shape. One day after we wrestled in practice, did our drills, and ran up and down stairs until we were ready to drop, I told Frank, "Mr. Stagg, I just love this sport. I love to sweat." He got a kick out of the fact that I loved to sweat.

I also loved wrestling because it was so manly, so basic and so primitive. Grappling is the oldest sport known to man, its origins going back 15,000 years. Some people say running was the first sport. But we wrestlers know that the runner was probably running from a wrestler!

Being tough was rewarding to me. If you're a good baseball player, you're good on the field. But if you're a good wrestler, you can carry that with you all the time. Baseball players, like hockey players or tennis players, use other artifacts, such as bats and sticks and rackets, to assert their supremacy. But a wrestler has only the most primitive tools available: his legs, his body, and his arms and hands. If you're a tough wrestler, you're tough, period. People don't mess around with you.

Lacking a father figure, I had spent my childhood searching for something to fill that void. I was attracted to manliness. And because I had been brought up by my mother, I rebelled against the possibility that I might become a mama's boy. In wrestling, I knew I could be tough. Even as a 13-year-old I could appreciate that.

In Frank Stagg I found my first male influence who represented discipline, morality and success. Frank wasn't a harsh man, but he was firm in his beliefs. He emphasized human kindness and he took a firm stand against smoking, drinking and using drugs. Frank caught me smoking once, right after the eighth-grade season. I was with my girlfriend, a cute girl named Colleen who smoked and was well liked by a lot of guys. She was just as rough as the neighborhood she came from. I was walking home from school with her one day, holding her hand, a cigarette dangling from my lips, when Frank drove by and saw me.

"So you're smoking, huh?" he said, the next time he saw me. I knew he was upset with me, but he never condemned me for what I had done. Frank ran the lunch line at school, and for the next month he frisked me every day, looking for cigarettes. I'm happy to say he never found any. I had already stopped smoking. His opinion of me meant more to me than cigarettes.

The summer after eighth grade, I started to go through a growth spurt, and the effects of the weight lifting I had done as a sixth-grader were suddenly apparent in my strong, muscular arms. When I went out for the wrestling team as a ninth grader, I weighed 145 pounds. Seniority, experience, hard work and my new build helped me earn a starter's role in my weight class, and I had a very good year. I lost my first match to a tough, muscular kid, but I went undefeated the rest of the year, finishing with a 16-1 record. I won the Little Oak League title at my weight, and I received a medal. But if you think I was on my way, guess again.

The next year, my sophomore year at Hazel Park High School, I suffered the greatest curse of wrestling: cutting weight. Always an accepted part of wrestling, cutting

VICTORY

weight is based on the theory that a wrestler will have a physical edge if he cuts some weight and drops down to wrestle a person without as much muscle mass.

I weighed 165 pounds that fall when I played on the football team, and I was hoping to wrestle at 155. But that didn't happen. After one or two matches, the wrestler who weighed 145 came up to my division and beat me. If I wanted to wrestle for the varsity team, I would have to wrestle at 145 pounds, some 20 pounds below my normal, healthy weight. The experience was the worst I ever had in wrestling. But it was also one of the most enlightening.

I hated every waking moment of it. When I was cutting weight, I spent the entire day thinking of what I would like to be eating. Everything I did, everything I saw, reminded me of food. Watching television advertisements about food made me ravenous. I even dreamt about food. I dreamt about strawberry shortcakes and banana splits.

But I didn't starve myself every single day. Like all wrestlers who competed below their normal weight, I gorged myself immediately after a meet. Then, the next day, I started fasting again. What did I eat during that week-long fast? Almost nothing. I skipped breakfast, had a grapefruit or an orange for lunch, and had another grapefruit and maybe a couple of poached eggs for dinner. It drove my mother crazy. "Oh, surely you can have a little salad," she'd say. But I just couldn't eat anything. I couldn't drink much, either. Just a few sips of water.

Meanwhile, the practices I had loved so much became pure torture. I frequently would go into the hot wrestling room looking like a mummy, dressed in one or two T-shirts, a plastic sweatsuit, and a thick sweatsuit over the plastics. If I had a lot of weight to lose on a given day, I might also pull my hood up, put a wool hat on over the hood, and wear gloves or socks over my hands. After 10 minutes of calisthenics, I was mentally exhausted. The pain I felt was compounded by the bitter knowledge that after all this work, I couldn't even look forward to going home to a well-deserved meal.

You might wonder how I could have been physically and mentally sharp at the end of a week of starving and suffering. Well, I wasn't. I wasn't sharp at all. But I fasted because that was the accepted practice in wrestling, and I believed it was the right thing for me to do. My coach, Robert Morrill, hadn't pushed me into dropping 20 pounds. He had left the decision up to me.

I ended up having a very ordinary year. My overall record was eight wins, nine losses, and one tie. My big successes were that I made the varsity team and I made weight for each of my matches. But as a wrestler I was only average. I beat the below-average wrestlers, not the good ones, and finished fourth in the Southeastern Michigan Association League. I was sick during the district championships and couldn't wrestle, but it really didn't matter. I wouldn't have advanced to the regionals, anyway. The guys who beat me during the regular season would have beaten me in the district championships, too.

My experience cutting weight taught me several things. First, it taught me that a hungry, dehydrated wrestler probably isn't going to do any better at a lower weight than his normal weight. Second, it taught me that the fasting wrestler doesn't just lose his strength, he destroys his attitude as well. At a time when he should be trying to learn everything he can about technique and strategy, his main goal becomes making weight each day or losing a certain number of pounds.

I also learned that cutting weight can have a negative effect on a wrestler's education and home life. Good nutrition is vital to your performance in school, and going to school without breakfast is one of the worst ways to begin the day.

Finally, there was one last discovery I made. The conventional wisdom in wrestling suggested that by dropping down a weight division, I should have been able to outclass the little wimps who weren't as strong as I was. But, surprise; I learned that there are good wrestlers in all weight classes. At 145 pounds, when I was going 8-9-1, I didn't lose to any wimps.

Of course, you can't tell a kid not to cut weight. Sometimes wrestlers have to learn for themselves. And I must say I learned a lot from the experience. I learned that I would never cut weight again. I also learned to appreciate food, because I found out how painful it is to starve.

I should mention here that cutting weight is not bad in all cases. If a kid is 20 pounds overweight, he should make an effort to lose that fat, provided he still takes in the proteins and nutrients he needs to stay healthy.

But most kids who go out for wrestling are already lean, the way I was, and I would never advise them to cut anything over 10 pounds. My advice to those wrestlers is that they wrestle at or around their normal weight. If they can't make the team at their normal weight, I would advise them to move up a weight class before they consider moving down a weight class. I probably should have gone up to the 167-pound division my sophomore year instead of suffering through the season at 145 pounds. I might have surprised myself and found that I was quicker than the wrestlers who were 10 pounds heavier than I.

I proved that theory correct during my junior year in high school, when I wrestled in the 185-pound division while weighing 175 pounds. I went into my practices feeling wonderful. My goals were to improve and have fun, both of which I did. And while I was going all out in those practices, the wrestlers who were cutting weight were walking around with their chins hanging down to the floor, sweating and tired and mentally exhausted.

I also proved I could win. I remember so well the time we wrestled Southfield High School. I weighed about 167 pounds at the time, and as I was standing in the weigh-in line in my skivvies, Southfield's 185-pound wrestler looked around and asked in a loud voice, "Who's the 185-pounder?"

"I am," I said shyly.

He looked at me and said, "You're 185 pounds? You're kind of small, aren't you?"

"Yeah," I said. "Kind of."

That was the last time he laughed at me, because I beat the tar out of him. I was leading 18-3 before I pinned him.

I went on to have a great junior year losing only three matches the entire year. I won the very prestigious and very tough Oakland County Christmas Tournament, which was the best Christmas present I could ever have received. This was the beginning of my success. Winning this tournament meant so much to me and it gave me such a great feeling inside. It allowed me to experience how good it felt to have success in this wonderful sport. Now I wanted to feel this fantastic emotion again and again.

I also won the SMA League Championships in which I had to beat a tough senior

VICTORY

from Berkley High School in the finals. His name was Curtis Pope. He had beaten me early in the season accounting for my only loss of the year up to that point. The rematch victory was one of the hardest matches I had ever experienced. My win, which took place in my home gym of Hazel Park, was so close and I never had been that exhausted after a match.

I continued on…finishing the year by winning the district, the regional, and taking fifth place in the state championships where I picked up my second and third losses of the season.

My senior year I weighed about 185 pounds after winning all-league honors on the gridiron. I captained our football team that had not lost a game in three years. In fact, we ended up ranked second in the state my junior year. However, in this final football season we ended up losing three games.

Very disappointed with our team's football performance, I then turned my attention back to wrestling. I wrestled at 185 pounds that year, having my best, most successful season ever. I went undefeated, posting a record of 39-0. I did it! I achieved my ultimate dream! I became a state champion for Hazel Park High School.

I was recruited by a variety of colleges and finally made my choice to attend the University of Michigan in Ann Arbor. Then, another dream came true for me. The head coach at Michigan, Billy Johannesen, awarded me a full-ride scholarship to wrestle and get my college education paid for. I was on top of the world! I was going to go to the University of Michigan where I *knew* I was going to kick some butt!

Then, at the University of Michigan my freshman year, much to my dismay, I found myself back on the bottom of the heap. I was back to ground zero! How could this be? I was state champion one moment and now the next moment I am scratching, clawing and fighting just to score one single point in the tough Michigan wrestling room. Here we go… starting all over again. Ugh!

Learning From Failure

Failure, I know now, can be a blessing. A mistake can be the greatest teacher. But failure can be a blessing and mistakes can be a teacher only if they are followed by six simple but powerful words: <u>What can I learn from this?</u>

Those six words may be the most important words I ever learned from the sport of wrestling. But as with everything else in my long, grinding career, I did not learn them immediately. I did not know that failure could be a blessing disguised as hardship when I arrived at the University of Michigan as a naive and eager freshman. Nor did I know that mistakes would prove to be my greatest teacher. Had I understood that my failures in the short term were the key to my successes in the long term, I would not have been so bitterly disappointed my freshman year, when I came face-to-face with a brick wall named Mark Johnson.

Mark was a senior and the captain of the University of Michigan wrestling team when I arrived on the Ann Arbor campus. He had high status, an impeccable image, good looks, a friendly disposition, a solid academic record, strong opinions and a strong will. He had placed second the year before in the Big Ten and National Collegiate Athletic Association (NCAA) tournaments, losing both finals to Chris Campbell of the University of Iowa. Mark stood on a pedestal in the eyes of Michigan's wrestlers and coaches alike. Bill Johannesen, the head coach, treated Mark a little differently from the rest of us. He was always praising Mark for his disciplined training methods and his hard-nosed approach to competition. Mark was Billy Joe's boy.

In addition to being the star of the Michigan team, Mark Johnson was also in my weight class. This meant that for me to earn a position on the varsity, I had to dislodge him. The last thought on Mark's mind that fall was that an upstart freshman wrestler might come in and take away his place on the team. But, of course, I didn't see it that way.

I had wrestled him only once, several weeks earlier, during the summer after my senior year at Hazel Park High School. We had met in a low-key tournament in suburban Detroit. Mark had smiled and chatted with me beforehand, and then — I found out later — he had not beaten me as badly as he could have. Mark had legitimate reasons for not crushing me then. As a big-time collegiate athlete, he wouldn't have felt comfortable beating up on a new Michigan recruit who was still wet behind the ears. My ears were so wet, in fact, that I went home thinking I would be able to hold my own with him at Michigan.

I was full of optimism as I anticipated my collegiate wrestling career. I remember the rush of adrenaline I felt when I walked into the Michigan wrestling room, its walls covered with photographs of all the Michigan teams and champions going back to the 1920s. My pilgrimage to the 1976 Montreal Olympics a few months earlier had renewed my convictions, and I had dreamed ever since that someday I, too, would be a member of the United States Olympic Team. Naturally, I realized that such an accomplishment was many years away, but in the meantime I was going to add my name to Michigan's wrestling tradition. I really thought I had a good chance to make Michigan's varsity team.

But if the high school champ was fairly confident at this point, he was a far cry from being arrogant. Mixed in with the excitement of starting college were some very real feelings of trepidation. Like any freshman, I had no idea what college would be like; I had no idea how it would feel to leave my home behind, and I had no idea how good a student I would be. I was particularly concerned about my academic future.

Believe me, I was no bookworm. I hadn't taken all the basic college preparatory courses at Hazel Park High School. During my junior and senior years, I had spent three hours a day studying refrigeration, a course offered by the vocational department. To this day I have no clear idea why I chose to study refrigeration. I can't even fix my own refrigerator if it goes on the blink, because the models I studied are now out of date. I guess I picked refrigeration because it sounded more interesting than the other vocational courses the school offered, things like auto mechanics and electrical work. I was from a blue-collar neighborhood, and by going the vocational route, I was just doing what seemed natural. I remember that I maintained a 3.2 grade-point average on a scale of 4.0 in high school, but I rarely did any homework.

The shocks of my new world in college hit me immediately. Mark Johnson didn't just beat me to maintain his position as the 177-pound member of the varsity team, he devastated me. In Mark's eyes, I was just another freshman, a short fireplug of a kid who at 5-foot-9 was about three inches shorter than the average wrestler in my weight class. In my eyes, Mark was in another league, wrestling from a plateau that I could barely touch. He pummeled me in practice, day in and day out.

Those practices were brutal. Michigan's wrestling room was a warm, windowless, banana-shaped enclosure with large blue mats on the floor and the smell of sweat in the air. The heat hits you the moment you step inside. The room's temperature was kept at about 90 degrees, in accordance with the standard, worn-out philosophy that the more you sweat, the easier it will be for you to make weight. Never mind that your body is crying to replenish those liquids afterwards! Practicing for hours in that warm air would have been draining under any circumstances. Losing all the time made it even tougher.

Mark wasn't a spectacular thrower in the mold of Sweden's Frank Andersson, a great World champion in Greco-Roman wrestling, but he was stronger than Andersson. Mark was a serious weightlifter and bodybuilder, and through his rigorous training with weights he had developed into one of the strongest wrestlers in the United States. His body looked as though it had been chiseled out of stone. And when I wrestled him in that sweltering practice room, I really felt as though I were being crushed beneath a couple of stones.

Some days I wouldn't even get a good workout against Mark, because he was just too slow, too methodical and too good. I liked to wrestle at a fast pace, but Mark was never in a hurry. He had an unusually strong stance — moving him was like trying to move a boulder — and he maneuvered slowly and deliberately from within that stance, positioning himself for the strike which, when it came, was like lightning.

One of Mark's favorite ploys was to paralyze me with double underhooks. As we stood face to face, chest to chest, he would pummel me with his arms, maneuvering me around until he could force his arms underneath both of my arms, his elbows pointing toward the floor. He was invincible in this position, while I was utterly immobile, like a fly caught in the spider's web. Of course, the spider always determined what happened next.

Mark had several options from that double-underhook position. Often, he would lift me up and stretch me out, causing my elbows to rise above my shoulders. Then he'd finish me off. With my left arm resting on his right arm, he would give a sharp upward thrust of the right arm and then pivot around behind me, locking his arms around my waist. From this position, he had four or five more options, while I had no choice but to grit my teeth and suffer the inevitable. He would either lift me and throw me, or he would just dump me on the mat. Sometimes, I went down flat on my face.

Mark's double underhooks were like a recurring nightmare for me that year. When he pummeled in on me and raised my elbows up, I could feel myself start to panic. I was vulnerable in that position, and I knew I was only seconds away from being thrown. I knew I had to learn to defend those double underhooks somehow. Occasionally, I could fight my way out. But just as often, he would pummel his way back in. Our matches nearly always revolved around this double-underhook battle. And if the battle went on long enough, I eventually would get too tired to escape one more time.

Mark never let up against me. Not once. He took those practice "matches" seriously, just as I did. Wrestling is such a personal form of competition that losing in practice can hurt as much as losing in competition. Your pride is always on the line, in the practice room or in the arena. And Mark had far too much pride to allow some rookie to lessen his image as the kingpin of the Michigan wrestling room.

Mark outscored me during my freshman year about 10 points to 1, and the few points I did earn were hardly the most satisfying kind. In college wrestling, a wrestler is awarded one point for "escaping" his opponent's hold. Well, I escaped on numerous occasions, usually when Mark allowed me to escape. If he got me into a hold and then got tired of holding me, he would simply let me get back up. Then he would start pummeling me all over again.

But as much as I hated losing to Mark, I never avoided him in the wrestling room. I believed I would get better by wrestling the better guys. Each day, I'd think, "Maybe today's my day."

Mark, who is now the head coach for the outstanding University of Illinois wrestling team, says you can spot the truly dedicated wrestlers right away, because they keep coming back to wrestle the men who have beaten them. He respected me for that reason.

"There are ways of avoiding the good people," Mark says today. "You can always find other freshmen or walk-ons who aren't as good. You can say, 'Oh, I've already got a partner.' Or you can grab someone who's easy or smaller than you. That can happen on every level, from junior high to the Olympics. Some guys don't push themselves as hard in practice."

But I pushed and pushed. And while Mark respected me for that, he also sympathized with me. He knew I didn't have a chance. He was not just more experienced than I was, he was much further along in his physical development. He and I may have weighed the same, but his muscular strength was far greater than mine. There is a world of difference between a 21-year-old man and an 18-year-old kid. Mark Johnson had felt just as helpless when he was a freshman.

"I can remember coming into that practice room," Mark says. "I was the only freshman who started, and I had a hard time surviving in the room. Steve came in as a freshman and of course couldn't make the team. You kind of think back and realize that you're now at the other end of the spectrum. I was using him as a sparring partner. It's frustrating for every young kid. And it's especially frustrating in wrestling, because you're getting physically dominated. It's not as if you're getting outrun on a track."

I was oblivious to those laws of nature, however, and sometimes I became frustrated because I thought Mark wasn't helping me as much as he could have. I often asked him questions, and he would always look me in the eye and answer honestly. He would even drive me back to my dorm on nights when we both stayed late at practice, after the last bus had gone. But although he tried to be encouraging and helpful, I believed that he could have done more to help me through those tough times.

Obviously, my bitterness had colored my feelings about our relationship. While I did not see us as being particularly close, Mark remembers us as being pretty good friends. Clearly, it's easier to be friends with someone who isn't a threat to you. Years later, when I was on an equal footing with Mark, it was his turn to have difficulty being friends. Today, now that we have both retired from competition, our friendship really is a two-way street.

Looking back, I know that I couldn't have been more wrong in thinking that Mark wasn't helping me my freshman year. In truth, he played a vital role in my development. By trying his hardest and by beating me so consistently, he taught me how to accept failure and how to respond to it. He taught me that simply dreaming about the Olympics wasn't going to get me there. He taught me that I had to set realistic goals and develop a realistic plan.

After losing to Mark time and time again, I was forced to concentrate on a goal that was within my reach. For the moment, my goals of making the Michigan team (not to mention the Olympic team!) had to be set aside. My new goals were simple but specific: I had to work as hard as I could, try as hard as I could, and improve as much as I could.

The consolation I received during that frustrating period of my life came not from my peers at Michigan but from two treasured friends of long standing: my mother, who loved me whether I beat Mark Johnson or not, and Masaaki Hatta, the volunteer coach at Hazel Park High School who took me to the Montreal Olympics and who influenced my career more than anyone.

My mother had appreciated my involvement with wrestling when I was in high school, because she knew it was keeping me out of trouble. Now that I was in college, she no longer saw the same pot of gold I saw in wrestling. Yet she supported me just the same. Her words were always sympathetic and encouraging.

One dismal night I called her on the telephone. "Mom, I'm coming home," I said, barely able to get the words out. "I can't survive here."

"Yes you can," she told me firmly. "Hang in there. You can do it."

When I drove home to Hazel Park on a weekend to take my laundry to my mother and to see my girlfriend, I would also visit Masaaki and tell him how Johnson was beating the tar out of me. I revered Masaaki, who had wrestled for Japan and had won the silver medal in the 1968 World Championships at 125.5 pounds. He was the wisest man I knew. I would drive over to his little single-story home in Hazel Park, sit down with him in his living room, and open up my soul. As I told him about my failures, he listened quietly, with great politeness and professionalism. He could well understand how good a wrestler Mark was.

Masaaki Hatta never told me I wasn't cut out for wrestling. He never told me that I didn't have the physical talent, or that I didn't have enough heart. It was Masaaki's style always to find a technical solution to a problem, not a personal one.

"How exactly is Mark getting these double underhooks?" he would ask, in impeccable English with a thick Japanese accent.

I would tell him how Johnson powered his way in close to me and then pummeled those bear-like arms into me, raising me up on my toes.

"When he does this, I'm a goner," I would say.

Masaaki would nod wisely and then would give me fundamentally sound advice. "Keep your elbows at your side more," Massaki would say. "Keep those elbows tight, so that when he goes to dig underneath, there is resistance. Circle around him more to keep from giving him a stationary target. Attack one of his arms. Attack one side of his body. Capture one of his arms."

Then Masaaki would push the coffee table out of the way, move a chair or two, and show me physically how I should try to defend against Mark Johnson's vicious underhooks. We weren't actually banging into things, Masaaki only weighed 130 pounds, but I must admit that people normally don't conduct wrestling demonstrations in their living rooms. The average wife would probably be furious if she saw her husband wrestling on the living room floor. Heck, most people don't want their children wrestling in the house. But Mrs. Hatta, a typically deferential Japanese wife, never said a thing. I don't think she even considered it unusual. Having lived with Masaaki for so many years, she accepted the fact that Massaki's love of wrestling was destined to touch every corner of their lives.

Masaaki and I didn't always wrestle in the living room. If Masaaki really wanted to work up a sweat, he put on his headgear and we went out in the back yard instead. His technical skills were still very sharp. Occasionally, one of his wrestling buddies from Japan would visit, and we'd spend two hours out on the grass. Masaaki would still be in his street clothes. I'm sure the neighbors thought we were crazy.

I always left Masaaki Hatta's home feeling better about myself and my future. The Japanese wrestler never gave me fiery pep talks, the way my Olympic coach, Pavel Katsen did. He was entirely the opposite, unemotional. While Pavel inspired the heart, Masaaki touched the brain.

Masaaki never said, "You're getting better Steve. You're learning fast. You're going to win." He never even told me I was making progress. But the way he listened to me spoke volumes. His very interest in me was testimony to the progress I was making.

I have often wondered how many coaches would have gone to such lengths to help a struggling wrestler who was no longer a part of their team. During my freshman year I must have gone over to Masaaki's house once a month. I knew I could call Masaaki anytime with a question or a problem, and he'd be there to help me.

Masaaki's guidance enabled me to continue climbing higher at a time when frustration threatened to tear me apart. After each visit, I would go back to Ann Arbor and try to incorporate his suggestions into my game plan during my next confrontation with Mark Johnson. Some of Masaaki's ideas didn't work. Others did. But nothing enabled me to throw Mark. No matter what I did, he beat me badly.

I should add that Mark Johnson wasn't the only Michigan wrestler beating me up in practice. Some of the other underclassmen in lower weight divisions were beating me, as well. Mark Churella, a 150-pound sophomore who would be instrumental in my development, could beat me easily. The NCAA champion in his weight division, Churella was known for his powerful leg techniques. His moves were painful, really painful. They even had painful-sounding names, like "guillotines" and "the splits."

As I was coming to grips with my humble new goals and the fact that I wasn't going to make the Michigan varsity this year, I was confronted by something even more frightening than Mark Johnson. Physiology 101. Once again I was failing, but this time I was failing where it mattered most.

The University of Michigan had strict academic requirements for athletes, and I knew that if I flunked this physiology course, my wrestling career would be in jeopardy. If I couldn't make it at Michigan as a student, I certainly wasn't going to be able to fulfill my dreams as a wrestler. But to say I was in danger of flunking is putting it too mildly. We were nearly halfway through the term, and I had no idea what was going on. The text could have been written in Greek and I would not have understood it any less.

I was not academically oriented in high school, and my poor study habits had finally caught up with me. I had earned a D-minus on the first physiology test, an F on the second. Only two more exams remained. It was like being down on the mat, trapped in a suffocating headlock. It was a nightmare. I couldn't breathe.

For a few days I was in a panic. I felt I was too far behind to catch up, but at the same time I was willing to do anything I could to survive. So I started seeing a tutor, an athletic-looking graduate student at Michigan. Several other athletes, mostly football players, were in the tutor's class. I don't remember the tutor's name, but I'll never forget what he said.

"Steve," the tutor told me, "You're not going to be able to learn what's in these chapters by reading them once. And you're not going to be able to learn by reading them twice. You're going to have to read them three times."

When he said that, my heart sank. I can't read this stuff once, I thought to myself. How am I going to read it three times? When I had tried to read the physiology book in the past, I would start reading and fall asleep. But this time I didn't have any choice. I wanted to stay in school too badly. I wanted my wrestling career too badly. All of my dreams depended on my staying at Michigan. To survive I had to follow the tutor's plan.

Then the tutor gave me a second piece of advice.

"Go to the library and just stay there," he said. "The first time you read through the chapters, just read and don't try to figure everything out. Look at the diagrams, but if they don't make sense, keep going. The second time, start figuring out some of the words you don't know. Take a closer look at the diagrams. The third time through, look up everything you don't know and make sure you understand every diagram."

Just as the tutor advised, I went to the undergraduate library and sat down in a corner where no one would bother me. I had three chapters to read, one on the circulatory system, one on the reproductive system, and one on the respiratory system. The heart does interest me, I thought to myself. Maybe this won't be so bad.

Well, sure enough, the first time through the circulatory chapter, I didn't understand a single thing. Just as I figured. But as soon as I finished the chapter, I went right back to the beginning and started to read it again. And you know what? All of a sudden, a few of the concepts became clear to me. A few of the diagrams made sense. I finished the chapter a second time and, excited and hopeful, I went immediately to the beginning. This time it was like osmosis. Everything made sense. Words I had never heard before had meaning for me.

I can't tell you how inspired I was. During the next lecture, which I attended with about 300 other students, I sat in the auditorium and actually understood what the professor was saying. Sometimes I would understand concepts before he explained them. I remember turning to a friend sitting next to me, a hockey player, and saying, "Dave! I know what he's talking about. I honestly do!" Dave, who was also struggling a bit in this course, didn't believe me. He probably thought the pressure was getting to me.

You may not believe me either when I say that on the third test I got an A and that my score was among the top five in the class. I scored 95 out of 100 points. And with three of my five mistakes, I erred because I had misread the question. In truth, I knew the answers to 98 of the questions.

What my professor thought, I have no idea. He probably thought I had cheated somehow. Shortly thereafter, I stopped working with the tutor. I received an A-minus on the final, which brought my final grade for the class up to a B.

My main reactions to my stunning academic recovery were ecstasy, relief and pride. Going from F's to A's let me know deep in my heart that I could succeed at Michigan. I could graduate. I remember thinking that if I could succeed in physiology, I could succeed in anything. Finally, after twelve and a half years of schooling, I had learned the discipline necessary for academic success.

That success was represented not only by the grade on my report card but also by the lasting appreciation I gained for the miracle of the human body. The systems of the body, the respiratory system, the circulatory system, and the nervous system, work together in harmony as a complex machine. My physiology studies left me with a feeling of awe for the whole body, because so many sequences of events must occur for you to perform even the simplest task. Here I was an athlete, and yet I had never understood or appreciated what was happening within my own body.

My comeback from the brink of failure in the classroom also reinforced my belief that dreaming, goal-setting, planning and learning from your mistakes apply to everything in life, not just sports. Until my encounter with physiology, I had worried that I might not be cut out for academic life at Michigan, that perhaps I hadn't been born smart enough to succeed. I had worried that no matter how hard I worked, I wasn't going to make it in the classroom because I wasn't special. But Physiology 101 taught me that you don't have to be special to make it.

Not surprisingly, my improvement in the classroom was paralleled by marked improvement in the wrestling room. I never did beat Mark Johnson that year, but I began scoring on him more and more. Then when I went home to work out with my friends at Hazel Park High School, I noticed a major difference between them and me. Suddenly, my high school buddies did not seem so tough anymore. I could whip right through them, even those who would have given me trouble a year earlier.

I remember one incident in particular, a workout against Dave Evans, a 250-pound high school senior from Hazel Park who had won the state heavyweight title that year. When I was at Hazel Park, Dave always got the better of me. But now I was doing well against him. "Wow, you've really improved!" he told me. And I really had.

Seeing the improvement was exhilarating to me. So even when I returned to the Michigan wrestling room and took another beating from Mark, I was no longer quite so discouraged. My goals were to improve and to learn as much as I could, and all signs indicated that I was achieving those goals.

While my progress was cause for private celebration, it was not exactly the talk of the Michigan wrestling room. I was still a lowly rookie who had failed to make the varsity team, and thus I was not of prime concern to my coaches, Bill Johannesan and his assistant, Cal Jenkins. Billy Joe and Cal encouraged me in a perfunctory sort of way, but they didn't coach me the way Masaaki did. They were absorbed in the fortunes of their varsity wrestlers, and rightly so. At that time, I was still far down on their list of priorities.

After the school year had ended, Masaaki took me to the Junior National Greco-Roman Championships, which were for wrestlers 20 years old and under. The championship was in the form of a grueling, month-long camp, conducted in Mount Pleasant, Michigan, and Murfreesboro, Tennessee. During the camp, I discovered that my perseverance at Michigan had made a difference. I won the national junior title at 180 pounds and qualified for the Junior World Championships in Las Vegas, where I placed fifth. Winning the nationals was a big, big victory for me, especially considering the obstacles I had to overcome during the camp.

To begin with, I didn't relish working out in a suffocating wrestling room in Mount Pleasant and in hot, humid Murfreesboro during the summer. My girlfriend was back in Hazel Park, and most of the other wrestlers I knew were home, enjoying the summer. I was lonely and homesick, and I was working my tail off.

But even while I was feeling sorry for myself, I certainly wasn't alone. Masaaki was there, of course. And Mark Churella, my teammate at Michigan, was also there, jumping up and down and cheering for me during my matches. A friendship was just beginning.

To win the national junior title and make the world team, I had to beat a loud, arrogant wrestler named Don Brown. He was strong and musclebound, but his endurance wasn't the best. He was like a big puncher in boxing, who could knock you out of the ring early but ran out of gas in the later rounds.

Our tryout was supposed to be best two out of three, but we ended up wrestling four times. I beat Don in the first match, a close one, but the officials looked at the videotape afterward and decided not to count my victory. Don had not received any points after a particular throw, and the officials decided the match was too controversial to count. I felt cheated and devastated when they disallowed my victory. Obviously, they wanted Don Brown on the team, not me. Now I would have to beat Don Brown twice again, and I didn't relish the task. I didn't like him one bit.

We split the first two matches. Don won the first one, catching me with his one big throw and pinning me in about 25 seconds.

Our second match was a thriller. I began by wrestling too cautiously, and Don powered ahead of me, 9-0. Thinking the match was probably lost, I got so angry I told myself I might as well go out swinging. With that attitude, I was suddenly back in the match. I ended up winning, 14-13. Then in the third match I wrestled very well, beating Don soundly and making a berth on the Junior World Team.

All in all, my comeback victory wasn't a bad ending to a difficult year, and it really helped me place my freshman setbacks into perspective. I can see so clearly today that those failures helped make me a tougher wrestler and a more confident one at that.

"The Upset"

The 31st day of July, 1984, began quietly for me in my little corner of the Olympic Village on the University of Southern California campus, with no hint of the triumph and the fury to come. I arose at 6:30 a.m. and slipped out of my bunk in the comfortable, two-bedroom apartment I shared with seven other members of the United States Olympic Wrestling Team. I showered, shaved and dressed as usual. As I looked in the mirror and combed my hair, the face I saw looked just as it had a thousand times before, and just as it has a thousand times since. It was not a face of greatness that I saw. It was not the reflection of someone special. I saw only me, Steve Fraser, an uncomplicated, ordinary guy who had never set limits on what he could achieve.

Unaware that I was at the threshold of glory, I left my apartment at the Olympic Village and took the 45-minute bus ride to the Anaheim Convention Center, where the 1984 Olympic wrestling championships were being held. I had won my first two matches here, against Karolj Kopas of Yugoslavia and Toni Hannula of Finland. Now, upon arriving at the Anaheim Convention Center for the second day of competition, my first order of business was to check the pairings chart on the wall behind the weigh-in scale and find out who my third opponent would be. When my eyes fell upon the identity of that opponent, my stomach turned in a flutter of excitement and surprise. I was to meet Frank Andersson of Sweden, the man virtually everyone regarded as the favorite in the 198-pound division for Greco-Roman wrestlers.

Frank Andersson was a powerful, golden-haired athlete, who enjoyed the status of a movie star in Sweden and who had claimed the world championship in 1979, 1981 and 1982. With his great strength and technique, his quickness, and his superb sense of balance, Andersson had devastated his first three opponents in these Olympic Games. Each of Andersson's foes had served as a target for his most breathtaking and crowd-pleasing throw, the high-arching "back suplex," which we wrestlers pronounce "sou-play."

Frank Andersson would begin his suplex by locking his arms around his opponent's waist, when his opponent was lying face down on the mat. Andersson then would lift his opponent in the air and arch his back. Muscles rippling, his face contorted from the strain, the Swede would hurl his foe up in the air and back over his head. The victim would hit the mat with a thud, flat on his back. The throw was stunning from the spectator's standpoint. But as a wrestler, it made my stomach turn.

From the moment I saw us paired together on the chart, I knew our duel would be one of ultimate contrasts. Frank Andersson was "the natural," a brilliant athlete who had become internationally famous long before anyone knew my name. I was the boy next door, a wrestler from Hazel Park, Michigan, and now a sheriff's deputy in Ann Arbor, Michigan, who had gone from being ordinary to exceptional by a lot of hard work and unwavering focus. Andersson was flamboyant, a thrower who could literally hurl his foes out of contention. I was unspectacular, a grinding, physical fighter who pounded his opponents into exhaustion. Andersson was the international wrestling community's pick to win the Olympic title. I was considered a long shot, even to win the bronze. Andersson was a man who had always been given his due. I, Steve Fraser, was a man who had always been underestimated.

Under ideal circumstances, Frank Andersson and I would have wrestled each other much later, perhaps in the finals, with the gold and silver medals hanging in the balance. But that was not to be. The luck of the draw had thrown us into the same half of the championship, forcing us into a premature showdown. Deep in my heart, I had hoped our showdown would come later, rather than sooner. But when the pairings were drawn that morning, fate refused to accommodate my preferences. Even though the competition was still in its early stages, the gold medal would be won or lost when Frank Andersson and I met that afternoon.

With a hundred thoughts racing through my mind, I turned away from the fateful matchups on the pairings chart and went about doing what I knew I had to do. At the official weigh-in, an emotion-packed ritual attended by all of the Olympic wrestlers, I stepped up on the scale and was reassured to find I was right where I wanted to be, just a few ounces below the limit of 198 pounds for my weight class. Then I ate a good breakfast, carefully taking small servings of all the right foods. I had some fruit, toast, cereal, eggs, juice, milk and maybe one piece of bacon. I was careful not to eat greasy foods, and I didn't allow my stomach to get full.

After breakfast, I went to an area set aside for the various Olympic teams in a hall adjacent to the Anaheim Convention Center. Every team had an area, partitioned off by curtains. There was a private area for the United States team, just as there was a private area for the Finnish team, the Romanian team and the Swedish team. Preoccupied and alone, I lay down on one of the bunk beds. It was very quiet. There was no music. Those who spoke, spoke softly. Other wrestlers, like myself, were resting, immersed in solitude, preparing themselves for the matches ahead, perhaps the most important matches of their lives.

While I was lying on my bunk, I reminisced about my 13 years as a wrestler. I didn't know whether I would win or lose against Frank Andersson, but I did know that whatever the outcome, I would always be happy about my wrestling career. I knew I had done well to get as far as I had, and I knew I never could have done it without the energy and will that God had given me.

Unlike Frank Andersson, I was not a gifted athlete. Some people have the impression that champions just pop out of the womb, full-grown and bursting with natural talent. But I was anything but a champion when I began. When I played Little League baseball as a fourth-grader, I was afraid of the ball, and I used to hope the pitcher would walk me when I came up to bat. When I tried wrestling in the eighth grade, I didn't even make the team. As a sophomore in high school, I did make the team but I was no better than average. My humble record was eight victories, nine losses and one tie.

The story I'm relating to you now is not just a wrestling story, but a story of human potential. It is a story others can learn from, too. I became a great wrestler not because I was born that way, but because I made myself the best I could be. As I plodded through the ranks, rising from a state high school champion to a collegiate All-American to a national champion, I discovered a methodology for improvement and success. I allowed myself to dream, and I backed up my dreams with a plan of action, in both my practices and my matches. I trained with my goals constantly in mind, and as I met them I reset them higher and higher. I trained with a positive attitude; I developed a winning attitude, and I developed a mental toughness that short-circuited physical pain. In short, I developed a kind of <u>laser vision</u>. Like the laser beam, a burning concentration of light of a single wave length, my concentration was focused so fiercely on my goals that I never thought about defeat, and I never allowed myself to go astray.

My concentration was unwavering even in failure, because I learned that making mistakes is an important part of success. The most successful people in the world make mistakes, and they make a lot of them. I know I did. I was the freshman at the University of Michigan who failed to make the team. I was the college sophomore who was advised to drop to a lower weight class when I wasn't doing well. I was the college junior who was told I would never make it to the top if I continued to compete in two divisions of wrestling, freestyle and Greco-Roman, instead of just one. I was the sheriff's deputy who barely managed to make the United States Olympic Team. And I was the Olympian who was not expected to climb the highest mountain.

People underestimated me until the end, because they failed to understand me. Fired by intensity of purpose and concentration, I never entertained the thought of losing – not when I was at the University of Michigan, not when I was embroiled in the Olympic Trials, and not now, as I awaited my great moment with Frank Andersson. I had always done my very best, and I never – <u>never</u> – relinquished one inch. This focused intensity had been a part of my life for many, many years, through victory and defeat. And it brought me now to one of greatest moments of my career. It brought me face to face with Frank Andersson on July 31, 1984, in the Los Angeles Olympic Games.

As the hours ticked away and our confrontation neared, I did my best to relax. I didn't stay in the bunk all day, because I didn't want to let myself feel groggy. I walked around a bit and watched some of the other wrestling matches in the Convention Center. I also picked up that day's edition of the *Los Angeles Times*, and there, for me and everyone else to read, was Frank Andersson's best-known quote of the Olympic Games. The boycott-induced absence of one of Andersson's fiercest rivals, Igor Kanygin of the Soviet Union, combined with Andersson's victory over the outstanding George Pozidis of Greece, left the Swede confident that the gold medal was his to win. In his mind, he had already beaten his most challenging opponent.

With "the Soviets not here, I only count gold," the *Times* quoted Frank Andersson as saying. "If it's not gold, it's not worth anything."

Another opponent might have taken offense to Frank Andersson's comment, but I can honestly say that it didn't bother me at all. I didn't think Frank Andersson was putting me down. I just felt his words came out that way because he wanted to win the gold medal so badly.

The truth was, I liked and admired Frank Andersson. I had met him for the first time several years earlier, in the United States National Wrestling Championships in Albany, N.Y. He was a big star even then, and his image as a playboy was firmly established. I was a college sophomore and basically a nobody. I met Andersson through a friend of mine, Mike Chastin of Troy, Michigan, a very good wrestler who had been blinded in a childhood accident. Andersson beat Mike in the National Championships in Albany, and I think he felt sorry for him. In a gesture of friendship and sportsmanship, the Swede invited Mike up to his hotel room that evening for a visit. When Mike asked if I would like to accompany him, I didn't hesitate to say yes. So what if I was tagging along. I was eager to meet Frank Andersson too.

The Swede came to the door, greeted us warmly in English, which he spoke very well, and put his arm around Mike's shoulders, the way Europeans often do. Now that he had cleaned up and changed into his fashionable clothes and leather slacks, he looked even more like a movie star. He was good looking, with pearly white teeth and blond, curly locks that fell almost to his shoulders. His hair was layered in the back, like a movie star's. He was really a Hollywood type. His hair would have been in style in Hollywood, I suppose, but it was a radical departure from the clean-cut look favored by most world-class wrestlers. I could tell just by looking at him that he enjoyed his life, and that he lived in a much faster world than I did. When we sat down to talk and he lit up a cigarette, my eyes nearly popped out. I knew he couldn't have smoked very much, because wrestlers who smoke don't have the endurance to get very far. But to see him smoking even one cigarette was a shock for me.

In between puffs on his cigarette, Andersson showed us rookies a thing or two. In the middle of the room, all spiffed up in his leather pants, he grabbed Mike around the waist and showed him a tricky little move that might help him during some wrestling match down the road. In Greco-Roman wrestling, you're not allowed to use your legs, and when you're fairly inexperienced in Greco-Roman, as Mike and I were, you're very careful to obey that rule to a T. But Andersson had been around a while, and he was showing Mike and me a way to use our legs legally. Twisting in close to Mike, he used his own leg to raise Mike's thigh and throw Mike off balance. But in the flurry of activity, it was impossible to detect whether Andersson had really used his leg to lift Mike, or whether Mike, fighting for balance, had lifted up on his own accord.

Mike Chastin and I were in awe. Here we were with one of the best wrestlers in the world, and he was sharing the secrets of the trade he knew so well. We took advantage of his generosity and asked plenty of questions, and Andersson was kind and patient enough to answer them. One answer in particular I have never forgotten.

"What does it take," we asked, "to be a great wrestler?"

Andersson leaned forward and looked at us, his eyes gleaming. For a moment, he said nothing, allowing the suspense to build.

This was going to be the ultimate statement, I thought to myself. He's going to say something about running or lifting weights or strengthening your back.

Then Andersson answered.

"It takes drinking beer, getting in trouble with the police, and having sex with women."

My jaw must have dropped a mile. But I certainly didn't challenge him. Who was I to challenge one of the best wrestlers in the world?

Obviously, I never took Andersson's statement literally. But there was an underlying message in his words that has always been helpful to me. The Swede didn't really mean that you had to drink beer and get in trouble to be good; he meant that you must enjoy life if you want to succeed. Perhaps my idea of fun and Andersson's idea of fun were two different things. But he understood a truth that I did not fully appreciate at the time. He knew that if the long, hard path to success is not enjoyable, the pot of gold at the end is not worth having.

I can thank Frank Andersson today for helping me arrive at that truth, because if I had not truly enjoyed the long journey through my wrestling career, I would have quit far short of the Olympic gold medal. Wrestling is a tough, personal and often painful sport, and it is easy to let your sense of worth get tangled up in winning and losing. At times along the way, I also became overly upset by my failures. But with the help of Andersson's advice, I always came back to the realization that the journey itself was ultimately the greatest prize.

Frank Andersson and I crossed paths from time to time after that meeting in the hotel room in Albany, New York, but we never wrestled against each other until the Olympics. By this time, the Swede was even more famous than before, and I was no longer just another wide-eyed youngster. I don't think Andersson really appreciated how far I had come, however, because as I prepared for my second opponent of the Olympics, Toni Hannula of Finland, he came up to me and gave me a helpful little tip.

"You can get around him this way," he said, gesturing with his hands and shoulders. "You can beat him. Go after it!"

Andersson no doubt wanted me to beat the Finn for a couple of reasons. First, I don't think he perceived me as that much of a threat to him. Second, there was a natural rivalry between these Scandinavian athletes. And third, Frank was just being a nice guy. Even though he and I had very little in common personally, we were both Olympic wrestlers. We respected one another.

Helping me devise a strategy for the Swede was Pavel Katsen, an assistant coach of the United States team. Pavel was a Soviet nationalist who came to the United States in 1979 and became a United States citizen not long before the 1984 Olympics. Pavel and I understood that although I had some spectacular moves myself — including a crushing slam headlock — I was not the technician Andersson was. Conditioning was my forte. To win, we knew I had to get Andersson tired. I had to make him wrestle my fighting, brawling style. I had to wear him down. And if I was going to wear him down, I knew that somehow I had to break him.

I believed I could do that because I had never been in better condition in my life. If peaking is crucial for all athletes, it is especially crucial for an athlete whose success is founded on endurance. And I believed I had peaked perfectly. During the month-long Olympic training camp for the United States team at Big Bear Lake, California, I had followed every detail on the plan mapped out by Pavel Katsen and the Olympic head coach, Ron Finley, who was the wrestling coach at the University of Oregon. Pavel and Ron had devised an excellent plan, which called for short, intense workouts during that final month. Their goal leading into the Olympics was to kindle the wrestler's fire, not to burn it out with too much work. I followed that plan 100 percent, and I believed going into the Games that I was ready to reach my physical and emotional peak.

My strategy against Andersson sounded simple. I was to wear him down physically during our six-minute match and win. But it was a lot more complicated than that. Pavel and I agreed that I would go out sprinting in the first three-minute period and try to score on him. I would come at him like a grizzly bear, frantically and aggressively. Then I would pace a bit. Finally, at the end of the second three-minute period, I would finish as I had started, in a sprint, whether I was winning or losing. If I were losing, I would want to pick up the tempo in a final attempt to win; and if I were winning, I would still quicken the tempo in an effort to deny him any chance for a comeback.

This part of the strategy involved me. The other, more unpredictable part of the strategy, involved Frank Andersson. I was worried, believe me, about his high-arching back suplex. I was worried about the suplex the way a pitcher would have worried about Joe DiMaggio's power at the plate, or the way a defensive back would have worried about Joe Namath's ability to throw the bomb. The suplex, like the home run and the touchdown pass, meant big points. Four points to be exact. No other throw was worth that many. If Frank Andersson threw me once, I would be four points down. If he threw me twice, I would be eight points down, and I'd be in big, big trouble. If he threw me a third time to take a 12-point lead, the referee would halt the match and award him the victory.

The crowd loved watching the Swedish suplex, but I knew that it was sheer horror and humiliation for his opponents. I have been thrown on a back suplex for four points about 10 times in my career, and it was always a spooky experience. There is a point when you are safe and still fighting down on the mat, and then, suddenly, you can feel yourself being lifted, and you know there is no stopping what is about to happen. You see a big flash, a blur, and you worry during that split second when the world is turning and the crowd is roaring that you might get hurt, because you're going to land on your back and the back of your head. Wrestlers are rarely injured by the back suplex, but they have had the wind knocked out of them. Although the mat is two inches thick, it doesn't give much when you hit.

I knew Andersson would have at least one, and probably two, chances to throw me. The Swede executed virtually all of these throws when his opponent was in a "down" position, lying face down on the mat, and I was certain to be in that position during our match. The rules of international wrestling are designed to promote action and scoring, and if the referee thinks there is insufficient activity — even if both wrestlers are fighting as hard as they can — he will "caution" one of them. If you are the one cautioned, your opponent chooses whether you remain standing or whether the referee puts you in the down position. In 99 percent of the cases, your opponent will have the referee put you down. Andersson certainly would do this, because it would give him a perfect opportunity to play his trump.

In the minutes before our showdown, I visualized how the match would go. I visualized the pace I would set — fast at the beginning, slower in the middle, and fast again at the end. I saw myself winning with this strategy, although in my mind's eye I did not see myself throwing Andersson. Needless to say, I did not see him throwing me either!

I felt I was capable of beating Andersson, but I definitely felt like the underdog. I had seen him win so many tournaments over the years, and I knew he was the one to beat in these Olympic Games. Furthermore, he was wrestling at his peak. He was on fire. He had thrown everyone with that back suplex. I'm sure he expected to throw me, too.

You might wonder whether I was intimidated or nervous. Well, at various points during that long day I was both. But I did a good job of keeping my emotions under control. Every time I caught myself tightening up and thinking, "This is it; this guy is awfully good," I told myself it didn't matter. No one expected me to beat him anyway. I had never told anyone I was going to win a gold medal, or even a silver medal or a bronze. When people had inquired about my goals, I had said I would be honored to win a medal, any medal. My real goal, all along, was to do my best.

Finally, the time came. A tournament official approached me in the dressing room and escorted me to the tunnel leading into the Anaheim Convention Center's arena. Frank Andersson was also escorted to the tunnel, and there, in the half-darkness, we warmed up together. We did not say anything to each other, but we were definitely aware of one another. Although our eyes never met, I saw him, and I'm sure he saw me too. I was aware of how he carried his muscular frame, upright and sure, and I sensed that he was confident, as he always is. He did not strike me as arrogant, because he is not an arrogant person, but he seemed confident, strong and sure. I didn't dare pay too much attention to him, however, because I was concentrating hard and I didn't want to lose one fraction of that concentration. If ever I needed my laser vision – my Fraser's edge, as I sometimes call it – I needed it then.

As I walked out into the arena, the partisan crowd cheering wildly, I was thrilled to be where I was. Mingled with the sound of the crowd were the fiery words of Pavel Katsen, who had left me with a ringing exhortation. Pavel had a way of talking to me that sent my adrenaline flowing. In a raspy, intense, guttural kind of shout, he sought to evoke my fury by striking at my heart.

"You gotta go for it, buddy! You gotta be mean, you gotta be mean! You gotta go out there and get 'em!"

I was never one to make a big deal out of getting "psyched up," as so many athletes do. But upon hearing Pavel, I knew more than ever that I was going to give everything I had.

Frank Andersson and I came together in the center of the mat and shook hands. Then the referee blew his whistle, and the first period began. I came out sprinting, just as I had planned. And just as I had planned, I scored on Andersson almost immediately with my favorite throw, a slam headlock. Fifteen seconds into the match, I swung my right arm through the air and locked it, elbow bent, around Andersson's neck, and then hurled him down onto the mat. The blow came so fast and with such power that Andersson had no chance of stopping it. Having thrown him down, I was unable to hold him on the mat, he was so strong. Instantly, he was back on his feet. But I was leading, amazingly, three points to zero. My quick score was certainly unexpected, and the crowd, which was 95 percent American, screamed furiously.

Moments later, I tried the headlock again. But this time, he stopped me and I slipped and fell on my belly. My botched throw not only earned Andersson a point from the referee, it gave him a chance to try the suplex as I fought for position down on the mat.

What followed then, I believe, was the turning point of the match. It all happened so fast. Andersson got his hands underneath me and began to lift. The crowd was screaming.

I remember thinking, "I've just got to hold on!" For a second, my feet were off the ground, and then I adjusted and got my toes barely on the floor. At this point, all my knowledge of technique went flying out the window. I just gritted my teeth and got as tough as I could get. I was like a frenzied animal caught in the jaws of a trap. Survival was my only concern. And I was going to claw and writhe and do everything I could to survive.

I twisted and thrashed so violently that Andersson had to set me down. Then, deliberately, he lifted me again. And again he raised me slightly off my feet. This time I turned into him. I faced him. I didn't think to myself, "He's lifting me, so I have to turn into him." I just ended up there. It wasn't necessarily a classic defense, or the greatest defense, but it was the only thing I could do at the time. I think it shocked him. And it worked. We both fell back down on the mat.

Frank Andersson, his arms still locked around me, lifted me a third time and tried to turn me in a different direction. I fought like a tiger and for the third time I rebuffed him. It was furious and frenzied. The whole episode lasted 45 seconds. The match itself was only one minute old.

The referee then blew his whistle to stop the action, and Andersson and I separated. I had survived. Perhaps I had done more than just survive. As I backed away from him, my head up, he remained on his knees for a moment, holding his back. Then he stole a few seconds so he could catch his breath. I don't know whether he had really hurt his back or whether he just needed a little rest. But I do know that lifting someone like that three times without success can take a lot out of you. I knew it must have taken something out of him. And it said a lot to me, too. I thought, "Yeah, I stopped him."

Andersson didn't get much time to recoup. The referee immediately called him back into a wrestling position. Moments later I scored again. Gripping his left arm with both of my arms, I stepped in between his legs, turned my hips and threw him over my shoulder. Frank Andersson landed on his hands and the side of his face, with both feet in the air. I received only one point this time, for a correct throw, because Andersson, with his cat-like sense of balance, went through the air without exposing his back and was on his feet almost instantly.

I was leading now, 4-1. But that didn't mean I was cocky. He was still strong. And explosive. I was well aware that all he needed was one dramatic suplex and he would surge ahead of me, 5-4. I knew that if I let up one inch he could beat me. And I was really afraid that was going to happen. So I never let up, not for one second.

About two minutes into our match, the referee cautioned Andersson and put him in the down position. I used that time to burn up the seconds because I found it impossible to turn him. I was not at my best from this position, and he was just too strong for me to do anything with him. He was also getting slippery. We were both sweating profusely, and it is always harder to get a firm grip on a sweaty body than a dry one.

With about 15 seconds left in the first period, it was my turn to be cautioned. Andersson now had the option of putting me down on the mat with 15 seconds left, or of waiting until the start of the second three-minute period, when he would not have to worry about having the clock run out on him. Naturally, Andersson elected to wait. This also gave him the advantage of being rested, and it gave him a chance to try to throw me when I was nice and dry after I had toweled off during the break.

VICTORY

I was not hysterical when I went to my corner after the period ended, leading 4-1, but some people in the stands might have thought I was. I was wired with adrenaline, consumed by my stunning early success. Ron Finley, the Olympic coach, and Brad Rheingans, one of the assistant coaches, met me in my corner, but I hardly saw them. Everything was a blur. I was supposed to sit down so they could fan me with a towel, but I couldn't sit. Andersson was sitting, but I couldn't. I was too excited. I just kept standing and talking excitedly. Ron and Brad were supposed to be giving me advice, but they didn't need to. I knew what I had to do. And I told them.

"I've gotta stay on him," I rasped. *"I've gotta keep moving! I can't let up! I can't let up!"*

Finley asked me if I wanted to sit down, and I said no, I didn't want to sit down. I didn't want to relax. In my own mind, I remember, I didn't want my concentration to drop. Because I was afraid that if it did drop, Andersson was going to zero in and throw me. I knew that I was going "down" on the mat first thing during the second period, and if I relaxed — boom! — I'd be gone. Four points, and he'd be winning, 5-4.

We went out on the mat and they put me down. The whistle blew. He started to lift and locked his arms around my waist right away. He wanted to throw me fast because he had had so much trouble before, when he had taken his time. He got me in the air and as he prepared to throw me, I twisted my body around and faced him. His back arched and he fell onto the out-of-bounds line, hitting his shoulders and head. I fell, too, my chest on top of him. I was certain I had earned two points.

But I was wrong. I was given no points. The score was still 4-1, not 6-1, although I did not know it until about 10 seconds after we had started wrestling again. I was surprised when I saw the score out of my peripheral vision, but I didn't let it affect my intensity. It would have been easy to say, "I should have gotten that!" But in fact it helped me, because it made me keep thinking, "Don't let up! Keep going!" Perhaps I would have gotten a little lazy if I had rolled ahead, 6-1. I might have let up for a heartbeat of a second, and that's all it would have taken for him to pitch me.

Even though I had won no points, this was the second turning point of our match. Andersson, in his mind, knew he was lucky to escape without being scored upon. And he knew that in two attempts, he had failed to throw me.

With two and a half minutes now remaining, my strategy changed from trying to score to trying to burn up time. I would remain aggressive and would try to score if presented with a high-percentage opportunity. But I would not risk my victory. I didn't want to take any chances trying to create an opening and end up giving him an opportunity to score on me instead. My botched headlock early in the first period, which had given him a point and a chance to throw me, was precisely the kind of thing I wanted to avoid now.

At about this time I sensed that Andersson's movements were slowing down. About 20 seconds after he tried to throw me, I got underneath him with double underhooks, my arms locked, elbows bent, underneath his arms. It was an excellent position for me and a poor position for him, and it suggested that he was getting tired. Deep down, however, I thought he might be setting a trap. Perhaps he was faking fatigue so he could catch me by surprise. I refused to believe he was actually getting tired. He was a cagey competitor. Maybe, I thought, he's going to do something I've never seen him do before.

With about a minute and 45 seconds left in our match, the referee cautioned me for a second time. And for the third time in our match, I was down on the floor. This could be his last opportunity to throw me, I thought to myself. If only I could hold on one more time! And hold on I did. I blocked Andersson's moves by keeping my elbows in. The referee repeatedly slapped my hands, first one and then the other, in an effort to make me open up. But I didn't open up any more than I had to. I was like a clam opening his shell just a crack. I didn't dare open up completely, because I didn't want the Swede to grab me and take away the victory that seemed more and more within my grasp.

Andersson never got me off the ground this time. By the time he got his hands locked around me, 30 seconds had elapsed, and I met his challenge by twisting my body and forcing him so far out of position that he had to let go. The referee then blew the whistle, bringing me back to my feet.

Andersson was then cautioned for a second time, and once again I couldn't budge him. But the seconds were ticking away. When Andersson came back to his feet, only 35 seconds remained. For the first time, I thought in my heart that I could see the end and that I could beat him. I looked up at the clock and thought to myself, "I can burn for 35 seconds." He made some last, desperate attempts, trying to swoop in on me from underneath and then from above. But I was sprinting now, pummeling him from the right and from the left, and I never gave him a chance to set up a throw.

I know I was tired by this time, because it was a terribly physical and emotional match. But the funny thing is I don't remember being the least bit tired. Year in and year out, I had nearly always passed the threshold of fatigue when wrestling against my toughest opponents. As with other wrestlers, my ability to operate in that zone of pain was strictly related to how many times I had actually operated in that zone. And I had been there a thousand times before. So when I crossed the inevitable threshold against Andersson and reached that plateau where air comes hard and in stinging gulps, I was neither worried nor intimidated. I knew I wasn't completely spent. I knew I could go on.

By contrast, Andersson was exhausted. During the last 25 seconds, he couldn't even attempt a move. He was finished, and he and I and the crowd knew it. With 10 seconds remaining, the crowd began to chant. Ten, nine, eight... It was deafening. I will never forget that crowd. It was a sea of fury.

When the referee blew the whistle, I raised my arms but was too tired to smile. As I walked around the mat in a kind of aimless circle, I wanted to acknowledge the cheers, so I blew the crowd a kiss. It was only a little half-hearted gesture, but it was the best I could manage at the time. I was drained. My whole body felt numb.

Andersson felt even worse. The moment the whistle blew, he bent over in a gesture of utter exhaustion. I did not see him do that at the time, but I saw it later on a film given to me by ABC television. He was disappointed, obviously, and totally exhausted. My strategy had worked perfectly. I had worn him down just as I had wanted to. I had stopped him from throwing me. I had broken him, physically and mentally.

My victory over Frank Andersson, by a score of 4 to 1, was not the closest match I had at the Los Angeles Olympic Games. In the final round against Ilie Matei of Romania, I won via a tie-breaker with the score tied at one point apiece. Andersson, the bronze medalist, was, nevertheless, the toughest of the five men I wrestled in the Olympics. The

VICTORY

Los Angeles Times called my victory over him "one of the major upsets of these games."

Against Andersson, I wrestled the single greatest match of my life. I have never been so intense in a match from start to finish. All of those years of dreaming, planning, striving, and coping had yielded the perfect performance. My 13 years of effort had brought me to a point where I was so unyielding in my mission and so well prepared that every move I made was right. This, in the end, was my proudest moment of the Olympics.

My happiest moment of the Olympics came the next evening, at the awards ceremony. Just before Frank Andersson, Ilie Matei and I walked up to the awards stand, Andersson came up to me, smiling. "Congratulations," he said. "You wrestled well. You deserved to win. I'm happy you won in the finals."

"Thank you," I said, smiling back.

Then we stepped up on the victory stand. I stood in the center. Andersson was to my left. Matei was to my right. As we stood together, Andersson grasped my hand in his and raised my arm.

When the National Anthem was played, I had to blink several times to keep the tears from falling. I swallowed hard a few times and then began to sing. I had achieved my ultimate goal. I had realized all my dreams. I was stunned, completely stunned, and happier than I could say.

Quotes To Wrestle By

The #1 Reason Wrestlers Win is:

COMMITMENT!!

The best ways to improve / win / succeed:

STAY OPEN-MINDED AND HUNGRY

FOR KNOWLEDGE ALL THE TIME.

"When training I always tried to stay a little naïve - thinking there was always something else for me to learn."

— Dan Gable, Olympic and World champion

"The word "if" should be eliminated from a wrestler's vocabulary. I hear so many athletes lamenting their lack of success by its use:

'If I had more strength;

if I had better technique;

if I had a better coach;

if I had more experience.'

The success that U.S. wrestlers have achieved to date has been achieved because individuals accepted responsibility, dedicated themselves to excellence, and utilized whatever physical characteristics with which they were endowed. For future gold medalists, there is no other course except to take responsibility of one's own destiny."

— Stan Dziedzic

World champion, Olympic bronze medalist

VICTORY

LEFT: Steve was named "offensive lineman of the year" in ninth grade at Webb Junior High School. He was also all-conference in football his senior year at Hazel Park High School.

BELOW: During his undergraduate career at the University of Michigan, Steve earned All-American honors twice at 177 pounds.

In his sophomore season, 1978, Steve (far left) earned All-American honors at 177 pounds. The placewinners are (from left) Steve Fraser, sixth; Don Shuler, Arizona State fourth; Eric Wais, Oklahoma State, second; Mark Lieberman, Lehigh, champion; Charles Gadson, Iowa State, third, and Bill Teutsch, Florida, fifth.

LEFT: At Michigan, Steve Fraser made the varsity lineup for three seasons and earned a reputation for a non-stop and aggressive style of wrestling.

Before earning a spot on the 1984 Olympic wrestling team, Steve was featured on the cover of MICHIGAN magazine, a supplement of the Detroit News.

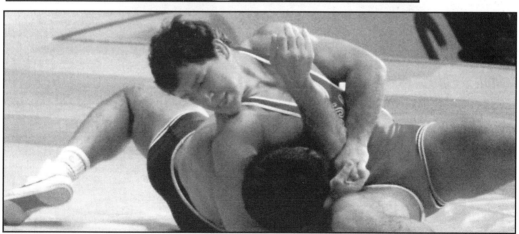

A bruising headlock was the key to many of Steve's victories in both the 1984 Olympic trials and at the Games in Los Angeles, where he is shown here punishing a foe. *(Photo by Steve Brown)*

In the final match, Steve battles with Ilie Matei of Romania. The match ended in a 1-1 tie, with Steve winning on criteria and clinching the gold medal. *(Photo by Steve Brown)*

VICTORY

In one of the most exciting matches of the entire 1984 Olympics, Frank Andersson of Sweden, a three-time World champion, tries to throw Steve for points. Steve won the crucial match, 4-1.
(Photo by Steve Brown)

Steve Fraser (left) celebrates after his final match, and then is interviewed (below) by announcer Russ Hellickson on national television.

(Photos by Steve Brown)

VICTORY

Steve is hugged by Dean Rockwell moments after becoming the first American to ever win a gold medal in Greco-Roman wrestling at the Olympic Games. Dean was the 1964 Olympic Greco-Roman coach and one of Steve's top supporters. *(AP/Wide World Photos)*

Part Two:
Columns by Steve Fraser

Reading the Columns

During the last several years, I have written a column for W.I.N. magazine, one of the nation's foremost wrestling publications. The columns were written to provide insight into a wrestler's mental and physical preparation during the course of his or her season(s) and career. The columns were meant to offer insight into an individual's journey, offering advice for all their endeavors in wrestling as well as in life.

The columns were written over a period of several years. The reader will want to take into consideration that the dates of each article are not composed or placed in chronological order. The dates of the articles have been identified where it was deemed necessary or helpful.

Because these articles were written over several years time, some may appear repetitive. However, the reader is encouraged to read and review each article. Drilling and repetition is the key to improvement and to absolute comprehension. Reviewing each article will help ensure your success on and off the mat. Additionally, some articles utilize similar or repetitive examples to reinforce different messages which are essential to success.

I believe that the overall message of each article is relevant and worthy reading material that will help any competitive wrestler and athlete be successful.

Hope you enjoy!

Steve Fraser,
April 15, 2005

Chapter 1
The Fundamentals

Attitude Makes the Difference

If you have never experienced the agony of defeat, then you had better get living. I pity the poor souls that have never felt the stinging pain of failure. Failing at anything is not pleasant. In fact, failing just down right stinks! However, experiencing failure is what propels us forward. Experiencing failure is what makes us strong.

To achieve success, especially in the sport of wrestling, it takes putting ourselves on the line. It takes stepping up to the plate and swinging the bat fiercely, maybe striking out several times. It takes exposing oneself totally. Exposing one's strengths as well as one's weaknesses.

Many people do not want to expose their weaknesses. They are afraid of what people might see. They are afraid of what people might think or what they might say.

There are a lot of ways to look at life. We can go through life cautiously, being careful not to expose too much. We can go through life with some degree of aggressiveness, taking some chances but still being careful. Or we can really Go For It!

And why not… why not really go for it? Why not try and be the very best at what we are doing? Why should we settle? Why should we settle for mediocrity? Settling is no way to live your life! Settling means you limit your opportunity to feel the greatest emotion that there is in life… the thrill of victory!

There is no better feeling in the entire world than accomplishing something that is so very difficult. Something that so many people may want but only a few can have. Especially in the wonderful sport of wrestling.

In wrestling, there is usually only one champion in each weight class…. each wrestler is striving to be the champ but only one will get the gold. And when you are the one that gets the gold, it is the greatest sensation.

The thrill of victory is the ultimate high. Whether it is the city, state, national or world championship, the thrill of victory is tremendous.

There is only one way to win the wrestling title or, more importantly, experience the thrill of victory. We must put it all out there. We must put everything we have on the line. When we put it all out there, we expose ourselves. And when we expose ourselves, we sometimes will stumble and fail. Sometimes we will lose. Sometimes we will be defeated. But that is life. That is what makes the thrill of victory so sweet.

There is no possible way to experience the thrill of victory without looking right into the eye of failure. We have got to challenge failure. We cannot be afraid of it.

Theodore Roosevelt once said, "Far better it is to dare mighty deeds, to win glorious triumphs, even though checkered by failure than to take rank with those poor spirits who neither enjoy much nor suffer much because they live in the great twilight of knowing neither victory or defeat."

<u>It is an Attitude!</u> An attitude that does not care what people may see, think or say. It

is an attitude that will not be satisfied with mediocrity. It is an attitude that says, "Life is too short to be middle of the road. Life is too short to be cautious about winning."

With my wrestling career I thought, "If I am going to do all the hard work that it takes to be successful in wrestling, then why not give it that little bit extra? It is that little bit extra that makes a huge difference in the final outcome. It is that little extra that separates the stars from the rest. A little extra energy and effort are the keys to success.

What do I mean, "a little extra?" Just what it sounds like; a little extra effort in every aspect of your life.

In regards to wrestling, it means a little extra wrestling, a little extra running, a little extra technique work, a little extra study of the sport and a little extra toughness. To bottom-line it… it means A Little Extra!

So, if you are waiting until tomorrow to give it your all…. STOP! Do it today, for tomorrow may never come. Take on each day like it was your last. Approach each practice like it was your final one. Take on each match like there is no tomorrow.

Start putting everything you have forward each and every moment, and you will advance very fast. You will move ahead in life with great enthusiasm and you will be excited about your progress. Happy are those who go for the gusto in life, for they will look back some day with no regrets.

Desire: The Biggest Key to Success

How did an average guy like me wrestle competitively for some fifteen odd years? Fifteen years is a long time. How did an "average Joe" like me win some of the lofty titles that I've won? You have got to realize I was terrible when I first starting wrestling.

How do average, everyday people accomplish the remarkable? Ask Matt Lindland or Rulon Gardner (Olympic silver medal winner and gold medal winner) how good they were back in the beginning. They will be quick to tell you that they were not any good.

So what is the answer?

We all know that to be successful at anything takes a lot of hard work and sacrifice. To be successful in wrestling takes discipline to practice the skills of wrestling over and over again. It takes conditioning the mind and body to withstand a tremendous amount of stress. It takes learning the strategies and tactics of wrestling so you can outsmart your opponents. It takes setting high goals, eating healthy, operating with a great attitude and being willing to overcome extraordinary adversity.

But first and foremost it takes desire... desire to be the very best wrestler that you can be. It all starts with *desire*. Do you desire to be the best? Do you want it bad enough? Are you willing to pay the price for the thrill of victory? If the answer is yes, then you are on your way. Only you can determine what you desire in life. For me, the thrill of wrestling victory is the ultimate high. For me, there is no better feeling in the world than to win the big one in wrestling. So needless to say, I had a great desire burning inside me.

For the elite guys that are on my national team I can see it clearly: they want it oh so bad! The Kevin Brackens and Jim Gruenwalds want it so bad they can taste it. These guys not only have the desire, they have learned to love the journey. They love the challenge. They love the training. But most of all, they love the battle!

The battle is how you get to the victory. Without the battle, without the struggle, the victory would be meaningless and empty.

Just like any wrestling technique or skill, enjoying or loving the battle must be practiced. It must be honed. This attitude must be cultivated daily. Having fun and enjoying the fight is what it is all about. Think about it – isn't life too short not to enjoy it?

So, do you love what you are doing? Do you enjoy wrestling? Do you look forward to the fight? Do you long for the moment when you can get into a battle with that other wrestler?

Loving success is easy. Loving the whole process of achieving success is really what helps one advance to a new level of competitive skill. We must constantly remind ourselves to love the battle. We must love the process; love the fight, and the struggle as well as the success. Learn to love the process and the success will take care of itself.

I encourage you to have some fun this month. Put yourself in the battle and practice

VICTORY

thinking humorous thoughts. Practice thinking how you love the combat. It doesn't matter if you are scoring points or getting scored on, just think about how much fun the battle really is. Yes, you can grit your teeth and be mean and tough but still smile deep down inside because you realize how much fun the fight really is.

If you tend to get nervous, think goofy or off-the-wall thoughts and your nervousness will disappear. When your emotions start to get the better of you, remember that internal laughter will put you back on track. Life is too short to be stressed out. You can and should learn to control stress.

Practice your mental focus in the present time. Operate in the here-and-now, especially during competition. This will enhance your "Ideal Competitive State" and your talent and skill will come alive. During the battle, if you think about the past or future, it may hamper your ability to really open up and go for it. Enjoy the present moment and your performance will flourish.

During the competition, how many wrestlers tend to only think about the results? They think about "If I can only win this next match," or "If I can only win this tournament," or "I should be able to beat this next guy so I will think about my subsequent match." NO! That is not enjoying the battle. We must look forward to every single match and live it like there is no tomorrow!

Think energy! Energy is everything. Generating a high level of positive energy will create that dynamic fight. It will help you to heighten those positive emotions that will make you strong and confident.

Think fun and positive energy will start to flow immediately. Say to yourself, "I love it! Isn't it great! Show me the pressure!"

When you get into those close matches, remind yourself how you love it. You love the pressure, you love the excitement and you love putting it all on the line. For you, life would be too boring if you did it any other way. No holding back, no excuses, you are going for it. You will do the best you can on this given day. You will wrestle to win at all cost and then be proud of whatever happens. You will accept the results and forge ahead to get even better the next day.

I have been in wrestling for over thirty years now. To this day, I still enjoy (more than just about anything) walking out of the wrestling room, drenched with sweat after a gut wrenching practice.

Am I crazy? Maybe, but I think if you asked Dan Gable, John Smith, Bruce Baumgartner, or any other of the great ones… they just might agree.

You've got to love it!

Do You Know WHY?

When up-and-coming wrestlers ask an accomplished wrestling star what it takes to become a champion, they usually are looking for the "how" they did it more then anything else. Not too many wrestlers ask "why" they did it. However, the "why" they did it is probably more important.

In fact, whenever I am asked how I did it — how I won the Olympic gold medal — I usually say, "it's not about how I did it, it's about why I did it." I say this because without the why, the how would have been impossible.

I could easily talk about how I did it, and with that I would discuss issues that dealt with: ways of increasing one's wrestling skills and knowledge; ways of conditioning the mind, body and your emotional state; ways of surrounding yourself with good coaches and athletes

However, for the sake of this article I would like to focus only on the why.

The "why" deals with desire and passion. Desire and passion to be the very best at something. I believe desire is the first and most important attribute one must have on the road to wrestling success. Desire is what ignites your engine. Desire is what gets you going.

Then there is passion. Passion is what fuels your fire. Passion keeps the flame burning even on the rainiest of days. If you do not have the intense desire and the fiery passion for wrestling success — then the "how" is irrelevant.

Did you ever have a moment where you were sick and tired of where you were at and where you seemed to be going with your wrestling career? Maybe even sick and tired of yourself? I remember one occasion in my career when I was at that point.

I had just completed my final season at the University of Michigan, where I had finished my college career with a disappointing fifth place at the NCAA tournament. My goal had always been to win the NCAAs, however it wasn't to be. Feeling pretty down and rather depressed I decided to take a short trip with some buddies of mine.

It was between my final NCAA season and the freestyle/Greco season when we jumped in my car and drove up to northern Michigan. We went to my friend's cottage that stood on a bluff overlooking Lake Huron. We had gone up north to getaway from it all and do some fishing and relaxing. It was here where I started thinking about where I was going with my wrestling career.

It was late March and there was still some wet snow on the ground with a winter chill still in the air which was common for that part of the state. We were sitting on the beach looking out over the vast sparkling waters of Lake Huron. I remember very clearly how I began to examine my feelings about wrestling. I really took a hard look at where I was going and what I wanted to do with this sport. Did I still have the desire and passion for the sport? Did I still want to achieve something great yet? I remember thinking about this very hard.

I had been wrestling for nine years up to that point in my life. Wrestling had consumed most of my thoughts and actions during this time and not winning the NCAA tournament was a very big disappointment and failure to me. So, it hurt! It hurt badly!

As my buddies and I were just kicking back on the beach, I began to think. I began to think of all the trials and tribulations of my past nine-year career. Yeah I had many failures and setbacks and this NCAA setback was big. Oh yes ... I was feeling mighty sorry for myself. Then all of a sudden I realized my "why"! I realized why I was going to change my attitude and continue wrestling.

I was sick and tired of my old self, and it was time to change. It was not just a mental change; it was a change that came from deep inside. It was time for a big change and I knew I could change because I found out why I wanted to change. The following are some of my personal whys — why I decided to commit to the dream of winning an Olympic medal.

- I was fed up with feeling sorry for myself.
- I was tired of being just average.
- I was determined to find the answers to my questions of how I could become the best.
- I loved the thrill of victory and wanted to experience it a lot more.
- I was tired of getting beat, especially when I was not totally committed.
- I wanted to challenge my own self-doubts, my laziness and my past.
- I wanted to be tough!

All of a sudden I got the urge to get up off my butt and, in my combat boots, I decided to take a run down the shoreline. I must have run for about a half mile when I started to think about how far I had come with my wrestling skills and, with a tad more effort, where I might end up. I also started to think about some of the victories and extreme highs that I had experienced in my career.

I knew I was pretty good at this sport and I thought to myself, why not really go for it? Why not give it everything I had — I knew I had to be close. Why quit now, when I was probably just around the corner from getting the true success that I deserved? Why not go all the way?

I thought to myself — the highs are so high, and it feels so good to succeed — this must mean that I still have the desire and passion for the sport. "Yeah (talking to myself) ... let's go for it! Let's totally commit and see where this thing might take me."

So while running in my army boots along the shoreline of Lake Huron, on that cold, Michigan March day, I decided to nourish my desire and passion for the sport of wrestling. I had my "why" which in turn allowed me to focus on the "how".

I learned years ago that passion is a combination of love and hate. Unless someone has the passion for something, it is difficult to accomplish anything. If you want something you must be passionate. Passion gives you the energy to your life.

If you want something you do not have, find out why you love what you want and why you hate not having this. When you combine those two thoughts, you will find the energy to get you off your seat and go for anything you want.

Chapter 2
Mental Toughness and Psychological Training

Learning What Toughness is All About

When talking about talent we must realize that every wrestler has talent. Some have it big and some not so big. This is the great gift given to you by Mother Nature. Theoretically, talent defines the potential of your athletic achievement. The idea is that if you are gifted, or a real 'natural', you can be great. If you are not gifted then nothing special can happen athletically.

I do not believe this theory. We've all seen wrestlers with limited talent become great performers. I consider myself one of those wrestlers who lacks natural talent. We've also seen wrestlers with great talent never truly reach their full potential. Why?

Next we look at the nature of skill. Whereas talent is a gift, skills are learned. The mechanics of running, jumping, shooting, hitting and kicking are skills. They are acquired through hard work, repetition and practice. Theoretically, skills affect achievement in wrestling in much the same way as talent does. If your skills are strong, you can be great! If your skills are weak, your potential is limited.

Again, I think we've all seen some successful wrestlers with skills that were marginal to good, at best. So how do wrestlers with no special talent and average-to-good mechanics become the best?

Talent and skill are important contributors to achievement in sport, but I don't think they are the most important factors. So many highly-successful athletes exist today who are not gifted or have not achieved mechanical perfection. They are everywhere in every sport – golf, tennis, baseball, basketball, football, boxing, skating, hockey, soccer and wrestling. So what is the critical factor in wrestling achievement?

It's called TOUGHNESS!

What is toughness? Toughness is the ability to consistently perform at a high level no matter what the competitive circumstances. In other words, no matter what happens, no matter what is thrown at you, no matter what adversity you are faced with, you will still be able to bring all your talent and skills to life on demand.

Toughness is being able to perform at your ideal competitive state of mind and body. It is simply the optimal state of physiological and psychological arousal for performing at your peak. You are most likely to perform at your peak when you feel:

- Confident;
- Relaxed and calm;
- Energized with positive emotion;
- Challenged;
- Focused and alert;
- Automatic and instinctive;

• Ready for fun and enjoyment.

Toughness is learned. Make no mistake about it. Toughness has nothing to do with genetics. It is acquired the same way as are skills. If you don't have it, it just means you haven't learned it yet. Anyone can learn it at any stage in his or her life.

Toughness is mental, physical and, ultimately, emotional. What you think and visualize, how you act, when and what you eat, the quantity and quality of your sleep and rest, and especially your physical conditioning level can all have a great effect on your emotional state. Tough thinking, tough acting, fitness, proper rest and diet are prerequisites for feeling tough.

Your emotions control your ideal competitive state of being. Some emotions are empowering, freeing your talent and skill. Other emotions are disempowering and lock your potential out. Empowering emotions are those associated with challenge, drive, confidence, determination, positive fight, energy, spirit, persistence and fun. Disempowering emotions are those associated with feelings of fatigue, helplessness, insecurity, low energy, weakness, fear and confusion.

Learning to access empowering emotions during competition, especially in difficult situations, is the basis for learning to be a great fighter. That's what toughness is all about.

Vering: Tough As They Come – 2003 World Championships

At the 2003 Greco World Championships in Creteil, France, there were some great displays of toughness. One in particular stands out in my mind. This was the performance of one of our younger Greco guys: Brad Vering at 185 pounds.

Vering, who has been in the United States Olympic Training Center (USOTC) Resident Program for less than two years, finished in fifth place for his second year in a row. Brad overcame and wrestled with a very painful groin injury that really hampered his mobility. Brad wrestled like a true American gladiator. Even with this serious injury, he wrestled fiercely and without hesitation.

In the quarterfinals, he faced the Norwegian wrestler Fritz Aanes, who is one of the top 185-pound wrestlers in the world. Brad battled back from a 2-0 deficit to tie the match, 2-2, in overtime. Brad had the Norwegian dead tired, crushing him with intense pummeling. He was moving him back and forth, dominating the fight. It seemed to be only a matter of time before Aanes would break down completely, giving into Brad.

Vering then hit a "duck under" and was almost all the way behind him, when his groin injury pulled and Brad stumbled a bit. A tremendous scramble ensued. When both wrestlers came up neutral, the official signaled one point for the Norwegian for a correct attempted throw (correct call). For me, as national coach, it was one of the most heartbreaking losses I have ever experienced. I'm not embarrassed to say that I had tears in my eyes for at least one hour after the match. Even though Vering lost this match it was a tremendous display of great courage and extreme toughness.

What does being tough really mean? Is it having the "Killer Instinct?" Is it being mean or cold? Is it being hard, insensitive, callous or ruthless? In a previous issue of WIN magazine in Wade Schalles's column, Wade identified who, in his mind, were some tough, hard-nosed wrestlers. He mentioned Doug Blubaugh, Wayne Baughman and the Brands brothers. I think most people would agree that these individuals all fit the bill of "tough".

So, would we describe these tough wrestlers with the adjectives above or do words like flexible, responsive, relentless, strong and resilient under pressure come to mind? Although they all have some of the above attributes (i.e. killer instinct), I think the latter words better represent what tough really is and these men are definitely all that.

Toughness is the ability to perform at your Ideal Competitive State, no matter what the competitive circumstances are. What is your Ideal Competitive State? It is your personal state of being that allows you to wrestle with the greatest potential. It is a state of being where you feel most energized, most confident, most strong. It is when you are generating positive emotions that help you to be most alert, instinctive, responsive and creative.

It is when you have that positive fight – when you are having fun and enjoying the battle. When all these positive emotions are flowing, you are going to wrestle to your greatest potential.

Toughness is being able to create these positive emotions upon command, thus enabling you to bring all your talent and skills to life at that moment.

Emotion is very important in wrestling, and all competitive sports, for that matter. The positive emotions mentioned above will empower you with great action and attitude. But some emotions can disempower you, blocking your potential. Negative emotions include such feelings as fear, confusion, low energy, fatigue and helplessness.

Which brings us back to toughness: Being truly tough means no matter what is happening that might be considered negative, you continue to operate in your Ideal Competitive State, generating positive emotion. This means during the match when you make that big mistake, you can refocus and be right back on track. When you get thrown to your back or taken down, you can refocus and get right back at it. When the referee makes a bad call against you, you can refocus and get back to business.

Being tough means that if your girlfriend breaks up with you, your mom is on you about keeping your room clean, your teachers are hammering you about your school work, it doesn't matter – when you step on the mat you kick into high gear, rising above all of the problems. You can adjust your mindset and, voilà… you are in your Ideal Competitive State. Nothing can break you. Nothing can stop you. You are resilient. You can bounce back. You are one tough cookie!

Toughness is physical, mental and emotional. Being tough involves all three of these areas. And make no mistake, toughness is learned. If you are not tough, it is just because you have not learned and practiced enough yet. Just like any wrestling technique or skill… toughness can be developed, practiced and honed to perfection.

So, how tough are you? Before one can improve his or her toughness, one must be able to face the truth! And, if you are unsatisfied with what you see you must be willing to take full responsibility to change it. Let's take a look at the truth.

On a score of one to ten, with ten being the best (strongest), rate yourself on some of the following issues:

resilient	disciplined	self-reliant	responsible
committed	coachability	confident	focused
patient	motivated	relaxed	physically fit

Be honest with yourself in regards to how you rate in the above areas. Remember that in the heat of the battle, when push comes to shove, you'll tend to break at your weakest points.

For example: If your weakness is discipline, in a tough match when it really counts for you to be disciplined – i.e you are ahead 3-2 with 30 seconds to go in the match – you must stay disciplined at keeping to your game plan of "sticking and moving" (not stalling) to burn seconds off the clock and secure the victory. But because your discipline is weak, you second-guess yourself, change your strategy and start backing up, and –

VICTORY

BOOM! – your opponent takes you down to win the match.

To improve your toughness, you should focus your training on your weakest areas. This is why it is important to know the truth about yourself and your needs for improvement. Getting feedback from your coaches is vital here. You need to be very open-minded about what your coaches see. This will help you get to the "real you".

<u>Addressing your needs for improvement:</u> Take two areas that you score low in. Now, let's create a **toughness training plan** to improve these areas. Here are some suggestions:

1. State your 'needs for improvement' in writing in a positive fashion.
    i.e. Discipline – "I have tremendous discipline" or Resilience – "I love being in a close match where I must come from behind to win."
2. For the next 30 days, make these positive statements the most important issues in your wrestling life.
3. Post these positive statements in your locker, near your bed or on your bathroom mirror.
4. Write a one-page summary on how you will improve each of these issues.
5. Just before you go to sleep and when you first wake up, take 30 seconds to visualize and see yourself successful at improving these issues. <u>Take the time to really feel it.</u>
6. For the next 30 days, track your progress in these areas. Note in your training journal the days you feel you improved and when you did not.
7. At the end of 30 days, take two new areas that you feel you need improvement in and repeat this process.

Remember, you must take control of your own wrestling career and commit to making changes. The sooner you take full responsibility for your actions and hold yourself accountable, the better.

No matter how old or young, weak or strong – you can get tougher. Never believe that you cannot achieve because you are not talented enough, not smart enough or that you were not given the gifts to succeed. Your future is much more dependent upon the decisions you make and what you do than what you are genetically.

And believe me, the level of toughness that you acquire through your focused training efforts will be the most powerful force in your wrestling career and your life.

As always… expect to WIN!

Men of Courage Do Great Things

The quote, "Men of courage do great things," has become one of my favorite quotes as of late. Of course, in my mind, the word "men" can be interchanged with the word "women." I first heard this quote from Hugh Suenaga of Pocatello, Idaho, who is a great man, friend, and coach/supporter to our USA Wrestling programs.

Let's look at the word "courage." Courage, as defined in the American Heritage Dictionary, means, "The state or quality of mind or spirit that enables one to face danger with self-possession, confidence, and resolution; bravery."

Being called "a man or woman of courage" is probably one of the finest compliments one can receive. It means you are brave in the battle...having the guts to fight ferociously and the nerve to be the best at what you are doing.

Very few people in the world have the audacity and valor to be daring enough to do great things. Most people are content with just living life as it comes. There is nothing wrong with living life as it comes; however, you must ask yourself the big question: "Is that good enough for me? Will I be satisfied with my life if I just take it as it comes?"

There is no better feeling in this life than the feeling one gets from accomplishing great things. Whether it is in the sport of wrestling or in life in general, accomplishing greatness or achieving something that many think is extremely difficult, or maybe even impossible, creates the most fantastic emotion one can imagine. Winning that big event or conquering that gigantic feat creates the highest of highs. The thrill of victory produces the most euphoric of sensations.

I have been fortunate over the years to have experienced the thrill of victory at times – the proud feeling of accomplishment makes all the hard work well worth it. This feeling is one that money can't buy, literally. It is the emotion that makes some think, "Oh yeah, I'm bad! I am the man! Don't mess with me!" It is the sensation that makes you walk proud, sticking your chest out, with your head up high.

Matt Lindland and Dennis Hall are two great examples of "men of courage." Matt won a silver medal in the 2000 Sydney Olympic Games and then followed it up by winning another silver medal in the 2001 World Championships. Dennis was World Champion in 1995 and then a year later won the silver medal in the Atlanta Olympic Games.

In the year 2000, countries had to pre-qualify their eight weight classes for the Sydney Olympics. There were five Olympic qualifying events that took place throughout that year. Going into the final qualifier, the U.S. Greco-Roman squad had yet to qualify four of the eight weight classes. Our last chance to qualify the remaining four weights would take place at the Pan-American Championships held in Cali, Columbia. And it was not going to be easy.

In order for us to qualify our entire team for the Games, we had to win the tourna-

VICTORY

ment in all four of these remaining weight categories. In two of the four weight classes, we had to beat very tough Cuban wrestlers, who were also trying to qualify.

Qualifying all of our U.S. weight classes for the Sydney Olympic Games was extremely important, as one might imagine. In prior Olympic Games, we had always had our full team represented. Our U.S. team did not want to go to an Olympic Games without a full contingency for the first time. We were fighting for our lives and, of course, feeling the enormous pressure.

The first of the two weight classes that we had to triumph over the Cubans was at 58 kilos, where Dennis Hall had to beat Gonzalez Monzon. Monzon was a world-class competitor. In fact, he was the eventual Olympic silver medalist in the 2004 Athens Olympics. He had beaten us on previous occasion, but we had defeated him, too. Monzon was definitely an Olympic medal contender in the year 2000.

The other weight class was at 76 kilos, where Matt Lindland had to defeat the former two-time world champion from Cuba, Nestor Almanza. Almanza was very strong and very experienced.

So, the pressure was on and it was on big!

After a tough day of wrestling all the preliminary bouts, Hall and Lindland made it to the finals and faced off with their Cuban adversaries. Both Cubans needed to win to qualify and the U.S. had to do the same. Earlier, we had qualified our other two, previously un-qualified, weight classes. So now the stage was set for Hall and Lindland.

Dennis Hall went out and wrestled a great match against Monzon. However with just 12 seconds left on the clock, as the fierce action took both wrestlers out of bounds, Hall found himself tied in the match score. Unfortunately, Monzon had the tie breaking criteria, thus giving the Cuban the eventual victory if Hall did not score again.

The situation looked very bleak for the U.S. It looked all but lost. The atmosphere was electric in this small, heat-filled South American gymnasium. All of the Cubans were crowded around the mat screaming in Spanish to their teammate. They could sense they were just seconds away from victory and the qualification of 58 kilos for their homeland.

All of the U.S. team and delegation were also surrounding the mat screaming, obviously screaming for Hall.

And then it happened. With only 12 seconds left on the clock, a man with great courage hustled back to the center of the mat. When the whistle blew to continue the bout, Dennis sprinted, flurried, scratched and clawed like an animal fighting for his life.

Eleven, ten, nine, eight... as the seconds clicked off the clock, Hall, in a full dash for the finish line, moved left, right, up, then down creating such a scramble that his attack gained him great momentum and superior position.

Seven, six, five, four... Hall, still striking fiercely; spun, twisted, controlled and finally subdued Monzon; miraculously taking him down to the mat, scoring with just three seconds left on the clock to win the match. It was unbelievable! It was thrilling! It was spine-tingling! Dennis Hall did it. He qualified the 58-kilo weight class for the Sydney Olympic Games.

Then it was Matt Lindland's time for courage. This made him the only guy left on the U.S. squad with the awesome challenge of qualifying our last weight class for the Sydney Olympics. Every category was now qualified, except for 76 kilos. The pressure was on!

I remember in the warm-up room where Lindland was getting ready for this great confrontation. Even though we were trying very hard to be calm and show great confidence, the coaching staff was very nervous; especially Rob Hermann, who was the assistant olympic coach.

In fact, at one point Lindland actually said, "Can someone tell Coach Hermann to relax?" Lindland joked, "His nervousness is making ME uptight." This was an extremely intense time for everyone.

It was a very hot mid-summer evening with extreme humidity and enormous tension filling the air. I will never forget the attitude Lindland had during this very anxious time. He looked totally laid-back, confident, and ready for the battle. He did not show even an ounce of doubt, nervousness or hesitation in his demeanor. This was a true warrior getting prepared to go into combat for his life. It was extraordinary!

As a coach, I have experienced many athletes preparing for competition and never have I seen someone in such a tough, high-pressure situation handle it so well. Matt was as cool as a cucumber. He was focused only on what he was going to do. He spoke to me about his tactics and strategy and the different scenarios that could possibly occur; and then how he would react and adjust to them. He was a man on a mission.

Lindland wrestled one of the most calculated and intelligent matches of his life. He wrestled with tremendous poise and determination. The score was very close, and the match was extremely exciting…all of us were on edge the entire bout. One mistake against this Cuban world champion would mean utter disaster. However, Lindland controlled the match from beginning to end and was victorious. His enormous courage on this pressure-filled evening was remarkable.

The U.S. team was victorious in qualifying all eight of our weight categories for the Sydney Olympic Games; where we went on to have our best Olympic performance ever.

It takes great courage to do what Dennis Hall and Matt Lindland did for themselves and our country. These two wrestling superstars exemplify the true meaning of the quote "men of courage do great things."

Expose Your Weaknesses To Stress

The idea that our muscles become stronger and more resilient when they are exposed to physical stress is usually easy for most athletes to understand. For example, when you stress your muscles by lifting heavy weights, you stimulate growth in these muscles which, in turn, will make them grow stronger. What is more difficult for some athletes to understand is how this same toughening principle can be applied to our mental and emotional weaknesses.

Here's how it works: Remember that stress is energy expenditure. Muscle stress, then, is generated by expending energy. Lifting heavy weights requires more energy expenditure than lifting light weights; therefore, it is more stress producing. Likewise, the more repetitions one does, the greater the stress. The important thing to realize is that

> *Thoughts and emotions involve energy expenditures just like muscles do.*
> *Every thought, every image, every emotion is a form of stress.*

Very powerful thoughts, images and emotions are just like heavy weights. They require more energy and, therefore, are more stressful. With this understanding, how do you build mental and emotional weakness into strength? How do you attack negative thinking, low self-confidence, impatience or poor self discipline?

The first and most important step in strengthening mental and emotional habits is to expend mental and emotional energy in specific targeted areas. Just like you must target a specific motor skill to improve, you must target specific weak mental and emotional habits the same way. The more you think a particular thought, the more often you trigger the same image or emotion, the stronger it becomes. Like muscles, the more thoughts, images and emotions you stimulate, the more accessible they become.

Here are some practical examples:

<u>Weakness:</u> Negative habit of thinking…. "I hate close matches."

<u>Consequence:</u> This undermines your "Ideal Competition State" and results in repeated failure to perform to your potential in close matches.

<u>Toughening Process:</u> Expose yourself to new forms of mental and emotional stress.

<u>What to Do:</u> Any one or a combination of the following could be used to build a new, more adaptive response:

- Constantly think the affirmation "I love close matches."
- Constantly say to yourself during close matches, "I love it."
- Repeatedly visualize performing well during close matches and see yourself loving it. Visualize with strong positive emotion.
- Write about how much you now enjoy close matches and all the reasons why.
- Combine mental practice with deep relaxation.

The two key things to remember in toughness training are: (1) Growth requires stress, and (2) Stress is energy that you expend.

Expose your weaknesses to stress – physically, mentally and emotionally – and you will gain tremendous toughness.

Keeping Cool When the Pressure Is On

Have you ever watched the Olympics on television and wondered how the athletes can be so calm under pressure? With millions of people watching, the Olympic stars seem so nervousness-free and relaxed. How can this be? How can these athletes compete anxiety-free under such pressure-filled conditions? Well let me tell you a little secret…they don't.

If you could come back with me at the Olympic Games, you would see some very, very nervous athletes....pacing back and forth; looking very tense and uptight; smiling but with clenched teeth; constantly going to the restroom. The tension so intense, you can almost feel it.

The truth of the matter is that elite athletes do in fact get nervous before they compete. They react to stressful situations just like you and me. In fact, I don't know any of our world-class wrestlers that don't get a little nervous before wrestling. All the great ones do.

The big difference is that they know how to manage their nervousness. They know how to control their emotions. They have learned to stay cool and focused under these pressure situations. They don't panic when they get nervous, and they use specific strategies, ones that they have practiced, to help them cope with the anxiety. Despite the pressure they are under, they can still achieve at the highest level. They know how to keep cool.

By learning how to "keep cool," you can be calm and look confident when performing; you can handle stressful situations in a productive and professional way; and perform at your best, even when the pressure is great! Gold medals are not won by chance. Gold medals are won by athletes who are fully prepared for the pressures they encounter. In fact, many successful athletes will use their nervousness to help push their performance to even greater heights.

This reminds me of a situation in my wrestling career. Back in 1984 at the U.S. Final Olympic Trials in Grand Rapids, Michigan, I was in one of the most stressful predicaments of my entire wrestling career. In the final leg of the Olympic Trials procedure, I had beaten 1980 Olympian Mark Johnson two matches in a row the day before. This advanced me to the final series of matches against my long-time nemesis, Mike Houck of Minnesota.

In the first of the two-out-of-three match series that morning, I defeated Mike in a close 2-0 match. The second match took place that afternoon where Mike beat me 3-0. The third and final rubber match was scheduled to take place one hour from my 3-0 loss. Here

I was just 60 short minutes away from having to wrestle the biggest match of my entire life. This was it! My whole career hinged on this final deciding match against my fiercest American opponent. Was I going to make the 1984 Olympic team or not?

I remember feeling extremely down after my loss. I was very nervous. The anxiety was so great I could barely keep from crying. I remember feeling very sorry for myself. I was confused and tense. I felt very drained and weak. And now the minutes were flying by. It was just 30 minutes from the start of my final bout with Mike.

The moment of truth was upon me! What was I going to do? I had to get hold of myself. I had to get my mind ready for battle. It was now or never!

I remember going over to Joe Wells, who was one of my coaches at the University of Michigan at the time. Joe is a great coach and is currently the head coach for Oregon State University. Right away, he saw my state of mind. Right away, he gave me some great words of advice and encouragement. He helped me to relax, telling me that I just needed to forget the last match and look at this next bout as a brand new one. He helped me to rationalize and focus on the task at hand. Then he somehow managed to make me smile and all of a sudden I was back focused and on track.

The match began and in just a short time I found myself behind 3-0 after Mike scored on me from the parterre position. I knew it was coming but I just could not stop it. Now, I really had nothing to lose. In the many matches that Mike Houck and I wrestled, the person who scored first usually won. When I got back to my feet I let all anxiety go, figuring that I had nothing to lose now.

I went after Mike Houck with all my fury. For the next minute or so we were brawling like two street fighters. This was it for both of us. Years of preparation. Years of sacrifice. Years of dreaming of that one ultimate experience – making the United States Olympic Wrestling Team.

Then it happened! I pummeled in on Mike and was able to get double underhooks. With just seconds left in the first period I locked my arms around his upper torso, faked one way and threw Mike laterally the other way. This throw put Mike on his back and scored three points for me.

The score was now 3-3, but because I scored a three-point throw and Mike scored a two-point and one-point maneuver, I would win the tiebreaker if it ended up that way. The next three-minute period was yet to take place, though.

At the one-minute break, in between periods, I remember using all my experience in staying focused and controlling my emotions. I knew I had to keep up the intensity and concentrate on what I had to do to win the match. Any lack of focus or breakdown in my "keeping cool" would be sure disaster for me.

This is where years of training and practice came into play. I did, in fact, manage my mental and emotional state and proceeded to wrestle the last three minutes of this life-altering match wonderfully. The match ended up 3-3, which meant I won the tiebreaker. I did it! I was on the Olympic Team. I was going to Los Angles to wrestle in the event of my life.

Staying calm in pressure situations is one of the keys to keeping focused on your wrestling tactics and strategies. Keeping cool and concentrating on the competition at hand is vital to performing at your best. I have written about this a lot over the years. It is called your "Ideal Competitive State" – the mental, physical and emotional state of being that allows for you to wrestle at your best potential.

There are things you can do to practice "keeping cool."

First, realize that it is okay to be nervous. We all have experienced match anxiety and nervousness at one time or another, especially in the individual sport of wrestling where it is so "hand-to-hand" and "one-on-one." Having sensations of freezing or your mind racing are common. You may feel out of control or tend to make bad choices. You may rush things or have feelings of negativity.

If you care about your performance, it is natural to worry. Knowing that being nervous is normal and common allows you to approach this in a "matter of fact" way. If you know that many great athletes tend to get nervous before a big event, then you can manage these feelings with confidence.

Getting a little nervous can actually help your performance. Why do you think there are so many records set at World or Olympic events? It is because athletes will use their nerves to push themselves to excellent performances. The nervousness your body experiences before the big event is a way of preparing yourself for the battle.

Second, learn to relax your mind and body. There are many exercises and activities that one can do to help relax. Deep breathing exercises, muscle relaxation techniques, centering, visualization and using affirmations are all ways to help one relax and keep cool.

Finally, the main secret in learning to deal with nervousness is to expect it. Remind yourself that it is not only a normal thing but a good thing, as well. With practice you can learn to make nervousness help you perform even better. It can help you concentrate more sharply, it can make you react faster, and it can give you more energy when you need it.

So, just like practicing a wrestling technique, practice dealing with nervousness in a positive way. Everyone has the "butterflies" from time to time; the trick is to get those "butterflies" to fly in formation.

As always, "Expect to Win with Relentless Intensity."

The Most Powerful Computer on the Planet!

Imagine for a moment that you are relaxing in your favorite lazy chair one afternoon and you fall asleep. You start dreaming about a magical coach that comes up to you and gives you a small computer device that he calls a success machine.

He tells you that this success machine will allow you to have all the success you could ever imagine in the sport of wrestling. But he warns you to be very careful. He tells you to read the owner's manual very thoroughly, for if you misuse it it can cause great failure and disappointment.

The magical coach then suddenly disappears and poof — you wake from your nap very disappointed, realizing that this was only a dream. Darn, it seemed so real! One minute you had the solutions to all of your problems and challenges and then the next moment, reality takes it all away from you.

Not true! The fact is that we already own this success machine. The success machine is in reality our "mind."

Unfortunately, our mind does not come with an owner's manual and that is one of the reasons it is often unused, misused, and abused. Most of us don't realize the great potential that is in the computer between our ears. We truly can achieve anything we want in our lives and, more specifically, in our wrestling careers if we take control of the most powerful computer on the planet — our "own mind."

Most people rationalize the success of others with thoughts like:

"They are gifted."

"They are a special case."

"They have all the right connections."

"They were in the right place, at the right time."

And most of all:

"They are just lucky."

What keeps most wrestlers from achieving the success they want is not the lack of a high I.Q., family history, level of education, race, age, or bad luck! <u>It is the way we think.</u>

Life is a game played between the ears. What we think determines the decisions we make. The decisions we make determine what we do, and what we do determines how successful we become. Change our thinking and we change our decisions. Change our decisions and we will change our behavior. Change our behavior and we will change our life. Unfortunately, a lot of wrestlers don't realize this, or they are just unwilling to change. A lot more people would be willing to change if they only realized the success and riches that come with this realization.

Of course, this leads us to the very important question: What kind of thinking does it take to become the best in wrestling? What kind of thinking does it take to become a city, state, national, world and Olympic champion?

This is the main question. The answer to the question is that you must develop a champion wrestler mindset. If you have a champion wrestler mindset, you will make more of the right decisions. If you make more of the right decisions, success will follow as surely as Tuesday follows Monday.

It is crucial that we believe "our present life is the result of the choices we have made in the past and our future life will be the result of the choices we make in the future." We are the sum of our choices. Becoming successful in wrestling begins with the understanding that we have total power in the hundreds of choices we make daily.

We all have what it takes to be the best. All we have to do is make good decisions each and every day. The most important decision that we will ever make is the choice to take control of our mind. What we choose to focus our mind on is critical because we will become what we think about most of the time. The late Earl Nightingale, one of the foremost success experts of the 20th Century, called this discovery the "Strangest Secret."

To quote some great philosophers and thinkers regarding this concept:

"A man is what he thinks about all day long." – Ralph Waldo Emerson

"We become what we contemplate." – Plato

"The mind is everything. What you think, you become." – Buddha

"As a man thinketh in his heart, so is he." – Proverbs 23:7

Whether you realize it or not, we create the life we live through our choices and our thoughts. If in our thoughts all day we think wrestling, then we will become wrestlers. If we think about how to become great wrestlers, then we will make better decisions, which will lead to better choices, which will lead to better wrestling behavior, which will lead to better wrestling results.

Most people think that life is something that just happens to them. They feel powerless when it comes to success. We must realize that this is not true! We create the life and success we have by the power of our thinking. We can be as successful as we can imagine and believe.

So let's not settle for anything less than being the very best we can be. Take control of your wrestling success machine. Realize life and your wrestling career are a self-fulfilling prophecy and as you think, so shall it be!

And remember – "Expect to Win!"

Staying Cool, Calm and Collected

Why do some wrestlers choke or get crazy with anger in adverse competitive situations and other wrestlers stay calm and focused on the job at hand? Why do some get negative emotion flowing and others remain positive?

In another article, I discussed what I think toughness is, and what it means in wrestling. It means "that no matter how difficult the situation – no matter what is happening either on or off the mat – you can generate positive emotion that allows you to get to your 'ideal competitive state' of being, the state of being where you are challenged, energized and excited about the fight."

Along with that you have the physical, mental and emotional strength of conditioning and discipline to bring you through. This is toughness in wrestling.

Toughness, however, can be sabotaged by negative emotional thoughts or responses. These can include the following:

1. Tanking – The act of quitting or giving up inside and/or making excuses.
2. Getting angry and negative.
3. Choking.

All of these negative responses tend to relieve the pain and fear that accompanies competitive adversity or failure. Quitting and/or giving up is the biggest example of "tanking." Excuse making and reducing your amount of effort is another common form of tanking. Subconsciously, some athletes tend to realize that if they reduce their emotional involvement it will reduce fear and nervousness during the match. Here are some specific examples of "tanking:"

1. "The ref keeps making bad calls, how can I possibly win?"
2. "My coach is a jerk; I'll never wrestle well with him around."
3. "I didn't really try today, otherwise I could beat him easily."
4. "I hate wrestling overseas. The food stinks, the hotel was bad and my time clock was off."
5. "My opponent cheated. That's why I lost."

Getting angry during the heat of the battle or after a loss is another form of negative emotional response to adversity. Like tanking, the anger response to competitive situations also acts as a protective mechanism for the wrestler. It can be used to protect one's self image.

As a coach, I have seen this happen many times to some of my athletes, as well as to others. Some very successful wrestlers tend to fall into this trap after they have experienced major accomplishments and now are struggling with what, in their mind, should be a lesser opponent. They forget that every match should be wrestled with the same challenged attitude that got them their previous victories.

Some accomplished wrestlers tend to think that now that they have succeeded, every opponent should just lie down for them and that every referee should give them all the close calls, always giving them the edge.

The moment you start thinking that things should always go your way is the time you are in trouble. You have to wrestle every match like you love it. Enjoying the competition of each match is what will keep you sharp and passionately into your career.

Anger can be directed in two directions — inward or outward. Inward means you get angry with yourself, saying such things as, "Boy, I am terrible," or "That was stupid, man, what an idiot I am." This inward anger is sure death for you.

The outward directed anger, I contend, is also in the long run detrimental to your performance. You may get away with it on occasion but, more likely than not, it will blow up in your face.

I believe to be at your best you must be having fun. Being angry all the time goes against the idea of enjoying the battle and living your career to its fullest.

Two great examples of being calm and focused in the face of competitive adversity come to mind:

1. **DAN GABLE:** In 1970, he lost the last match of his senior year, after winning 181 straight matches and going undefeated his entire high school and college career. I never had the privilege of speaking to Dan about what he was thinking after this historic defeat, but I did watch the video of his match with Larry Owings and saw how Dan reacted after the loss. He was calm, collected and respectful. He shook Larry Owings's hand and then went back to work at preparing to win his Olympic gold medal in 1972, when no one scored a single point on him.

2. **RULON GARDNER:** At the 2001 World Championships in Patras, Greece, he had to defend his historic Olympic gold medal performance when he beat the legendary Alexander Karelin from Russia. In Patras, he had the toughest draw of any weight class. The pressure was on! In the quarterfinals he met up with the new Russian superstar, Patrenkeev, who had beaten Rulon twice previously. It was an extremely intense match, with the whole wrestling world watching. With one minute remaining in the match, Rulon found himself down 0-3. Very calmly and with great focus, Rulon rose to the occasion. His continued and relentless attack on the Russian allowed Rulon to secure a good body lock where he then threw his foe through the air directly to his back – pinning him for the comeback victory. Rulon, of course, then went on to defeat his next two opponents and win the 2001 World Championships.

Tanking, anger and fear are all normal responses to the pressure of competition. Responding to crisis, adversity and pressure with a sense of challenge and love of the battle takes intense practice and should be the goal of all wrestlers who strive for the ultimate success. The true champions and leaders of our great sport have mastered this toughness skill that helps them to be champions not only in wrestling, but also in all aspects of their personal life.

Creating Positive Images, at Night

Often, I've wondered how an "average Joe" like myself from Hazel Park, Michigan, could win a gold medal at the Olympics. You have to realize something – when I first started wrestling I was terrible. I was the worst wrestler on the team. I was pathetic.

The reason I was able to have some success in this sport, and in some other areas of my life, was due to some common things. It takes a lot of hard work to succeed. I figure it took me approximately 16,000 hours to be good enough to compete at the world level. Now if you compute that into 40-hour work weeks, that comes out to about eight years. It takes hard work, dedication, and making certain sacrifices to be successful.

I want to share with you the one thing that helped me and can help all of us when we are trying to achieve whatever it is we're going after. The one thing that I believe can help you achieve your dreams is the simple act of goal-setting.

Now, when I talk about goal-setting, I'm talking about getting the pictures in our minds of exactly what it is we are trying to accomplish. And then taking it one step further and actually seeing ourselves accomplish these visions or pictures.

Right before I fell asleep at night, when I was in that nice, relaxed state of mind, I would lie in bed and I would visualize locking up that Russian wrestler and I'd throw him – a high spectacular throw right through the air to his back.

Or I might visualize what it would look and feel like to stand up on that award stand and have them place that gold medal around my neck. I might visualize the crowd cheering or the national anthem playing or the U.S. flag rising to the ceiling, as it does in the Olympics. And not only would I think about these things once or twice but I would go over and over in my mind what those images looked like until I could see them and they were etched clearly in my mind.

And sometimes that can be a difficult thing to do, because if you've never thrown that Russian or stood on that award stand you may not be sure what it looks like. But that's when I believe you use your creativity, your imagination and invent these pictures in your mind until you have a vision, have that picture. And what that does is it, in turn, helps you achieve it.

A famous author and motivator, Norman Vincent Peale, calls this process "positive imagery." Basically, it takes these positive thoughts and plants (inputs) them on our subconscious mind. Studies have shown that our subconscious mind can't tell the difference between what is real and what you have just imagined. It just takes whatever you put in there.

So, the idea is that you put in all these positive thoughts and you practice them on a regular basis and before long your subconscious mind helps you achieve them. Your subconscious mind helps you do all the little things right that help you get closer to achieving your goals. So set your goals; set them high and set many of them. Goal setting gives you the target to shoot for. I encourage you to shoot for the moon. Why not try to be the best that you can possibly be? See yourself climbing to the top and, believe me, you will get there!

Two Types of Goals

There are two types of goals. **Outcome goals** give you direction, such as winning a match or tournament. **Process goals** include mastering the mechanics and strategy of a particular move or tactic.

You dramatically increase your chances of taking your opponent down by focusing on the process and letting the outcome take care of itself. When you focus on the outcome, you open yourself up to the fear of poor execution or losing. If you have bad technique or make a mistake, it is easier to become angry.

Fear and anger are negative emotions that adversely affect your brain's chemistry and performance. You will be more relaxed and efficient by focusing on instinctive execution rather than thinking about scoring or winning.

While you may not be able to control the outcome, you can control your thoughts and actions to improve the process. Success in mastering the process builds confidence and makes it easier to achieve your desired outcome.

Chapter 3
Preparation

What Does It Take To Be the Best?

What does it take to be the best in the world? First, it takes desire. Desire is the catalyst that propels us forward. We must first really want success before we can achieve it. The difference between successful people and others is not the lack of strength, not the lack of knowledge, but rather the lack of will. The spirit, the will to win, and the will to excel are the things that really make the difference when it comes to succeeding.

After desire it takes a variety of other things for different people to achieve success. There are a few principles, though, that seem to fit into all successful plans. Here are my Top Ten principles of success:

1. **Dream Big! Have a Vision and Set Goals**

We all must start with a destination in mind. This helps us to stay focused on the results we desire. Like a good coach, good goal setting gives wrestlers an edge by providing direction, feedback and support. (A) Direction – Goals tell you where you need to go and how to get there. (B) Feedback – Goals tell you when you are making progress. (C) Support – Goals keep you going when you might otherwise give up.

And if you are going to go for something why not go all the way? Why not be the very best that you can be? Think big! Why settle for making a million dollars when you can make 100 million? Why settle for becoming city champ when you can become state champ or national champ or even Olympic champ? Shoot for the moon and even if you don't reach it you will end up in the stars!

2. **Plan a Relentless Execution**

All great accomplishments start with a plan of attack. The plan allows us to break the big picture down into little (more manageable) pieces. How do you eat an elephant? One piece at a time.

A good plan acts like a good road map. It helps to guide us to our destination. Doing a training schedule, where you are planning your practices and training routines, will be very helpful in showing you the way to the top.

3. **Use Time Effectively (Good Organized Time Management)**

Organizing your efforts is the key to training smart. Using good time management skills will advance your wrestling skills quickly and will keep your wrestling career on the move.

Great organization allows for effective use of your time. There are only 24 hours to each day, so the better you use this limited resource the better you will become. God gives all of us only a certain number of hours to live our lives. We choose how to use those hours. Choose wisely.

4. Track Continuous Evaluation of Progress

Things that are not tracked aren't usually considered important and will not be improved upon. This is why I always keep a training journal. Keeping a journal is probably one of the most effective ways to improve your training methods and help develop your overall plan.

Recording information about your training, such as food you eat, hours of sleep, training activity, how you feel, etc., can really help you to identify certain trends that can greatly effect how you feel during competition. This information can help you customize your training methods/plan and will make you very confident in your plan of attack.

Because every individual is different, it is especially important to find out what makes YOU feel fresh, hungry and powerful. This continuous tracking and evaluation of your wrestling career will help to advance your skills and knowledge tremendously.

5. Use Positive Thinking

A positive attitude helps to keep you focused on your mission. Having a positive attitude will help you to stay on track through the tough times. Negative thinking will undermine your efforts and will tend to make you feel that you are not able to achieve your goals. Plus, life is too short to not be positive and happy with your journey to the top.

6. Work Hard and Wrestle A Lot

Nothing makes up for hard work. If you spend a lot of time at something you tend to get very good at it. No athletes work harder than wrestlers but it is also important to work smart. The combination of working hard and smart is the key to success.

"Condition comes from hard work during practice and proper mental and moral conduct between practices." – John Wooden, legendary UCLA basketball coach.

7. Overcome Adversity

Overcoming problems, obstacles and hardship is what makes one become mentally tough and will build great confidence. Therefore, we must pit ourselves against the most tough, grueling problems that we can find and then overcome them. This practice of overcoming great problems helps us to strengthen our mind and spirit. Overcoming great adversity builds a mental toughness that will be unstoppable during the heat of the battle.

8. Believe You Can Do It

Believing in your plan and goal will get you through the hard times. Believing in yourself will help you to have the courage, determination, dedication and the competitive drive to achieve anything you set your mind to. Believing in yourself will help you to commit to the goal whole-heartedly.

9. Commit 100 Percent

One hundred percent commitment means you are totally into it. You want it "Oh, so bad!" and will do whatever it takes. A total fanatic!

VICTORY

Commitment to doing what it takes to succeed is really one of the most important attributes one can have. Committing means that you will think of your dream first before life pulls you in other directions. Committing means you will prioritize your daily actions ensuring that you focus on the tasks that will help you achieve your goals. To be the very best in the world you must fully commit to your dream.

10. **Have Fun!**

You need to have fun! Life is too short not to enjoy it along the way. Plus, if you enjoy what you are doing you will be better at it. Yes! You can train hard and have fun doing it.

In fact, still to this very day the thing that is most fun for me is getting a tremendous wrestling workout with some tough, young stud who is on his way to becoming the world's best wrestler. Leaving the wrestling room after a sweat-filled, completely exhausting physical battle is euphoric and extremely satisfying to me.

Acquiring this fun mindset – regarding a grueling workout being fun and enjoyable – took practice. Just like practicing a wrestling technique, you must practice enjoying the battle. Once you master the mindset of having fun with your training and overall wrestling career, you are on your way to becoming the best you can be.

The wrestler who is capable of generating great enthusiasm cannot be beat. Live your wrestling career with passion each and every day and your memories will be grand.

The Grind Match

It was the beginning of my sophomore year at the University of Michigan when Mark Churella started taking a bit of a liking to me. Mark, Michigan's only three-time NCAA champion, was a junior at the time. He was wrestling at 150 pounds and defending his first NCAA title, which he won in 1977.

I don't know exactly why he took a liking to me. We didn't talk to each other all that much, and we didn't have a whole lot in common. Mark was married and didn't hang with the guys too much socially. He was an extraordinary wrestler and I was pretty mediocre.

Maybe he took a liking to me because I was one of the only wrestlers in the Michigan wrestling room that would stay out on the mat and wrestle with him for as long as he demanded. No matter how long I took a beating from him I would just hang in there and keep wrestling.

I'll tell you one thing – Mark Churella could inflict a brutal beating. He was an expert leg wrestler and seemed to explode with excitement when his opponent would wince in pain. I was 190 pounds and he would beat the living tar out of me for one to two hours straight without a break. I was so impressed and honored that he picked me to go with him that I would not allow myself to think about quitting or asking for a break.

Thus, my introduction to the "Grind Match." Do you want to get tougher fast? Do you want to develop your technique in a hurry? Do you want to condition your mind and body to their maximum? Then consider implementing grind matches into your training regimen.

What is a grind match? The grind match is a continuous wrestling match that lasts one to two hours in length. It is a live wrestling activity where the score is not as important as some of the other benefits one gains when completing this exercise.

What are the rules? It is simple. Keep wrestling, non-stop, for the entire, pre-determined time. Absolutely no stopping is allowed. No sitting on the sidelines for a minute to catch your breath. No going to the drinking fountain two or three times for a water break. No lengthy tying of your shoe or adjusting your shorts. Wrestling takes place continuously on your feet as well as in parterre or mat position. The time the wrestler takes on top in parterre is totally up to the guy on top. Walls, if padded, are in-bounds (maybe even if not padded).

What is the goal? The main goal is to try and break your opponent's physical or mental limit (or perceived limit). The objective is to make him quit. Force him to take a break. Of course, if and when this occurs, you must immediately grab another partner and continue your grind.

It is great to have a partner like Mark who wouldn't think of stopping but it's also fun to try and break two or even three wrestlers during one grind match session. Only when you actually break someone can you feel what it is like. This feeling is tremendous. It inspires you to want to do it again, but this time sooner. Before long you are breaking wrestlers in less and less time.

What are the benefits? This long grind match helps to develop many wrestling attributes. First of all, it helps develop an overall base conditioning that one needs to establish a solid foundation. It will develop tough mental, as well as tough physical, conditioning. It will help to develop that "in-your-face" constant attack. It will improve the rhythm and fluid movement of your style. It will help teach you to relax and then explode. Your chain-wrestling skills will improve, and you will learn to keep moving, no matter what happens. And, most of all, you will learn how to break your opponent's will to fight.

What actually happens in a grind match? Normally when we wrestle, we tend to be very rigid in our stance and movement. It is not until we have wrestled to the point of exhaustion that our bodies are forced to relax. This is where the average wrestler stops and takes a break.

Instead of stopping, continue to wrestle but focus on relaxing yet staying in good, solid position. From this position, work on exploding with technique and movement. Training your body to explode from this relaxed state will increase your effectiveness.

Mark Churella and the "grind match" are two reasons why I was able to get reasonably good at the sport of wrestling. I encourage you to find *your* Mark Churella and grind away. I'm confident you'll get great results.

Expect The Unexpected

Wrestlers should always try and develop a consistent approach to competition and performance, but don't think that things will always go smoothly. Expecting the unexpected should be a big part of one's preparation. Things happen…. especially in tough competition. Things occur that force you to change your thinking or your actions. This is not only in sport but also in life.

I once knew of a state champion wrestler in high school who always listened to his favorite music tape in preparation for his matches. Believe it or not, it was the "Rocky" theme song. One day, before the league championship, he arrived at the competition site and realized that he had forgotten his tape. For a moment, I noticed that he was panicking. He tried to call his mother in hopes that she could bring it with her when she came but he could not get her on the phone.

Fortunately, he got hold of himself and decided that he could compromise. He found a quiet spot in the gym where he would usually listen to his tape but this time he closed his eyes and started humming the song in his head. Later, he told me this was even more effective than listening to his tape. As he closed his eyes and hummed he said he visualized scenes from the "Rocky" movie and this inspired and focused him even more. He ended up winning the league championship that day.

The lesson I have learned from many such incidents is to anticipate problems in your quest for success. No matter how well you prepare, it seems like something always happens to throw you off balance. The way to deal with this is to prepare for the unexpected. Use this strategy in your everyday preparation plan. Think about some of the "what if" scenarios and imagine how to handle them.

For example, say you always cut weight the day of weigh-in by using a stationary bike. This has been your routine and you are very comfortable with this method. As a part of your preparation, practice cutting weight without a stationary bike. Maybe use a jump rope and another wrestler to help you shed those last few pounds. Especially overseas, there are many occasions where stationary bikes are not available and you have to compromise.

Have you ever been at a tournament where you thought you would be wrestling later in the morning, but as you were sitting there on the bleachers, taking your good old time lacing up your shoes, they called you up immediately to mat one for your match? No time to warm up, no time to mentally prepare, no time to go to the bathroom. What do you do?

Well, if you have *prepared for the unexpected* during your preparation, then no problem. You simply adjust your thinking, take a few moments to loosen up your main joints, and you go out focused and ready to wrestle. This is why in training you should set yourself up in difficult or unexpected situations and practice dealing with them. Then, when the unexpected happens to you in real-life situations, you flex and go.

If you are versed in some of the problems that can occur then you will be less apt to be surprised or flustered when something unexpected actually happens.

Being able to flex and alter your routine or normal method of operation is critical in increasing your ability to wrestle at your peak performance every time. Having a resilient attitude, especially under high-pressure situations, is the key to maximizing your "Ideal Competitive State." As I have written about many times in the past, your "Ideal Competitive State" is the personal state of mind and body that you operate in with the most potential for peak performance.

I would like to share one last example of the power of being prepared for the unexpected. It was in the Summer Olympic Games in 1992, in the sport of gymnastics. American Trent Dimas was preparing to begin his rings routine in the men's competition when the event was delayed. The judges were discussing the correct score for a previous event. Dimas was delayed for several minutes, which is highly unusual.

Many athletes who experience such an unexpected delay might begin to get nervous or even panic. They might start to think about all of the things that could go wrong. They might tense up and perform poorly.

But instead of getting nervous and distracted by the delay, Dimas closed his eyes and rehearsed the somersaults and special moves he was about to perform. The television cameras showed viewers across the country Dimas's head and body movements as he visualized his entire routine. Then when it was time for Dimas to begin, he moved into position and began an unexpected, flawless routine. He ended up winning the gold medal, much to the delight of the many American viewers.

Obviously, Dimas and his coach had prepared for the unexpected situations that can occur in sport. You can too. Maybe you can't predict every possible obstacle that you may encounter but you can prepare how you will react to obstacles. You can practice what your attitude will be when faced with these inconveniences or problems. If you are willing to rehearse these many situations it will allow for you to react in a more positive and planned way.

Developing the mindset that "nothing can rattle you" will allow you to perform in a consistent and effective way. By creating a plan for the unexpected and practicing how you will deal with the unexpected, it will enhance your ability to wrestle at your full potential.

Legendary football coach Paul "Bear" Bryant once said, "Have a plan for everything. A plan for practice, a plan for the game. I try to have a plan and the guts to stick with it no matter what happens."

Even in high-pressure situations, when many wrestlers find it tough to perform at their peak, you will perform superbly if you stick to your game plan for success. People will marvel at how strong your confidence is. So, expect the unexpected as you plan your work, and work your plan.

"Expect To Win."

Build a Team of Mentors and Coaches

A single conversation across the table with a wise man is worth a month's study of books. – Chinese Proverb.

The dictionary defines the word mentor as "a wise and trusted counselor or teacher." Another common definition is "a coach."

Many successful people achieve success by surrounding themselves with mentors and coaches. This article addresses the importance of seeking out and building relationships with mentors and coaches in your wrestling life. For the sake of simplicity, I will refer to the mentor as a coach, but realize that mentors come in all forms and may not always be a coach.

A coach can give us perspective. We wrestlers are often caught up in the emotions of trying to improve and win in our wrestling careers. We are often too close to the action to really see the big picture. Emotions – fear, excitement, anxiety, confusion, disappointment and frustration – can often cloud a wrestler's perspective and overwhelm them.

Coaches can detach themselves from the emotion and see the athlete and situation from a distance, thus giving them a better view of what is really happening and what needs to be done. Coaches give us the wisdom of a lifetime of experience, saving us many hours of trial and error.

A coach can give us proficiency. Proficiency is the way we train and learn new techniques and strategies. The coach can fill in the gaps of knowledge. They can help us to understand complicated situations and issues. A coach can save us a lot of time and energy. In short, they can help us take a short cut and speed up our journey to the top.

A coach can help us learn patience. It takes patience to get to the top of any field. Wrestling is no different. To be the best in wrestling it takes patience – patience which allows us to stay committed and focused for a long enough time to make good things happen. Learning a new skill always requires some learning curve. A good coach helps us to struggle through the frustrations of learning new techniques and skills. A good coach helps us to struggle through failures and set backs, failures and setbacks that are inevitable in anyone's quest for success.

Most successful wrestlers have had good mentors and/or coaches. Personally, I have had numerous mentors, coaches and role models that have proven invaluable throughout my wrestling career.

There are many kinds of mentors and they are everywhere! If you are open and teachable, each person you meet could potentially teach you something to help advance your wrestling career. Every encounter you make, no matter how trivial, has the potential to be a positive learning experience. Accidental mentorship happens every day for the people who are open to learning.

Mentors can be coaches or training partners but they can also show up in many other forms. Parents, aunts, uncles, sisters, brothers, friends and, yes, even enemies can be great mentors. Some relationships may last for years, others may only last for minutes. Some just show up out of the blue and some you may have to seek out.

Mike DeGain, now a very successful high school wrestling coach in Clarkston, Michigan, was one of my first great training partners/mentors. When I was a junior in high school, Mike was already a state champion. I searched Mike out and started training with him throughout the spring and summer.

Mike was much better than I was when we first started training together. I tried to absorb all I could from this accomplished wrestler. I studied his style, learned the techniques he knew, trained like he did and sought out his wrestling secrets. By the end of the summer I had improved immensely!

Mark Churella, a three-time NCAA champion at the University of Michigan, was my biggest mentor. In college, Mark and I trained together daily. Mark was a tenacious wrestler who would try to tear his opponents from limb to limb. He pinned more NCAA champions than I can count.

With Mark, I tried to absorb his entire body of information. I tried to meet all of his wrestling training partners and friends. I studied every aspect of him, from the technique he used to the way he trained. I learned his intense style, his tenacity, his motivation and his discipline. I learned to think like he thought and do what he did to obtain the results that he obtained.

On your journey between where you are now and where you want to go, there will be many points along the way that will require mentorship and coaching. It may be dealing with an issue in the area of your attitude, a technique, a tactic, a strategy or a habit. Often this will require a hands-on, in-the-trenches kind of mentor or coach.

Most wrestlers will have a coach that they can consult with, but sometimes you may want to solicit a new perspective in order to get another opinion or viewpoint. Some of you may not have a person capable of filling this role in your life. If this is the case you must seek him or her out. How do you go about finding a mentor?

1. List specific issues you need to address – the areas of your wrestling that need improvement so when you approach a potential mentor you have a clear, concise idea of what you are asking for.
2. List missing resources necessary to achieving your goals – coaches, training partners, videos, books, magazines etc.
3. Network with your own circle of contacts. You probably know someone who knows someone that can help you with the answers you need on issues you have.
4. Have a bold and open attitude about finding solutions to your needs. Do not be bashful about asking for help.
5. Widen your search for help. Do not be afraid of traveling some distance to get specific mentorship, coaching or training. I used to drive two and a half hours almost every weekend for a couple of years to get additional training and coaching from some other experienced wrestlers and coaches.

Please be advised… you are seeking more than specific answers to your problems. You want to establish great mentoring relationships, relationships with people who can coach you to success. But remember, many of the potential mentors are very goal-oriented, busy people themselves so respect whatever time and resources they may be able to share with you.

Another source can be found in your heroes, your champions and your role models. Your heroes may or may not be accessible, but still can be a great source of inspiration and learning. Become an avid student of their lives and their teachings. Access their courage, wisdom and insight through alternate means. Read their biographies and autobiographies. Watch the documentaries that chronicle their lives. You will learn that most successful people's lives have been full of challenges and setbacks that were overcome through commitment, persistence and focus.

Most successful people will tell you that they could not have done it alone. They had a great support team helping them achieve their goals. A support team includes family, friends, coaches, training partners, advisors, role models, etc. I encourage you to build your own personal "team" of supporters who you can count on for help, a team of experts and non-experts that will enhance your learning process and accelerate your career.

See you at the top!

Be Ready for the Main Event

The high school state championships and NCAA tournaments are an exciting time for all wrestlers who will compete for the prestigious title of state champion or NCAA champion. This is the time to get your mind and body feeling hungry for the battle which lays ahead.

Think back to your competitions the past few years. Remember the tournament or match at which you really felt great – where you were hitting on all cylinders, feeling powerful, fast and smooth! Did you taper your workouts before that event? How did you prepare your body and mind for the big match?

Now is the time to search your personal journal for answers to these questions:
- What activity did you do to make weight?
- How was your diet? What foods were you eating?
- What about your sleep, were you getting eight hours a night, more or less?
- Were your wrestling and running workouts short in duration and high in intensity?
- What routine made your body and mind feel invincible? Do you need to make any adjustments?

Being fully recovered before the battle is of critical importance. You trained extremely hard over the past year. Now with just a couple weeks before the big event it is time to reduce the physical and emotional stress. This needs to be done no matter how talented, skilled, physically fit or mentally tough you are. If you are not recovered sufficiently to meet the energy demands of competition, you'll make it more difficult for yourself.

Choose your recovery techniques carefully. Disciplined wrestlers will follow sensible rules regarding sleep, diet and rest. Undisciplined wrestlers, who veer off from their recovery habits, will tend to break under pressure. In other words, they will crack first. Disciplined athletes with the same ability as their undisciplined opponents will usually win.

Remember, you are more likely to perform at your peak when you feel:

Confident, relaxed and calm, energized with positive emotion, challenged, focused and alert, automatic and instinctive, and ready for fun and enjoyment. This is where your thinking, visualizing and acting skills can really enhance your ideal competitive state. No matter what your real state of mind is, you must use all your power to create these positive, performance-enhancing emotions. Be ready to play the hand you are dealt and do what you have to do to succeed. Focus on great execution of your technique, match strategy and plan. Keep the pressure on your opponent and break his will to fight.

Polish your tough-acting skills, focus on your competition goals and pay attention to your pre-tournament rituals. Understand how everything is interconnected. Sleep, diet, fitness, free time, tough acting and emotional toughness are all interrelated.

Dream about becoming a state or NCAA champion. There is no better time than right now. But treat it just like another tournament.

Even the most elite competitors and coaches can get caught up in the hype of the state championships or NCAAs. It is the big event which so many have been dreaming about. For many coaches and athletes the pressures of the tournament can produce feelings and behaviors which haven't surfaced in quite a while. Some first-time state championship or NCAA competitors may experience feelings which are similar to the feelings they had when they just started out in sports – thinking too much, worrying about the results and being distracted by stupid stuff.

At the United States Olympic Committee High Performance Summit, held in 1996, coaches discussed factors which have interfered with athletic performances in recent Olympic Games. Many of these factors also interfere with the performance of younger athletes facing other high-level competition for the first time. Recognizing, understanding and handling these factors is important for coaches at all levels. Many issues were discussed, but the main issue which I think is relevant to high school coaches, college coaches and athletes is as follows:

Big-event situations such as the state championships or the NCAAs may cause some coaches and athletes to think their normal way of preparing is somehow inadequate. This thinking can result in a tendency to stray from approaches which have been successful for past competitions. There are three harmful attitudes which might develop in big events:

(1) A feeling that the performance has to be perfect because it is the state or NCAA championships. Athletes who tend to be perfectionists may be pushed to new heights of over-thinking, over-correction and over-analysis.

(2) A focus on not losing or not looking bad instead of focusing on winning. The knowledge that thousands of people state or nation-wide may be watching can result in a less confident athlete who worries about messing up. This usually results in an athlete who is unable to take the risks necessary to succeed in elite sporting events.

(3) A tendency to "save" for later or final rounds. Occasionally, overconfident athletes, too focused on winning a medal, will outsmart themselves by saving something for later. These athletes are often upset in preliminary competition.

And here are some messages for the coaches to keep in mind: Anticipate changes in your athlete's thinking and stress the importance of consistency. Emphasize to your athletes that they need to do what got them to this championship. Try to shift focus from only the outcome to excellent execution. Don't allow your thinking to change. Do not change the way you coach. Two common coaching errors are as follows:
- Coaching too much, not wanting anything left unsaid which may make a difference.
- Being afraid to coach, not wanting to say something which messes up the athlete.

Athletes notice behavior changes and they can worry that these behavior changes are due to a lack of confidence on the coach's part. As a coach, you need to trust yourself since you must have done something right to get your wrestlers to this point.

Coaches taking wrestlers to a new level of competition should remember most athletes are surprised by their reaction to the big event and they are often nervous about being nervous. By anticipating these new behaviors and attitudes, you can let your athletes know those are common feelings. Discuss them ahead of time and teach athletes how to respond to get the best results in big competition.

Expect to win and have some fun!

Periodization: The Art of Peaking

All athletes want to maximize their success by being at their best when it is most important. We all want to wrestle to our fullest capacity when it counts. Whether it is the city championship, state championship, national championship or the world championship, we want to be at our peak. Understanding training cycles and periodization is critical in helping us get our minds and bodies ready to perform at the very best level.

Periodization may sound like a complicated, scientific word; however, all athletes and coaches must understand what it means and how it works. By following sound periodization principles, athletes will not only learn how to peak when it counts, but they will also learn how to avoid over- and under-training as well as reducing the risk for injury.

The simple definition of periodization is – "a long-term training plan, which is designed to optimize your chances to perform at your peak, when it most counts." It involves alternating periods of stress with periods of recovery in a strategic and planned-out manner.

The idea is that you properly balance episodes of physical, mental and emotional stress with the same episodes of physical, mental and emotional rest. It is the balance of this type of training that allows for an athlete to maximize his or her peak potential. Again, by following a good periodization plan, you will reduce the risk of injury, burnout, feeling stale and poor performance.

The concept of periodization came many years ago from the former Soviet and Eastern Block athletic programs. A lot of their Olympic success in a variety of sports was attributed to understanding and applying the principles of periodization. Now, most all countries involved in sport practice some sort of periodization plan.

In his book, *The New Toughness Training for Sports,* author James E. Loehr states that periodization is an organized plan for implementing the following training principles:

1. **Adaptation** – This is the process your body goes through to get stronger and tougher. This is where your body becomes more resilient. It is the time when your body actually improves. The stimulus for adaptation is training stress.

2. **Frequency** – This term refers to how often you should apply specific training activity; how many times a week or a day should you apply training stress.

3. **Intensity** – This refers to how hard you should be working. What intensity level is being applied? How much weight should you be lifting, how fast should you be running, how intense should you be wrestling? What percent of maximum effort should you be exerting?

4. **Specificity** – This involves training activity that closely simulates your actual event. It is the specific movements and actual demands of the competition. Generally speaking as you get nearer to your main event you would focus more on the specificity of your training.

5. **Variety** – This refers to changing the pace and activity in your training. It involves altering your training routines, which will usually lend itself to better recovery and less staleness and boredom.

6. **Recovery** – This refers to how much time you should allow for adaptation and growth. At this time of year, considering the frequency, intensity and duration of your training regimen, how much time should you schedule for rest and recovery?

In wrestling, I like to follow a periodization plan that involves three main training cycles or phases. The first cycle is called the conditioning phase. The second cycle is called the preparation phase. The third cycle is called the competition phase.

The **conditioning phase** takes place in the pre-season. Looking at a high school or college program, this may be in the months of October, November and early December.

In this training phase, the focus should be on learning new skills and perfecting favorite skills. The intensity level of your training activity should be on the lower side. The duration of practice should be on the longer side. The wrestling practice could be two or two and a half hours long. This is a good time to wrestle grind matches (one- to two-hour straight wrestling matches with no stopping). Running should be of longer distance. Weightlifting should include power lifting (heavier weights with lower reps).

In the **preparation phase** (end of December and January), generally speaking you would start to transition from lower intensity to higher intensity activity. The duration of your practice time should start to decrease maybe from two and a half hours to one and a half hours. The wrestling activity should start to increase on the intensity level. More "situation" goes, more matches, more fast-wrestling activity. Your running should transition from distance to intermediate running (shorter and faster). Weightlifting should change from power lifts to more circuit type lifting (lighter weight with more reps).

The **competition phase** (February and March, depending when your state or national tournaments are) is the highest intensity focus. Wrestling activity should be at its highest level. The focus should be on very fast and intense wrestling. A lot of regular matches, micro matches and pummel matches. The duration of practice should decrease to 45 minutes or an hour. In and out of the wrestling room is better. Short and sweet practices would be the focus. Running should be sprints only. I personally like sprint/jogs because there is less risk in pulling a hamstring if you are not starting your sprint from a dead stop. And by the way, protecting from injury is one of the main goals in this phase. Weightlifting in this phase is optional; however, if one wants to continue lifting in this period, the lifting should be lighter weights (circuit training/maintenance).

The main idea in this final training phase is to increase the intensity level to the extreme, but at the same time decrease the length of practice so as to refresh the mind. The goal is to feel hungry for the competition. The athlete should feel refreshed and anxious to compete. Time should be spent only on the wrestler's individual strengths and skills. Strategy and tactics should be emphasized. Staying healthy and getting the proper sleep is very important too.

The last 10 days before your desired peak should be very individual and flexible. As a general rule, rest is better than activity, especially wrestling activity. Wrestlers should pay attention to issues such as diet, sleep, naps, fun, relaxation and recovery. The days immediately preceding competition should be less demanding and less stressful, both physically and emotionally. You want to enter the peaking phase well recovered, rested, eager, enthusiastic, healthy, motivated and confident.

Training with a good periodization method in mind requires more planning, more discipline and more thought than simply doing whatever comes to mind at the time. Peaking your mind and body is no easy task and rarely occurs by accident when you need it most. By designing a good, year-long training plan, it will help you to prepare for the most important events in your season and will reduce the risk of injury, burnout and boredom.

Most athletes and coaches find that following a good periodization program makes all the difference in the world when it comes to moving forward with one's progress. It is the key to having more great performances when you most want them.

Expect to Win!

Rulon Gardner made Olympic wrestling history by defeating the Russian super star, Alexander Karelin in the 2000 Sydney Olympic Games. He etched his name in the chronicles of world sport by achieving this spectacular feat. Rulon did it! He did the unthinkable. He beat the guy that no one thought could be defeated. And, he did it to win the most honored medal there is, the Olympic gold!

How did this average kid from Afton, Wyoming, who grew up on a farm among his eight brothers and sisters, grow to this magnitude? How could this boy, who was picked on and ridiculed most of his young life, develop into one of the toughest wrestlers on the planet? How could Rulon Gardner possibly achieve this great wrestling status?

Our U.S. national Greco-Roman wrestling team went from basic obscurity 10 to 15 years ago to being the second-best team in the world. When comparing Olympic medals over the past three Olympic Games, our U.S. Olympic Greco squads have won seven Olympic medals in the Atlanta, Sydney and the Athens Olympic Games combined. We are second in the medal count only to Russia, which has won eleven. All other countries in the world have won five, four, three or less Olympic medals. How could our U.S. Greco wrestling team do this?

Besides Rulon Gardner, in my tenure as national coach for USA Wrestling, we have had six other medalists win world or Olympic medals. These world and Olympic medalists are: Brandon Paulson (Olympic silver, world silver); Dennis Hall (Olympic silver, world gold and bronze); Matt Ghaffari (Olympic silver, two-time world silver and world bronze); Garrett Lowney (Olympic bronze); Matt Lindland (Olympic silver and world silver); and Dremiel Byers (world champion). How could these guys do this in Greco-Roman wrestling when our country's developmental system is geared toward folk/freestyle?

I think most of these guys would admit they were average kids growing up, with no special talent as sportsmen or wrestlers.

The challenges that we are faced with in the U.S. with our Greco-Roman program are enormous. We are competing against powerful countries that train their Greco-Roman wrestlers from the age of five, as opposed to most of our past medalists who were only able to focus on the style of Greco-Roman for a few years.

When I first started wrestling in the eighth grade I was terrible. I was the worst wrestler on my Webb Junior High School team. I too was a very average kid from a little city called Hazel Park, Mich., a north suburb of Detroit. However, most of my life I have searched for the secrets of success and have studied greatness and accomplished people.

Besides being blessed with great mentors and coaches, for many years I have read personal development books, listened to audio tapes, attended personal achievement seminars and heard keynote speakers. I have always been fascinated by the principles of success and by the people that were able to achieve greatness in their particular fields or areas of life.

As the National Greco coach for the past 10 years and through my experiences in becoming an Olympic gold medalist, I have learned a lot about what it takes to be successful in wrestling and in life.

So, what does it take to be successful and to accomplish greatness? My nine principles to success in sports and life are as follows:

1. Desire
2. Hard Work
3. Setting Goals/Vision
4. Having A Plan of Attack
5. Commitment
6. Discipline
7. Toughness
8. Overcoming Adversity
9. Believing in Ourselves

Desire ... The first question we must ask of ourselves is, "How bad do we want it?" The answer is, "We must really want it bad!" We have got to dream about our success. Desire is the catalyst that propels us forward. We must first really want success before we can achieve it. Having the will to win and the will to excel are the things that really make the difference when it comes to succeeding.

Hard Work ... I look back on my career and calculated that it took me approximately 16,000 hours of training to become good enough to compete at a world level. I trained for over 13 years with one purpose in mind and that was to be the very best I could be in the sport of wrestling. However, even though I worked very hard I always tried to make it fun. Life is too short to not enjoy it every step of the way. Plus, I believe if you are having fun you will perform better.

The Olympic Games are serious business these days. There is great pressure to win at this level. However, as national coach, I try to make our very tough and intense training regimen fun for our athletes.

Is it possible to make hard work fun? I believe it is! It is all in our attitude. In fact, for me to this day the most fun thing that I like to do is get a great wrestling workout where I leave the practice room drenched with sweat, completely exhausted, sore from the battle. Call me crazy, but this is true. I have learned through the years to enjoy the battle and the harder I work the more I enjoy it.

Setting Goals/Vision ... Setting goals and creating a vision of what we want to accomplish is vital to our success. We must start with a destination in mind. This helps us to stay focused on the results we desire. Goals give us our direction. They give us feedback and a way to monitor how we are doing. Goals give us support which helps to keep us going in tough times. But how do we stay focused on our goals when we get pulled on by so many people and in so many different directions?

One way is to use the skill of visualization. I would do this by lying in bed at night. Right before I would fall asleep, when I was in a nice, relaxed state of mind is when I would visualize how it would look like to be locking up that Russian wrestler and throwing him in a high spectacular throw through the air and onto his back. Or I would visualize how it would look like to stand on the top of the awards podium at the Olympics. I would see them draping the gold medal around my neck. I would hear the national anthem playing and the crowd cheering. I would see the United States flag rising to the ceiling like it does at the Olympic Games.

I wouldn't just think about these things once or twice, I would visualize these images over and over in my mind until I could actually see myself accomplishing these goals.

Dr. Norman Vincent Peale, who was a famous writer who authored many books about positive thinking, terms this principle as positive imaging. He claims that we can organize the positive thoughts about ourselves in a way that programs our subconscious. Peale goes on to say that our subconscious cannot tell the difference between what reality is and what is imagined. Our subconscious just takes in anything we put in there. By programming our mind with these successful images, our mind will in turn help us achieve these things. Our mind will help us do all the little things correctly that in turn help us to succeed.

Our minds are very powerful. There have been studies to show we only use a small percentage of our mind's capacity. Probably the most important decision we can make in our lives is to take total control of our mind's power. Here are a few quotes that refer to our mind's power:

"A man is what he thinks about all day long" – Ralph Waldo Emerson

"Our life is what our thoughts make it" – Marcus Aurelius

"We become what we contemplate" – Plato

"The mind is everything; what you think, you become" – Buddha

"As a man thinketh in his heart, so is he" – Proverbs 23:7

Having A Plan of Attack ... We must design our strategy and organize our plan. We must seek out great coaches and mentors and model ourselves after these successful people. Our plan of attack is our road map to success. Having a great plan which involves great coaches and mentors will direct us toward our ultimate destination.

Commitment ... We must commit to our plan each and every day. We must strive to get better each and every day as well. The whole world is getting better. We have got to advance continuously or we will be left behind.

Take the NFL, for example, 15 years ago a 230 pound linebacker was considered big. These days linebackers are weighing in at 270 pounds. NFL players are getting stronger and faster every year. The same with the NBA, a short point guard these days is 6'5" verses 15 years ago when the average height was below 6 feet tall. In the world of wrestling there are more countries winning medals all the time. The entire world is getting better every day. We must commit to this as well.

Discipline ... We must have the discipline to act and stay focused on our dreams. Having strong discipline is essential in keeping us on track with the tasks at hand.

Toughness ... We have got to practice being tough physically, mentally, and emotionally. I don't care what sport we participate in or if we are in business, we have got to be tough! Why? Because when adversity strikes, AND IT WILL, we will need toughness to overcome it. Toughness means that we will be able to overcome any obstacle that gets in our way.

Does anyone actually think that one can achieve greatness at something without experiencing the most agonizing, excruciating, painful problems and set-backs? No Way! I have NEVER seen it. Never in wrestling, business or sport! We have got to be tough so we can fight through these frustrations.

Overcoming Adversity ... We have got to be willing to meet adversity head on and overcome it! If we are afraid of making mistakes, stumbling or experiencing setbacks, then we will inch ahead cautiously, not ever really letting go of our fears. It is our fear of failure that holds us back. We must realize that obstacles and adversity are a part of success. In fact, the act of overcoming agonizing, excruciating, painful problems is actually what makes us tough!

Believing in Ourselves ... Believing in ourselves is very important in our quest for glory. Believing will help us to get through rough times and difficult situations. Don't get me wrong, we all have doubts about ourselves at times. This is natural. However, we must understand that "believing" plays a vital role in our performance and advancement.

My favorite example of someone who had strong belief in himself was Muhammad Ali in the 1974 World Heavyweight Boxing Championship, "Rumble in the Jungle." Ali was challenging George Foreman, who was the reigning World Heavyweight Champion. George Foreman was crushing all of his opponents. He knocked out most of the top contenders prior to this big event in Zaire, Africa. No one thought that Ali could beat Foreman. In fact, even his own trainers and coaches thought that Ali was going to get destroyed against the seemingly unstoppable Foreman.

As described in the documentary, "When We Were Kings," before the fight, Ali's dressing room was like a morgue. It was like Ali was going to his "last supper." At one point Ali noticed that everyone was down and sad. Ali turned and said, "What is the matter with you people? Why is everybody so unhappy?"

They, his support team, believed that Ali was going to be defeated. And, they were terrified. They thought with his pride that he would take one of the world's worst beatings ever and he would not give up. They thought that Ali would be destroyed in the ring. They thought he would even possibly be killed. They were deeply frightened.

Then Ali looked to Drew "Bundini" Brown (his trainer) and said, "We're gonna dance, we're gonna dance and dance!" Then he turned to them and said "What are we gonna do?" And they said "You're gonna dance, you're gonna dance and dance!" Ali chanted, "We're gonna dance tonight, aren't we...and Foreman...he is going to be bewildered!" Ali repeated this over and over until his dressing room of trainers and support team members were crying. And with that Ali built them up so as to make them half happy.

The atmosphere at the beginning of the fight was as intense as ever before a championship bout. Ali was expected to dance, however, at the start of the first round Ali didn't dance. He came at Foreman with a different strategy. He threw 12 right hand leads in that first round, trying to knock Foreman down or out. But instead of knocking Foreman down or out, Foreman went crazy. He started throwing powerful punches, over and over again, a lot of them connecting with Ali.

The bell rang ending the first round. Ali went to his corner. The nightmare that had awaited Ali finally came to visit. Ali was in the ring with a man that he could not dominate. He was in the ring with a man who was stronger, not afraid, determined, and could punch harder and was unstoppable.

Ali had a look on his face that for the first time showed fear. Then as he stood there catching his breath, you could see him look into himself and he seemed to be thinking, "This is the moment you've been waiting for. It is that hour." He seemed to be thinking, "Do you have the guts, boy?" Then he nodded his head, seemingly saying to himself, "You have got to get it together. You ARE going to get it together. You WILL get it together." And as he continued to nod and nod to himself, as if he was looking into the eyes of his maker he turned to the crowd and chanted "Ali boma ye!" which means "Ali, kill him!" And the crowd started chanting "Ali boma ye!, Ali boma ye!" and Ali went back out in the ring as if he had new focus and energy and picked up the pace.

The next four rounds George Foreman, with his powerful punches, continued to wallop and bash at Ali as Ali went to the rope-a-dope. Foreman hit Ali time and time again with tremendous blows to Ali's body and head. Again and again Foreman pummeled Ali against the ropes. Ali was bobbing and weaving taking most of the powerful punches and sliding a few. As Foreman whacked ferociously at Ali, Ali kept talking to him, "George, you're not hitting hard enough. I thought you hit harder. George you are not even breaking popcorn." As Ali kept taunting him, George continued to slug at him. By the end of the fifth round George Foreman had punched himself out. It took five rounds for George to tire himself out.

Then in the eighth round, Muhammad Ali spun Foreman around in the ring and threw a combination of punches which, in a spectacular fashion, knocked Foreman down and out!

Ali was world heavyweight champion again!

I think this is one of the ultimate examples of a man who had to believe in himself. When no one else did, he still believed.

It is really not important that Rulon Gardner beat Alexander Karelin or that Muhammad Ali knocked out George Foreman or that Steve Fraser made his dream come true. What IS important is that YOU can make your dream come true. You can achieve anything you want in this life.

Have the attitude "expect to win." Set your goals high and see yourself winning. Enjoy the battle and the journey along the way. Get tough and make it fun, and you WILL get to the top in wrestling and in life!

How Jet Lag Can Be a Big Negative

There is a clear relationship between sleep and human performance. NASA, the aerospace industry, the U.S. Department of Transportation, thousands of physicians, and 100 years of scientific research support the conclusion that significantly-disturbed sleep can have adverse effects on human performance. Anecdotal reports from athletes and research on athletes have also supported this view.

The timing of the sleep/wake cycle, and many other biologic processes, is regulated by a biologic clock located in the brain. When we rapidly cross time zones in airplanes, the biologic clock cannot readjust quickly enough. As the body clock scrambles to catch-up, the timing of our biologic process becomes disrupted and we feel the symptoms identified as "jet lag" including:

- fatigue
- excessive sleepiness
- disorientation
- lightheadedness
- loss of appetite
- gastrointestinal disturbance
- insomnia
- difficulty concentrating

The severity of jet lag is dependent upon several things: the number of time zones crossed, the direction traveled (east or west), and individual susceptibility (some people are more severely affected than others). For example, you may not notice any symptoms after crossing one or two time zones, but you will certainly have some jet lag after crossing 12 time zones.

Jet lag does not occur if you stay within the same time zone because you do not need to readjust your biologic clock. However, other unpleasant consequences of travel – such as dehydration, stress and muscle soreness/stiffness – can still occur.

Jet lag often causes sleep deprivation and circadian rhythm (body clock) disruption. These, in turn, may lead to adverse consequences that may affect athletic ability such as:

- prolonged reaction time
- decreased short term memory
- decreased concentration
- reductions in anaerobic power and capacity
- increased accident and injury rates
- reduced dynamic strength
- decreased alertness
- cognitive slowing

VICTORY

The degree of these consequences ranges from imperceptible to very significant. With such a narrow margin of victory in today's competitive sports, it makes sense for athletes, coaches and trainers to consider jet lag's potential effects on performance.

You should learn more about jet leg and its treatment if:
- you are interested in optimizing performance
- you are traveling by airplane across more than two to three time zones, or
- you have had problems with jet lag in the past.

IS JET LAG DANGEROUS?

Not really, but jet lag often includes excessive sleepiness and many studies have shown that humans are at greater risk for accidents and injuries when sleepy. Many automobile accidents in the U.S. are related to sleepiness/fatigue each year. Please be careful when traveling or changing your sleep patterns. Drive only when you are fully alert. Avoid alcohol when you are sleepy, it may make your sleepiness worse.

HOW IS JET LAG TREATED?

A considerable amount of inaccurate information has been written on jet lag. Suggested treatments have included everything from strict dietary recommendations to potentially harmful advice that could worsen the symptoms of jet lag.

A rule of thumb states that it takes one day for the body clock to adjust to each time zone you cross. Complete readjustment to a trip from the States to Europe often takes six to ten days. Luckily, we can shorten this adjustment process through our understanding of the body clock's physiology.

In general, jet lag is treated by gradually shifting the sleep/wake cycle (bedtime and wake-up time) and by exposure to bright light at certain times of the day. The details of this treatment are determined by the direction of travel (east or west) and the number of time zones crossed. The general jet lag guidelines presented below have been simplified for ease-of-use.

CAN MEDICATIONS OR SUPPLEMENTS HELP?

Medications or supplements can help sleep, but none have been approved for jet lag. If you are considering the use of a sleep aid, keep the following in mind: Check with the USOC regarding policies on medications or supplements prior to use. Call the USOC drug hot line at 1-800-233-0393 for more information. Check with your physician or pharmacist regarding potential side effects. Some medications or supplements may worsen the symptoms of jet lag if taken at the wrong time.

HOW ABOUT MELATONIN?

Melatonin is a neurohormone that is not regulated/tested by the FDA. The risk of taking melatonin has not been clearly established yet. Some studies suggest that it helps with jet lag, but until more studies can demonstrate its safety profile you should probably avoid melatonin. This section will be updated when new information is available. Again, check with the USOC regarding policies on medications or supplements prior to use.

HOW ABOUT CAFFEINE?

Most athletes, coaches and trainers have heard about the performance-enhancing debates regarding caffeine. Obviously, you need to check the USOC's policies on caffeine prior to use. Caffeine acts as a mild stimulant and in smaller amounts has been shown to decrease sleepiness. Try to avoid the use of caffeine close to bed time as it can disturb your sleep.

GENERAL GUIDELINES TO REDUCE JET LAG

Follow these steps for help in dealing with jet lag and common travel-related problems:
Step 1: Read the General Travel Tips
Step 2: Read the Light Exposure and Shifting Your Sleep/Wake Cycle sections
Step 3: Find the time zone change paragraph that best fits your trip in the Guidelines section

GENERAL TRAVEL TIPS

Some unpleasant feelings are blamed on jet lag but are really due to other things. Dehydration, physical inactivity, noise, hunger and stress frequently occur with long-distance travel and often cause the traveler to feel poorly. Anticipating and addressing these problems may make your trip more enjoyable and successful. Let's look at how you can avoid mere problems:

DEHYDRATION – Many people do not consume enough fluids when they are traveling and they become mildly dehydrated. Dehydration can make people feel lightheaded, dizzy, sick to their stomach, and can cause headaches and constipation, etc. To avoid this situation, drink adequate amounts of non-caffeinated, alcohol-free beverages such as fruit juice, fluid replacement drinks and water.

INACTIVITY – A lack of physical movement or activity frequently accompanies air travel. This decreased activity can produce muscle and joint stiffness, backaches, etc. Regular physical activity counteracts these problems and even helps our immune system function properly. Try to get up and stretch or walk at least every two hours.

STRESS – Traveling is often stressful, and stress can cause all kinds of trouble! Muscle tension, irritability, anxiety, headaches, stomachaches, insomnia, etc., can be signs of stress. There are many books and professionals available to advise you on the topic of stress reduction and coping skills. In general after you recognize the signs of stress, reduce the stress with something that you find relaxing.

NOISE – Noise can disturb your sleep (without you even knowing about it) and noise can increase your stress level. One of the best travel investments known to humankind is a set of foam ear plugs. The foam ear plugs you can get from your local hardware store cost about a dollar, and can be used many times. They are even easy to sleep with.

DIET – Finding food of sufficient quality and quantity when you are traveling can be difficult. Try to carry some of your favorite portable foods with you. Some version of an energy bar is a decent choice as it travels well and gives you a variety of nutrients.

NAPPING – Brief naps (no longer than about 15-20 min) can decrease sleepiness, improve performance and induce a sense of well-being (that nap felt good). Longer naps, on the other hand, can confuse the body clock and can produce the opposite effect.

Be sure to test any major changes in your travel strategy prior to implementing them on your next important trip.

LIGHT EXPOSURE

Light exposure is arguably the most powerful tool we have for readjusting the body clock. There is a direct neurologic connection from the eye to the body clock which allows light to adjust the clock every day. We can use this physiologic knowledge to readjust the clock more quickly.

Obviously, you should never look directly into a light source because you may hurt your eyes. Simply being outside (even on a cloudy day), or in a brightly lit room is usually enough light exposure. The timing of the light exposure is important to try to follow the specific directions for each travel situation. This may sound obvious, but it is also important; it should be light when you want to be awake, and dark when you want to sleep.

SHIFTING THE SLEEP/WAKE CYCLE

The body clock can't make large time changes rapidly, but it can handle small changes slowly. Therefore, if you start shifting your sleep/wake cycle (bedtimes and wake-up times) a few days before you leave and finish shifting the first few days after you arrive, the effects of jet lag will be reduced or eliminated.

NATIONAL GRECO-ROMAN CREED

"Those who totally commit will be tempered by hardship – confident there is virtually no physical or mental demand that can't be handled or accomplished. The hot pain of our wounds will become a warm glow of pride for giving everything we have! To win on the mat you need to outsmart and outlast your opponent. The more you sweat in practice, the less you bleed in a match."

Steve Fraser
National Greco-Roman Coach

VICTORY

Here it is, the Clash of the Titans! In one of the biggest upsets in Olympic history, Rulon Gardner (right) defeats the legendary Alexander Karelin of Russia at the 2000 Olympic Games in Sydney.
(Photo by Tim Tushla, courtesy of W.I.N. magazine)

Emotions run wild as Rulon Gardner is congratulated by coaches Steve Fraser (right) and Dan Chandler (left) following Gardner's stunning win over Alexander Karelin in Sydney. *(Photo by Tim Tushla, courtesy of W.I.N. magazine)*

VICTORY

Rulon Gardner acknowledges the crowd (above) after his historic triumph and later waves to friends (below) after receiving his gold medal.
(Photos by Tim Tushla, courtesy of W.I.N. magazine)

ABOVE: Garret Lowney (left) has his hand raised after defeating five-time World champion Gogi Koguouachvili of Russia in the 2000 Olympics. Lowney earned a bronze medal at 213.75 pounds in the Games. *(Photo by Sonja Stanbro)*

Coach Fraser (left) works out with Dan Henderson, a veteran Greco-Roman star who also has been very successful in the world of mixed martial arts. *(Photo from Fraser collection)*

VICTORY

ABOVE: Steve gets a greeting from Muhammad Ali at the Sydney Olympics. Ali won a gold medal in boxing as Cassius Clay in 1960 before winning the world heavyweight boxing championship three times as a professional. *(Photo from Fraser collection)*

Olympian Kevin Bracken (left) and his coach spend some time "cross training" and enjoying the mountains.

(Photo from Fraser collection)

ABOVE: Matt Lindland (left) faces the crowd after winning a silver medal at the 2001 World Championships in Patres, Greece.
BELOW: Coach Fraser consoles Jim Greunwald after a shoulder dislocation knocked him out of the 2001 World Championships.

(Photos courtesy of USA Wrestling)

Coach Fraser (above) offers instruction during a summer clinic, and (bottom) enjoys the wilderness with his three chilcren, Kellen, Kerrin and Hannah. *(Photos from Fraser collection)*

Chapter 4
Coaches Corner

Become an Effective Corner Coach

I polled my senior coaches and athletes and asked them to give me some of their top tips on successful corner coaching. These dedicated coaches and athletes were quick to send me some great suggestions. I received approximately 200 tips and suggestions from around 20 coaches and athletes. Here is a summation of what I received.

Most coaches and athletes feel it is important to be very positive with corner coaching comments. All cited the need for a lot of positive affirmations before the match, as well as positive feedback during the match.

Rob Hermann, *1996 U.S. Olympic coach,* says he yells comments such as "looking good, nice move, stay focused, keep wrestling." He tries to stay away from yelling specific moves because he wants the wrestler to be thinking on his own.

Ike Anderson, *National Developmental Greco-Roman coach,* suggests, "When you shout instructions from the corner, don't expect your athlete to physically look at you. This may break his focus and concentration. Realize that your wrestler can hear you without actually looking at you. You may want to train your athlete to periodically look to the corner during natural breaks in the match (out of bounds or injury breaks). Another thing you can do is train your wrestler to nod his head to acknowledge your instructions."

Another key tip is to "know your athletes." Know what their technical capabilities are and what they want from a corner coach. Coaches should ask their wrestlers what specific information they want to hear from a corner coach. Each of your wrestlers may want and need to hear something different.

Knowing your wrestlers' pre-match routines are very important. Do they like to be massaged and loosened up or do they like to be left alone? Do they like to be yelled at and pumped up or do they prefer quiet rational talk? Do they prefer not to be talked to at all?

Jay Antonelli, *U.S. Marine coach,* states, "Knowing your athlete's opponent and stressing some of his weaknesses is a major help to most athletes. First of all, it instills confidence in the athlete about his coach. And secondly, it obviously gives some openings for technique and tactics."

Les Gutches, *1997 U.S. Freestyle World Champion,* states, "Keep me informed on the passivity calls and time left. Shout general things instead of intricate techniques, i.e., 'pick up the pace, looking great, keep working, you need a turn.' If I am getting frustrated or something particularly irritating happens during a match (such as a bad call or late takedown tying the match), remind me to keep my composure and cool. Only positive things from the corner coach no matter what – including the body language."

Dale Oliver writes about hearing from a kid he used to coach telling him about the guy who took over for him when he moved to Sweden. The wrestler would come to the side of the mat during injury time or something, behind by two points or so and the new coach would say something like, 'you got him right were you want him.' The young man would wonder what he was talking about? He was losing and all the coach would say was, 'he's getting tired, that single is working, you can take him down and get ahead and win.'

Matt Lindland, *2000 Olympic silver medalist,* suggests some great tips: "Say everything in the positive. For example say, 'good defense or tough defense,' as opposed to, 'don't get turned.' Say, 'short arms, elbows in,' as opposed to, 'don't get arm thrown or watch the arm throw.'"

John Morgan, *1988 Olympian,* says, "Always use positive verbiage. For example, 'You're doing great. You almost had the underhooks. Keep working it.' Do not use negative language like, 'Don't do that or stay away from such and such.' This puts a sense of fear or uncertainty in your wrestler."

All athletes (with the coach's help) should have a match strategy. The corner coach, just prior to the match, can ask his/her athletes about their general match strategy. This will get his/her athletes thinking of the specific tasks or tactics on which to concentrate. For example, getting your athlete to identify his/her "pace strategy" will help them to focus. Remember that all athletes are different and should design their own match strategy. When the coach knows his athlete's basic strategy he should coach to that strategy.

Masaaki Hatta, *Freestyle World silver medalist from Japan and NCAA champion from Oklahoma State,* has this perspective: "All coaching should be done in the wrestling room and well ahead of time. The coach in the corner should be calm and confident with a poker face. Show your emotion only if you think it will help the wrestler. You represent the confidence of your wrestler on the mat.

"It is important for the coach to focus on coaching and for the wrestler to wrestle. Leave officiating to the officials, especially when they understand your language. Do not get the officials angry with you or it will hurt your wrestler. Make sure that your wrestlers wrestle and do not worry about the officiating.

"One way to keep yourself and your coaching staff from irritating the officials is to encourage your wrestler by saying something like, 'good job' or 'way to wrestle', instead of calling points or being critical of their judgment. Say anything to make your wrestler feel better and it may make the officials feel good and encouraged, too.

"Coach to win, wrestle to win and leave the officials alone. If the officiating gets too bad, you may have to formally protest for future matches. But it is much better for the wrestler to win and not to protest. I know you will sometimes protest and you should if things get very bad. Regardless, the original purpose is to win."

An athlete's perspective: "Do not depend on your coach in the corner. He cannot wrestle for you. But it will be helpful if he can tell the score and time."

Coach James Miller, reiterates, "I believe that 99 percent of coaching should be done away from the corner. Chance favors the prepared mind, Louis Pasteur. Therefore, corner coaching to me is a misnomer. I believe once you get to the corner, the coach's main role is to be a representative and, at most, supportive and positive. I would clearly discuss with the athlete what he believes my role in the corner should be before we get to the mat."

Dave Dean, *assistant coach at Michigan State,* put it simply. "In the spirit of being a good corner coach, I won't give much information at all. 'Go get 'em!' That's my tip."

VICTORY

Steven Woods, *a current athlete,* writes, "I believe that the coach should not spend too much time discussing or arguing over a bad call. This seldom benefits the wrestler on the mat and, in team situations, can hurt other team members. Instead of disputing a bad call, a coach should help his athlete to re-focus and center himself."

Wade Genova, *of USA Wrestling,* says, "Do not antagonize the official by pointing out all his bad calls. It is better to be friends with him or her. Talk to your wrestler, not the official. If you want the official to put up some points for your wrestler, don't become confrontational with him. Instead, try to move him with the power of suggestion. You might start clapping your hands and talking to your wrestler, saying something like, 'way to go, good score' etc. Talk to the officials after the match. Tell them what a great job they are doing. You may see them on the mat later. Read *How To Win Friends and Influence People* before the tournament."

Keeping your instructions from the corner "simple" seems to be another common tip. Trying to communicate too much or too complicated information to your wrestlers only breaks their concentration and focus. Remember, most coaching should be done in the practice room prior to the competition.

Chip Bunker, *Napoleon, Michigan, high school wrestling coach,* writes, "One of the things I do in the corner is to keep a small notepad with me at all times. I jot down things my wrestlers need to work on. This way I do not forget them before we have an opportunity to go over them. I also have very brief, one-word terms which have been explained to them in practice. Often times, by the time instructions are completed (during the match) the opportunity has passed. I try to keep them short. I also try to know the strengths and weaknesses of my wrestlers to avoid asking them to do something which does not fit their wrestling style."

Dan Chandler, *Olympian and 2000 Olympic coach,* highlights the importance of staying calm. "This simple step helps your athletes stay relaxed." Dan also lists, among other things, "keep your athletes aware of their mat position. During a break advise your wrestlers of changes in strategy. Always, always keep track of technical points, passivities and cautions on paper. And always have a towel."

Darren Petty says, "As a coach in the corner my philosophy is to meet the athlete's needs, not mine. This is his match, his career, and his goals. In the practice room is where my beliefs play a bigger role in helping the athlete achieve his goals. But in the corner it's a different story."

Doug Reese, *head wrestling coach at the University of Minnesota-Morris,* says, "Ask the athlete what they want, what they need from you. Some athletes don't want too much information. They don't want to know too much about their opponent so they are focused on their opponent's offense rather than their own attack. Other athletes want entire scouting reports. Everyone is different so it is best to know what your athlete wants. Then try to work within his or her individual needs."

Ted DeRousse, *of USA Wrestling,* states, "When two coaches are in the corner, only one coach should be giving instructions technically. The other coach should be keeping track of time, passivities, cautions, the score etc."

So there you have it, a variety of tips from a variety of coaches and athletes. We must remember that we are all individuals with our own personalities and coaching methods.

Knowing your athletes and their needs, knowing your opponents and their weaknesses, and being there for your wrestlers with positive reinforcement seem to be some of the most common and most important tips for corner coaches. One should consider these tips and blend them with his/her own coaching personality to be most effective as a corner coach.

    Thanks to the coaches and athletes who took the time to send me some great tips on corner-coaching issues.

Coaches Do Change Lives

I was eight or nine years old when I got my first introduction to organized sports. I was the tenth guy on the midget baseball team. Another guy and I alternated playing right field. They always put the scrubs in right field. I hadn't had too much experience with ball games. When I came up to the plate I was afraid I was going to get hit by the ball. I was also afraid to swing and miss. I always hoped the pitcher would walk me.

I did get a little more coordinated in baseball as I got older. A man my mother dated before she remarried (my mother and father divorced when I was five years old) taught me how to catch one-hop grounders, the kind that bounce right in front of you and shoot up in your face. But my first faint glimmer of athletic talent became apparent in gym class when I was in the eighth grade.

Wrestling was one of our required activities and I kind of enjoyed it. I was strong because I had lifted a lot of weights in order to have muscular arms like my older sister's boyfriend. While wrestling in gym class, I'd get kids in headlocks. They were actually illegal headlocks that I was using, but I didn't know any better at the time. I squeezed and squeezed because I was pretty strong, and when my opponent quit I figured I was the winner.

The gym teacher and wrestling coach, Frank Stagg, saw that I liked to wrestle and encouraged me several times to come out for the junior high school team.

"Yeah, I'd like to," I told him. But I didn't follow through. Why, I really don't know.

One day I was standing at my locker between classes when Mr. Stagg came up behind me and grabbed me, right in the middle of the hallway, in a sleeper hold…. which is a kind of chokehold around the neck. Lifting me off the ground, he was careful not to hurt me. But as you know, a chokehold isn't exactly like shaking hands.

"Steve," he said in my ear, still choking me a little bit, "I want to see you at practice tonight!" Of course, I didn't have any choice but to say, "Okay."

I wasn't really surprised that Frank had grabbed me like that. He had a special way of relating to kids. He was a teacher who cared and he represented everything that was right in the school system. In those few moments, as he was simultaneously choking me and caring about me, he changed the direction of my life. If he had not given me that extra little push, I might never have gone out for wrestling.

I wasn't nearly as good as the other wrestlers at Webb Junior High. I wasn't even the No. 2 man in my weight division and I didn't make the team. I wrestled only one match for the varsity that year at 126 pounds. But I loved the sport immediately. I liked the training and I liked the combat. The physicality of it was exhilarating to me.

Frank Stagg was a great teacher and motivator, and he knew how to get you in shape. One day after we wrestled in practice, did our drills and ran up and down stairs until we were ready to drop, I told Frank, "Mr. Stagg, I just love this sport. I love to sweat." He got a kick out of the fact that I loved to sweat.

I also loved wrestling because it was so manly, so basic and so primitive. Grappling is the oldest sport known to man, the origins going back 15,000 years. Some people say running was the first sport. But we wrestlers know that the runner was probably running from a wrestler! And being tough was rewarding to me. If you're a good baseball player, you're good on the field. But if you're a good wrestler, you can carry that with you all the time. Baseball players, like hockey players or tennis players, use other artifacts such as bats and sticks and rackets to assert their supremacy. But a wrestler has only the most primitive tools available: his legs, his body, his arms and hands. If you're a tough wrestler, you're tough, period! People don't mess around with you.

Lacking a father figure, I had spent my childhood searching for something to fill that void. I was attracted to manliness. And because my mother had brought me up, I rebelled against the possibility that I might become a mama's boy. In wrestling, I knew I could be tough. Even as a thirteen-year-old I could appreciate that.

In Frank Stagg, I found my first male influence that represented discipline, morality and success. Frank wasn't a harsh man, but he was firm in his beliefs. He emphasized human kindness and he took a firm stance against smoking, drinking and using drugs.

Frank caught me smoking once, right after the eighth-grade season. I was with my girlfriend, a cute girl named Colleen who smoked and was well-liked by a lot of guys. She was just as rough as the neighborhood we came from. I was walking home from school with her one day, holding her hand, a cigarette dangling from my lips, when Frank drove by and saw me.

"So you're smoking, huh?" he said, the next time he saw me. I knew he was upset with me but he never condemned me for what I had done. Frank ran the lunch line at school and for the next month he frisked me every day looking for cigarettes. I'm happy to say he never found any because I had already stopped smoking. His opinion of me meant more to me than cigarettes.

The summer after eighth grade I started to go through a growth spurt and the effects of the weight lifting I had done as a sixth-grader were suddenly apparent in my strong muscular arms. When I went out for the wrestling team as a ninth-grader, I weighed 145 pounds. Seniority, experience, hard work and my new build helped me earn a starting role in my weight class and I had a very good year. I lost my first match to a tough, muscular kid, but I went undefeated the rest of the year, finishing with a 16-1 record. I won the Little Oak League title at my weight and I received my first medal ever. Today, after almost 25 years of coaching myself, I think that sometimes coaches and teachers don't always realize the great impact they have on our kids. Although very rewarding, our jobs at times can seem thankless and immaterial.

To Mr. Frank Stagg and all the other great people who work with our young kids, I'm here to say, "Keep the Faith and Stay on Track." Believe me, you are making a difference. No matter what level you are at, know that you are affecting our kids positively. Keep up the good work and thank you for a job well done!

Why Greco-Roman is Important, too

As most everyone in the United States knows, freestyle is more popular in the USA largely due to our high school and college programs being folkstyle. We seem to have a pretty good freestyle development system in place today. We are pretty successful in freestyle at all age group levels, especially at our senior level.

So why not just focus on freestyle? It would be a heck of a lot easier for us as an organization to do this. Well, besides the fact that I would be out of a job, we can't do this. As long as the two styles of wrestling are contested at the Olympic Games, it is our American duty to try and become the best in both freestyle and Greco-Roman. We are Americans! We cannot and will not ever settle to be anything else than the best in whatever we do.

Wrestling is wrestling! We are judged by the rest of the world in both styles. It has been extremely embarrassing in the past for foreigners to think that the U.S. is good in freestyle but terrible in Greco. That hurts! There is no reason that the U.S. should not dominate both styles. It is a matter of U.S. pride that we are the best!

We have the athletes needed to be the best in both freestyle and Greco. American wrestlers are the toughest wrestlers in the entire world. The potential is there. We just need to fine tune our developmental systems to maximize our efforts at exposing and educating young wrestlers in Greco-Roman.

Listed below are some other benefits derived from exposing young wrestlers to Greco-Roman wrestling.

- Greco-Roman technique, training and skills will greatly enhance our freestyle wrestling and will give more American athletes a chance to win Olympic/World medals.
- Our overall USA Wrestling organization will become stronger and grow more if we can dominate internationally in both styles.
- Our membership will grow.
- It will attract more fan support and interest.

The way I see it, wrestling is wrestling, upper body or lower body. To be the best wrestler you need to be good at all wrestling attacks and counters. Wrestling Greco-Roman helped me tremendously in many areas of my wrestling. It allowed me to develop skills that I used in freestyle and folkstyle.

Learning how to pummel was probably one of the biggest benefits I gleaned from wrestling Greco. Pummeling enables you to set your opponent up for upper- or lower-body attacks. Pummeling enables you to get your opponent tired. Pummeling enables you to destroy your opponent's offensive attack. Pummeling enables you to control your opponent.

Pummeling enables you to burn seconds off the clock while still looking aggressive. Pummeling enables you to break your opponent's mental and physical conditioning. Pummeling enables you to get in great position and keep your opponent in poor position. Pummeling enables you to set the pace of the match. It allows you to get momentum going in your favor or stop his momentum.

All in all, pummeling is the actual wrestling of wrestling! It is the fight of wrestling! I use pummeling to get my National Team in great wrestling shape. Pummel matches are a great exercise for wrestling conditioning.

The year I won the Olympic Gold Medal in Greco (1984) was the same year I won the U.S. National Freestyle Championships. Like I stated earlier, wrestling is wrestling. Learn techniques, tactics and strategies in both upper- and lower-body attacks and you will be unstoppable!

Through the years, we have made great strides in Greco-Roman and have been growing stronger and stronger internationally. We have a lot to be proud of, but we need to build on these accomplishments and continue to grow.

Keep in mind we are competing against countries like Russia which probably have 10 times the amount of wrestlers and coaches that we do. With some intensified efforts throughout our entire U.S. wrestling community we can start to win soundly and dominate the sport.

Some plans are already in place. We have a Greco-Roman Resident Program at the United States Olympic Training Center (USOTC). This program is specifically designed to help Greco-Roman athletes and coaches in the U.S. to achieve their goals. This resident program is a great asset to our overall success. It has already proven to be an extremely important piece of our overall Greco movement.

Plus, the OTC allows us to have the senior training camps, three junior training camps, as well as our Big Brother Program training slots. All in all, we use the OTC programs to their fullest. The fact that the USOC pays the cost of all room and board for these athletes and coaches confirms that this program is a great asset to our U.S. team.

Coaches Influence Careers

I was a senior in high school when I witnessed my first Olympic Games. It was in 1976 in Montreal where I set my goal to become Olympic champion someday. Why not? Four months prior I had won the Michigan High School State Championship at 185 pounds and won a full scholarship to wrestle at the prestigious University of Michigan.

So, I set some goals. Besides becoming an Olympic champion, I wanted to become NCAA champion and Big Ten champion. Of course, before I could accomplish these dreams, I had to earn a spot on the varsity team at Michigan. Well, after about two or three months of getting beat up by just about every upperclassman on the team, I was forced to concentrate on a goal that was more within my reach.

For the moment, my goals of making the Michigan team (not to mention the Olympic team!) had to be set aside. My new goals were simple but specific — I had to work as hard as I could, try as hard as I could, and improve as much as I could.

The consolation I received during that frustrating period of my life came not from my peers at Michigan but from two treasured friends of long-standing: my mother, who loved me whether I beat my opponents or not, and Masaaki Hatta, the volunteer coach at Hazel Park High School who took me to the Montreal Olympics and who influenced my career more than anyone.

My mother had appreciated my involvement with wrestling when I was in high school, because she knew it was keeping me out of trouble. Now that I was in college, she no longer saw the same pot of gold I saw in wrestling. Yet she supported me just the same. Her words were always sympathetic and encouraging.

One dismal night I called her on the telephone. "Mom, I'm coming home," I said, barely able to get the words out. "I can't survive here."

"Yes, you can," she told me firmly. "Hang in there. You can do it."

When I drove home to Hazel Park on a weekend to take my laundry to my mother and to see my girlfriend, I would also visit Masaaki and tell him how my teammates were beating the tar out of me. I revered Masaaki, who had wrestled for Japan and had won the silver medal in the 1968 World Championships at 125.5 pounds.

He was the wisest man I knew. I would drive over to his little single-story home in Hazel Park, sit down with him in his living room, and open up my soul. As I told him about my failures, he listened quietly, with great politeness and professionalism. He could well understand what good wrestlers my teammates were.

Masaaki Hatta never told me I wasn't cut out for wrestling. He never told me that I didn't have the physical talent, or that I didn't have enough heart. It was Masaaki's style always to find a technical solution to a problem, not a personal one.

"How exactly are your opponents getting these double underhooks?" he would ask, addressing my most recent problem in impeccable English with a thick Japanese accent.

I would tell him how my opponents would power their way in close to me and then pummel strongly into me, raising me up on my toes.

"When they do this, I'm a goner," I would say.

Masaaki would nod wisely and then would give me fundamentally sound advice.

"Keep your elbows at your side more," Masaaki would say. "Keep those elbows tight, so that when they go to dig underneath, there is resistance. Circle around more to keep from giving them a stationary target. Attack one of their arms. Attack one side of their body. Capture an arm."

Then Masaaki would push the coffee table out of the way, move a chair or two, and show me physically how I should try to defend against vicious underhooks. We weren't actually banging into things – Masaaki only weighed 130 pounds – but I must admit people normally don't conduct wrestling demonstrations in their living rooms. The average wife would probably be furious if she saw her husband wrestling on the living room floor. Heck, most people don't want their children wrestling in the house. But Mrs. Hatta, a typically deferential Japanese wife, never said a thing. I don't think she even considered it unusual. Having lived with Masaaki for so many years, she accepted the fact that Masaaki's love of wrestling was destined to touch every corner of their lives.

Masaaki and I didn't always wrestle in the living room. If Masaaki really wanted to work up a sweat, he put on his headgear and we went out in the backyard instead. His technical skills were still very sharp. Occasionally, one of his wrestling buddies from Japan would visit and we'd spend two hours out on the grass. Masaaki would still be in his street clothes. I'm sure the neighbors thought we were crazy.

I always left Masaaki Hatta's home feeling better about myself and my future. The Japanese wrestler never gave me fiery pep talks, the way my Olympic coach, Pavel Katsen, did. He was entirely the opposite — unemotional. While Pavel inspired the heart, Masaaki touched the brain.

Masaaki never said, "You're getting better, Steve. You're learning fast. You're going to win." He never even told me I was making progress. But the way he listened to me spoke volumes. His very interest in me was testimony to the progress that I was making. I have often wondered how many coaches would have gone to such lengths to help a struggling wrestler who was no longer a part of their team. During my freshman year I must have gone over to Masaaki's house once a month. I knew I could call Masaaki anytime with a question or a problem, and he'd be there to help me.

Masaaki's guidance enabled me to continue climbing higher at a time when frustration threatened to tear me apart. After each visit, I would go back to Ann Arbor and try to incorporate his suggestions into my game plan. Some of Masaaki's ideas worked, and some didn't. Regardless, I always knew I had someone to turn to for help with my wrestling career. Having a coach like this was a tremendous blessing for me.

Wrestlers, I encourage you to go to your coaches and mentors to seek knowledge. They can provide a wealth of information. Coaches, continue to nurture these relationships that come your way. Win or lose, you are helping create champions.

Building the U.S. Greco-Roman Program: A Call To Coaches

This is a call to all my coaching colleagues across the USA. Whether you are one of our most valued grass roots coaches or one of our country's most successful university coaches – Greco-Roman wrestling needs your support!

The GOAL: To win the Beijng Olympic Games in Greco-Roman wrestling, in 2008 in China.

In the Sydney Olympics, Greco had our best ever performance. This performance followed the previous Atlanta Olympics best-ever performance.

In Sydney, we won three medals (gold, silver, and bronze). An added plus was Rulon Gardner beat the seemingly-invincible Russian superstar Alexander Karelin! As a team we ended up in third place behind Russia and Cuba.

If you combine results of the past two Olympics (Sydney and Atlanta), the Greco team won six Olympic medals. No country in the entire world (in Greco) has won more than five medals combined in these two Olympiads; except Russia (they won seven medals). So in Olympic competition, based on the past two Olympiads, the Greco team is doing great.

We slipped a bit in Athens, for sure. We had just one medalist, in Rulon's bronze medal. However, the United States Greco-Roman team is still the second-best in the world when measured by medals from the past three Olympics.

But to win the team title in 2008, we must pull together even more. As the national coach I humbly ask all U.S. coaches (age group through college) to help. How can you help?

1. Simply be aware that as a country we are trying to be the best in the world at both freestyle and Greco-Roman.
2. Encourage your kids to wrestle both international styles (Greco and freestyle) in the spring/summer.
3. If you see a wrestler who seems to like the Greco style, encourage him to pursue the style. Put him in contact with me or Ike Anderson (National Developmental Coach-Greco). We at USA Wrestling have many resources and programs which can help your wrestler improve his skills.

The worst case scenario is that wrestling some Greco will help your kids win more for you in folkstyle. In the following article, Dan Chandler writes about the benefits of Greco. He quotes Dan Gable, Kevin Jackson, and Marty Morgan, among others, who cite some of the benefits of wrestling Greco.

In the end, I hope all American wrestlers, coaches, and supporters will feel a part of our Greco-Roman successes. We can all be proud of our boys who make the many sacrifices they do to be the world's very best. When the team wins, we all win!

"Coaches: Take time to learn Greco"
By Dan Chandler

Even though the USA is widely recognized as a world power in wrestling, it is no secret that if we have a weakness, it is upper-body wrestling. The vast majority of our wrestling coaches, from youth coaches to collegiate coaches, are afraid to touch Greco-Roman for a fear of the unknown. And in the United States, upper body techniques are pretty much just that, unknown. However, listening to a cross-section of athletes who know how to utilize their upper body skills will lead the average wrestler into pursuing Greco-Roman wrestling. Wrestlers will see how Greco-Roman technique can benefit them.

Dan Gable is the dean of all coaches. His success as a competitor and coach is legendary. When Gable became a college coach, his influence changed the sport. College wrestling became more physical than it ever had been in the past, due primarily to the Iowa style, which swept across the nation.

Dan Gable loves to talk wrestling, and he is very enthusiastic about Greco and upper body wrestling. He considers upper-body skills crucial to being able to execute the basic folkstyle and freestyle leg attacks. His Iowa teams always did a tremendous amount of pummeling to create openings for lower-body attacks. Dan's concept was to control your opponent with constant movement and skills which force your opponent off balance.

As an athlete, Dan wrestled as many matches as he could, whether they be folkstyle, freestyle, or Greco-Roman. From his perspective the goal was always the same – pin the other guy's shoulders to the mat.

"I noticed the more freestyle and Greco-Roman wrestling I did, the better my folkstyle got," he said. No matter what specific style you are wrestling, key elements of the different styles are incorporated. It's all wrestling."

Kevin Jackson is our national freestyle coach. Kevin has won Olympic and World freestyle gold medals. Not too many know it, but he was also a Junior National Greco-Roman champion. Kevin emphasized the importance for young wrestlers to try all styles to become well-rounded wrestlers.

"You may not be able to see the effects early in your career, but later you will," he said.

Kevin also recognized the importance of Greco to complete the basic skills.

"Where else will you learn to control tie-up situations and to defend upper body attacks? It is vital for a wrestler's development to be put in those situations."

Steve Fraser is the national Greco-Roman coach for USA Wrestling. He was an Olympic champion in Greco-Roman and a national freestyle champion in the same year. Coach Fraser sang the praises of learning how to pummel.

"Learning how to pummel was probably one of the biggest benefits I gleaned from wrestling Greco. Pummeling enables you to set your opponent up for upper-body or lower-body attacks. Pummeling enables you to get your opponent tired and to destroy your opponent's offensive attack. Pummeling enables you to control your opponent and burn seconds off the clock while still being aggressive.

Pummeling enables you to break your opponent's mental and physical conditioning. Pummeling allows you to get in great position and keep your opponent in poor position. Pummeling enables you to set the pace of the match and allows you to get momentum going in your favor, or to stop his momentum. All in all, pummeling is the actual wrestling of wrestling! It is the fight of wrestling!"

Marty Morgan is the head assistant coach at the University of Minnesota. As an athlete, he was an NCAA champion and a national Greco-Roman champion. He also represented the United States in the World Championships twice.

"Although Greco-Roman is commonly known for spectacular throws, it really is more about hand fighting and basic positioning," said Marty. "Greco-Roman can offer a freestyle or folkstyle wrestler a chance to learn how to utilize his upper body, use under hooks, arm ties and snap downs. These techniques can enhance a wrestler's hand-fighting ability, which can greatly improve any style of wrestling."

Morgan also stresses the importance of the parterre position. "Greco can also enhance a freestyle wrestler's parterre defense as well. The ever-important gut wrench and gut wrench defense are cornerstones of Greco-Roman wrestling. Strengthening these parterre positions will add a distinct advantage to a freestyle wrestler in the top or bottom position."

Dan Russell is one of only two American wrestlers to ever win the prestigious Podubny Cup in Russia. He has also won numerous Junior National titles in freestyle and Greco-Roman. Wrestling for Portland State, Dan won four NCAA Division II titles. Taking advantage of Oregon's outstanding international youth programs, Dan started to learn Greco at an early age.

"To have the Greco knowledge that I had at an early age was a tremendous advantage," said Dan. "I had a very aggressive, offensive upper-body style. My Greco skills made me very unorthodox for my opponents to wrestle."

Garrett Lowney won a bronze medal in Greco-Roman wrestling at the Sydney Olympics. He was a five-time Junior National champion (three in freestyle and two in Greco-Roman), a Greco Junior World Champion, and a three-time Wisconsin state champion. Garrett was also an All-American at Minnesota.

"I am a firm believer that young wrestlers should experience all styles of wrestling, especially Greco," said Garrett. "Because I was exposed to so many different styles and situations when I was young, I feel comfortable under any circumstance that occurs on the mat. I didn't like Greco much as a kid, but it always taught me things that I can draw from when a match is on the line. Wrestling Greco in the Olympics gave me the tools I need to reach a whole new level for my college wrestling."

Where can coaches go to learn more? USA Wrestling has a variety of outstanding programs for coaches looking to gain more information. The national Greco-Roman coaching staff consists of Steve Fraser (national coach), Ike Anderson (national developmental coach) and Anatoly Petrosyan (Olympic Training Center Resident Coach).

You can learn more skills through videotapes and on-site programs available through USA Wrestling and its staff. You may also contact your state junior coaching staff to acquire additional information on these programs. Wrestlers who like to participate in an intensive Greco-Roman program while attending college should contact Ivan Ivanov at Northern Michigan University.

Also, please consider taking part in the Coaches Summer Study Workshops that the national Greco-Roman staff offer during the summer.

Greco-Roman wrestling needs more active and dedicated coaches nationally! And, we want to hear from you!

For more information on Greco-Roman wrestling or to be a part of the Coaches Summer Study Program please contact Ike Anderson at: ianderso@usawrestling.org, or, please call USA Wrestling at (719) 598-8181.

**Chapter 5
How To Train**

Training Tips

Taking full responsibility for your training as a wrestler is really important when trying to become the best you can be. When you become totally accountable for your actions as well as your results is when you are truly on your way to reaching the top level in this sport. Are you ready to take on that total commitment and be completely responsible for your wrestling career? If so, here are some key things to remember while you are training.

1. Time: The one sure thing we have in common with our competition is time. Don't waste it; if we use our time more efficiently than our opponent does, we will be better prepared than he is. It isn't the hours you put in; it's what you put into the hours. Train smart!
2. Conditioning: When you have an opponent who is fast or quick – realize when he gets tired he is no longer fast or quick. If your opponent is really strong – realize when he gets tired he is no longer strong. If your opponent has great technique and he gets tired – realize he no longer has great technique. If you can make an opponent tired, while you are not, you will be faster, stronger, and your technique will work better. Work hard on your conditioning and learn the techniques which make your opponent tired.
3. Take care of your injuries: Don't neglect treatment on an injury, no matter how minor you think it is. Listen to your trainers and your body; don't let a small injury become a large one. Protect from injury by getting proper rest and staying alert in every practice.
4. Goals: Set specific goals for each practice. Use your drilling and technique practices to solve specific problems. Do a scouting report on yourself (I have a self-evaluation form available) to identify any problem areas and work hard to improve them.
5. Flexibility: Wrestlers must be able to produce and absorb forces under conditions where your muscles are "ballistically" stretched and loaded. Lack of dynamic flexibility can cause injury and limit your execution of technique. You should stretch often and very aggressively. Your warm-up and cool-down should be a priority and include good stretching methods in each.
6. Agility: Agility is the ability to change directions while maintaining balance, body control, and speed. It is a trainable motor skill, and having good feet is probably a better asset than having blazing speed. Agility work can be incorporated with wrestling-specific skills.
7. Nutrition: Nutrition might sound unimportant, but is actually one of the most critical aspects of a workout program. Because wrestling is governed by weight classes, athletes must be constantly aware of their diet and what kind of training

effect it will have on competition preparation. Keep your weight under control. Keeping a daily journal or recording what you eat daily will give you great knowledge of what makes you feel great and what makes you feel tired and unresponsive.

8. Daily journal: Keeping a daily journal is probably one of the most effective ways to improve your training methods and help develop your plan. Recording information about your training such as food, hours slept, training activity, how you felt, etc. can really help you identify certain trends which can greatly affect how you feel during competition. This information can help you customize your training methods/plan and will make you very confident in your plan of attack. Because every individual is different, it is especially important to find out what makes you feel fresh, hungry and powerful.

9. Rest: The fundamental part of the recovery process takes place during night sleep. During sleep, changes occur in the core of the brain, reducing the excitability of the centers in which the various senses are located: hearing, sight, touch, etc. Sleep brings calm and rest for the brain cells, replenishing their work capacity, enabling the accumulation of nervous energy for future activity.

10. New limits: Every time you work out, get a little better...push yourself to new limits.

11. Situations: Situations you need to be aware of and good in are as follows. Make sure you take time in practice to work on these issues.

    A. Scoring situations (use different time - 15 sec, 30 sec, 1 min., 2 min.)
    - Behind by 1 point
    - Behind by 2 points
    - Behind by 3 points
    - Behind by 4 points
    - Behind by 5-9 points
    - Ahead by 1 point
    - Ahead by 2 points
    - Ahead by 3 points
    - Ahead by 4 points
    - Ahead by 5-9 points

    B. You have to pin your opponent
    C. Wrestling in or near the zone and out of bounds. Tactics.
    D. Overtime, risk situations, passivity, cautions, time, score, etc., know the situation.
    E. Wrestle from a scramble position when you and your opponent have a hand around each other's waist. Face opposite your opponent.

12. Study: Study and make sure you know all of the current rules.

    A. Cautions, fleeing hold, fleeing the mat and false starts, three cautions and match is over.
    B. Know what fleeing the hold and mat are.
    C. How officials look at a 0-0 score, 1-0, etc. in relation to the time left in a match.
    D. What is an escape? How do they call it?
    E. When is a match over?
    F. Can you score out of bounds, offense and defense?
    G. If you go out of bounds in parterre, when do you start on your feet and when do you go down in parterre?

      H. What should you do if your opponent is greased?
      I. Overtime criteria.
13. Competition and Matches:
    A. You must be ready to play the hand you are dealt and figure out how to win.
    B. Work on developing a sense of each particular match and what it will take to win it. This means knowing your opponent, the referee, and yourself.
    C. Develop the ability to plan and visualize whole matches. Create and follow a plan to win.
    D. Key points in a winning plan: Do not put yourself in a position where the referee can beat you; be prepared physically and mentally; keep pressure on your opponent; break your opponent's will; make thought and action one; be able to break your opponent's balance and control the center of the mat; be able to attack and counter attack.

There you have it. A few tips to think about when designing your training plan and thus your wrestling career. Do it now...take your career into your own hands and live it with passion! See you at the top!

Iron Sharpens Iron

At the 1998 NCAA Championships held in Cleveland, Ohio, I went to an FCA (Fellowship of Christian Athletes) breakfast program where I heard John Peterson, 1976 gold medalist, use the quote, "Iron sharpens iron." He was talking about people pushing each other toward excellence.

Competing against tough wrestlers is how one gets better. This is how you sharpen your skills. It is so true: "Iron sharpens iron." Tough wrestlers sharpen tough wrestlers.

I can say our American wrestlers did just that. One year, our schedule included the Vehbl Emre Tournament in Turkey, Gramma Tournament in Cuba, Hungary G.P. in Hungary, Trophee Milone in Italy and then the Pan-Ams in Winnipeg, Canada. The one trip I did not go on was the Peer Gynt Cup and Sweden Cup tour. But I heard the same things at these tournaments as I saw in my travels. We wrestled very tough! Very aggressive! Very intense!

The Swedish coaching staff even presented an award to me in honor of how tough we fought and how tough our guys are. The Swedish staff has a goal to make the Swedes as tough as Americans. For example, Dan Henderson was wrestling Martin Lidberg of Sweden, a world champion. They were in a tough, close match when Lidberg tried to throw Dan. Dan countered physically and they bashed heads, resulting in one inch gashes on both their faces. Blood spurted all over; both guys looked like warriors.

Dan jumped up right away and said, "That hurt! Tape me up quick so I can get back out there." But Lidberg, who was holding his face still lying on the mat, never got up. Dan was ready to go again but Lidberg did not want any more. That is the difference between an American Greco-Roman wrestler and the rest!

Our foreign opponents know that when they wrestle an American they are going to be in the battle of a lifetime. They know they need to score early before they start to get tired. They know they must slow the match down to a pace that is comfortable to them. They know they must get on top in parterre and try to score.

We can't let this happen! We must force our style and our strengths. We must use our superior conditioning to our advantage. We must be physical right from the start of the match, not allowing them to set up their moves, not allowing them to think straight, not allowing them to pace themselves. We must out-fight them like we know how.

But at the same time we must learn to take hold more and score off the fight. We must get the underhooks and score! We must get to the body and score! We must get the front headlock and score! This is how we can beat them all. But, of course, we must continue to improve our parterre offense and defense, as well. We've come a long way but still need to be better here.

Athletes all need to take some time to analyze their matches. They need to study how they may have gotten turned, how they may have been taken down. They need to study and examine their pace… to ask themselves, how did I secure the victory in the latter seconds of the match? How did I get him tired? Did I break my opponents?

If our wrestlers put their "street-fight attitude" together with their technique, they will dominate.

And remember, "Iron sharpens iron," so continue to look for the toughest workout partners that you can fnd so that you can become razor-edge sharp!

Cutting Weight – Is It Worth It?

Cutting weight for a wrestler is a personal decision. For some wrestlers, cutting a few pounds makes them feel leaner, stronger, faster and mentally tougher. For others, cutting weight can make them feel slower, weaker and not as sharp. The big question is, "How does cutting weight make you feel?"

As I described earlier, my sophomore year at Hazel Park High School in Michigan, I suffered what I thought was the greatest curse of wrestling: cutting weight. Cutting weight was always an accepted part of wrestling and is based on the theory that a wrestler will have a physical edge if he cuts some weight and drops down to wrestle a person without as much muscle mass.

I weighed 165 pounds that fall when I played on the football team, and I was hoping to wrestle at 155 pounds. But that didn't happen. After one or two matches, the wrestler who weighed 145 pounds came up to my division and beat me. If I wanted to wrestle for the varsity team, I would have to wrestle at 145 pounds, 20 pounds below my normal, healthy weight. The experience was the worst I ever had in wrestling. But it was also the most enlightening.

I hated every waking moment of it. When I was cutting weight, I spent the entire day thinking of what I would like to be eating. Everything I did, everything I saw, reminded me of food. Watching television advertisements about food made me ravenous. I even dreamt about food. I dreamed about strawberry shortcakes and banana splits.

But I didn't starve myself every single day. Like many wrestlers who competed below their normal weight, I gorged myself immediately after a meet. Then, the next day, I started fasting again. What did I eat during that week-long fast? Almost nothing. I skipped breakfast, had a grapefruit or an orange for lunch, and had another grapefruit and maybe a couple of poached eggs for dinner.

It drove my mother crazy. "Oh, surely you can have a little salad," she'd say. But I just couldn't eat anything. I couldn't drink much, either…just a few sips of water.

Meanwhile, the practices I had loved so much became torture. I frequently would go into the hot wrestling room looking like a mummy, dressed in one or two shirts, a plastic sweat suit and a thick cotton sweat suit over the plastics. If I had a lot of weight to lose on a given day, I might also pull my hood up, put a wool hat on over the hood, and wear gloves or socks over my hands. After 10 minutes of calisthenics, I was mentally exhausted. The pain I felt was compounded by the bitter knowledge that after all this work I couldn't even look forward to going home to a well-deserved meal.

You might wonder how I could have been physically and mentally sharp at the end of a week of starving and suffering. Well, I wasn't. I wasn't sharp at all. But I fasted because that was the accepted practice in wrestling, and I believed it was the right thing for me to do. My coach, Robert Morrill, hadn't pushed me into dropping 20 pounds. He had left the decision up to me.

I ended up having a very ordinary year. My overall record was eight victories, nine losses, and one tie. My big successes were that I made the varsity team and I made weight for each of my matches. But as a wrestler I was only average. I beat the below-average wrestlers, not the good ones, and finished fourth in the Southeastern Michigan Association League. I was sick during the district championships and couldn't wrestle, but it really didn't matter. I wouldn't have advanced to the regionals, anyway. The guys who beat me during the regular season would have beaten me in the district championships, too.

My experience cutting weight taught me several things. First, it taught me that a hungry, dehydrated wrestler probably isn't going to do any better at a lower weight than his normal weight. Second, it taught me that the fasting wrestler doesn't just lose his strength. He destroys his attitude as well. At a time when he should be trying to learn everything he can about technique and strategy, his main goal becomes making weight each day or losing a certain number of pounds.

I also learned that cutting weight can also have a negative effect in other areas of your life, as well. Good nutrition is vital to daily performance, and going to school or work without breakfast is one of the worst ways to begin the day.

Finally, there was one last discovery I made. The conventional wisdom in wrestling suggested that by dropping down a weight division I should have been able to outclass the little wimps who weren't as strong as I was. But surprise – I learned that all weight classes had good wrestlers, and to beat the good wrestlers I needed to become a good wrestler.

Of course, it's hard to tell a kid not to cut weight. Sometimes wrestlers have to learn for themselves. And I must say I learned a lot from the experience. I learned that I would never cut too much weight again. I also learned to appreciate food, because I found out how painful it is to starve.

I should mention here that cutting weight is not bad in all cases. If a wrestler is 20 pounds overweight, he should make an effort to lose that fat, provided he still takes in the proteins and nutrients he needs to stay healthy.

But a lot of kids who go out for wrestling are already lean, the way I was, and I would never advise them to cut anything over a few pounds. My advice to those wrestlers is that they wrestle at or around their normal weight.

If they can't make the team at their normal weight, I would advise them to move up a weight class before they consider moving down a weight class. I probably should have gone up to the 167-pound division my sophomore year instead of suffering through the season at 145 pounds. I might have surprised myself and found that I was quicker than the wrestlers who were a few pounds heavier than I.

I proved my theory correct during my junior year in high school, when another high school coach, Masaaki Hatta, convinced me to wrestle in the 185-pound division while weighing only 170 pounds. I went into my practices feeling wonderful. My goals were to improve and have fun, both of which I did. And while I was going all-out in those practices, the wrestlers who were cutting weight were walking around with their chins hanging down to the floor, sweating, tired and mentally exhausted.

I also proved I could win. I remember so well the time we wrestled Southfield High School. I weighed about 170 pounds at the time, and as I was standing in the weigh-in line

VICTORY

in my skivvies, Southfield's 185-pound wrestler, a cocky kid, looked around and asked in a loud voice, "Who's the 185-pounder?"

"I am," I said shyly.

He looked at me and said with a chuckle, "You're 185 pounds? You're kind of small aren't you?"

"Yeah," I said. "Kind of."

Well, that was the last time he laughed at me because that night in our match I beat the living tar out of him. I was beating him 18-3 (I gave him three escapes) before I pinned him.

To become a great wrestler you need to learn the techniques, tactics and strategies of the sport. Then condition your mind and body to be able to execute those techniques, tactics and strategies. Body weight differences, especially when slight, are of little importance, in my opinion. I am totally convinced that this attitude I had about not cutting too much weight was one of the main reasons I wrestled as long as I did. I loved this sport and I don't think I would have loved it if I had cut too much weight.

I encourage all wrestlers to take a hard look at weight cutting, especially excessive weight cutting. Ask yourself, "How does it make me feel?" If you are cutting too much you will know it. Your mind and body will tell you so. Remember… having fun with the sport plays a big role in succeeding with the sport. In the big picture, life is pretty short. If you are not having fun, the answer to the question "Is it worth it?" should become very clear.

See you at the top!

12 Ways To Break Your Opponent

What do I mean, "Break your opponent?" When I talk about breaking your opponent, I'm not talking about causing an injury by breaking a bone or tearing a muscle. I am talking about breaking his will to fight. Breaking his confidence and his concentration. I am talking about pushing him past his comfort zone. I am talking about taxing his mental, physical and emotional capacities.

Breaking your opponent mentally means you have forced him to think negative thoughts like, "He's too tough, too conditioned, too good." I want him to think he is tired and have doubts about his chances of winning. Physically it means that your opponent is getting fatigued beyond his capacity. Emotionally breaking your opponent means that he is now completely exhausted and looking just to somehow survive. He has surrendered, giving up any thoughts of winning.

Breaking your opponent's will to fight. Making him quit. What does that look like? In a match or practice you will see many signs of this. Here is a list of some things to look for in breaking your opponent:

- <u>Backing up</u> — Your opponent or training partner starts giving ground as you attack him, back peddling.
- <u>Stopping as soon as you go "out of bounds"</u> — The moment you get close to or go out of bounds, he will stop wrestling
- <u>Takes a long time to get back to center (once you go out of bounds)</u> — Catching his breath, adjusting kneepads, shorts, etc. is a sure sign of breaking.
- <u>Inactivity</u> — Inactivity on the mat while wrestling or stalling.
- <u>Showing signs of desperation</u> — Your opponent will start making bad shots in desperation or giving up good position.
- <u>Complaining</u> — Complaining to the official or his coach, showing frustration.
- <u>Stumbling</u> — Staggering and showing signs of fatigue.
- <u>Adjusting knee pads, shorts, tying shoes</u> — Generally taking a lot of time, trying to recover whenever there is a break in the action.
- <u>Short bursts of anger with intensity</u> — This can mean he's desperate and frustrated. It can mean he is trying to give a last ditch effort before he breaks!

These can all be signs of your opponent breaking mentally, physically and emotionally. The more you do this to your wrestling partners the more you will learn to see the signs of breaking which will motivate you to experiment and expand these tactics. Understanding and developing these tactics will allow for many great options as far as offensively attacking your opponents. It will open up a whole new world of wrestling for you.

VICTORY

Here are 12 ways to make your opponent break in practice:

1. <u>Out-Pummel him:</u> This means you will dictate the pace. Physically you will move faster with a lot of change of direction. You will push and pull him, keeping him off balance and forcing him to move in a manner that he is not intending to move in. This pummeling attack should include many tie-up changes, i.e. collar tie left, then right, then two-on-one, then under hook, then shot, then arm drag attempt, then shot, then two-on-one, then collar his left, right, push, pull, under hook, circle him, snap, foot sweep.

 This is what I call your "dance." It is your physical wrestling movements that you have honed into your normal movement, your normal attack mode. You must create your own personal "dance" that in time becomes your natural method of attacking your opponent. This dance can be physical but at the same time it should be smooth and rhythmic to you.

2. <u>Out-hustle him:</u> In matches, when you do go out of bounds you always hustle back to the center of the mat, eagerly waiting for your opponent to arrive, then always making the first contact when the bout resumes.

3. <u>No stopping:</u> When you both go into the wall in the practice room, you spin him around and keep wrestling or you can use the wall to help you get hold and continue to wrestle (if your walls are padded). No stopping or walking back to the center of the mat. This is why in our room (the U.S. Olympic Training Center wrestling room) the padded walls are considered in bounds. Of course the added benefit to having the padded walls "in bounds" is that it teaches, very quickly I might add, the wrestlers who are backing into the wall to circle and stay in bounds. It only takes once or twice for you to get pinned into the wall and then get tossed on your back to realize you've got to stay off the wall and in the center of the mat.

4. <u>Keep scoring:</u> When you take him down you turn him right away (no stopping to let him up). When you take him down you always go immediately into a turning attempt. Most wrestlers will pause/relax after they get taken down. This is not only a chance to break him but it is a great time to score! If there is no action on the mat after you have taken him down, you don't just let him up, you,

5. <u>Pressure Option #1:</u> Gently or forcibly push him up from behind and as he stands up you spin him around, getting right back into his face; or.....

6. <u>Pressure Option#2:</u> If you go to push him up and he doesn't stand up (he stays down in the referee's position), then you circle out to the front of him and pull him back up to his feet by cupping your hand under his chin and pulling him up. Now you may just snap him right back down to the mat, going behind for another takedown or you keep him up on his feet getting right back in his face, pushing, pulling and pummeling him again; or.....

If you go to push him up and he doesn't stand up, you circle out to the front but instead of pulling him up, you just push down on his head with one of your hands, then with the other hand. You continue to push his head down two, three, four, five, six, seven, eight times alternating hands until he gets the picture that you will not just let up on him;

Or, you might push on his head and then pull him up using both of the afore-mentioned tactics in combination.

7. <u>Keep going:</u> If he takes you down and stops wrestling, you continue to wrestle,

jumping at the chance to reverse him or take him down when he pauses. The idea is that you continue to wrestle in all situations.

8. <u>Fight off your back:</u> If you ever get put on your back you always fight off no matter what; you never stop wrestling. If he stops wrestling to let you up, then you come up full force, immediately attacking him. Have the attitude "How dare you just let me off my back. You just robbed me of the chance to improve on how to get off my back."

9. <u>Keep him down:</u> If you turn him to his back and he stops wrestling, you don't. You either hold him for a time (loosely or tightly) or you tell him "Come on, keep fighting!" or, you loosen your hold up a great deal allowing him to fight off his back, then you immediately turn him again with either the same hold or a different one. As long as you are turning him and continuing to score, you keep him down. If and when you get tired of turning him is when you pull him up getting right back into his face with the fight.

10. <u>Keep going:</u> When you go out of bounds you continue to wrestle for two seconds after you hear the whistle. First, this will always leave an impression in the officials mind that you are more aggressive. Second, whenever your opponent stops wrestling and you don't, it will break him a bit more.

11. <u>Be like fly paper:</u> When he stops in the middle of your goes (in practice) to tie his shoe, adjust his shorts, fix his t-shirt, you continue to wrestle in his face. If you are kind enough to let him actually do this then at a minimum you hover over him, just inches away from his body, eagerly anticipating continued engagement. The moment he finishes tying, adjusting or fixing you immediately engage again in the battle. The main point is you become like fly paper on him. Always in his face, always attacking, always pulling him up, pushing him down, or spinning him around. He should feel like you are in his face or on him constantly. No pauses, no breaks, no rests.

12. <u>Stay in control:</u> If the battle ever gets heated where your opponent punches you (for whatever reason), you don't let it phase you one bit. You continue to attack him like you hardly even noticed him punching you. Now this doesn't mean you can't get more physical with your attack, but you always stay under control, never punching him back. Always just attacking him back. Remember, scoring points is the main objective and should be the ultimate payback for any un-sportsmanlike activity.

If he can punch you or foul you (for example, using legs in Greco) and that causes you to get mad and punch him back or complain, it is a sign that you are not focused and mentally strong enough to ignore it.

The idea is that nothing your opponent can do to you will take you out of your intense, focused game plan of attacking. Nothing will faze you. Nothing will bother you. Nothing will derail your tenacious, relentless attack.

Think about it. The normal reaction to one wrestler punching another is that the wrestler getting punched will get mad. But just imagine what your opponent will think when he punches you and you just keep on coming. This is not the normal reaction from most wrestlers. He will think that you are an animal. He may think you are crazy or that you are a fine tuned machine. This will break your opponent's will to fight, guaranteed!

Breaking your opponent is an attitude and it starts in practice. This attitude and tactic has to be developed, practiced and experimented with. You have to be willing to be a little rude. I don't care if he (your opponent or training partner) is a friend or not, you have to put everything aside and force this attitude. It will some times feel rude of you to stay in your wrestling partner's face when he is kneeling down on the mat, tying his shoes, catching his breath or adjusting his shorts but you must ignore this and stay in front of him pushing him to keep wrestling. Again, he may turn his back to you. Again, you must spin him around, never letting him rest. And, of course, if you master this in practice it will become your method of operation in your matches too.

Mark Churella, three-time NCAA champion from the University of Michigan, was the first wrestler to introduce this wrestling attitude and tactic to me. As teammates at Michigan, Mark and I trained together daily. For me it was "learn this intense style of wrestling or be gobbled up by this tenacious champion."

Three-time Olympian Dan Chandler from Minnesota was another example of a great wrestler who mastered the art of breaking his opponents. "Breaking your opponent has been the cause of some of the biggest upsets in the sport of wrestling, including Rulon Gardner's monumental upset over Alexandre Karelin at the 2000 Sydney Olympics," said Chandler.

As Dan notes above, Gardner beat the great Karelin from Russia with this wrestling attitude. Rulon broke him! No doubt about it! Matt Lindland won the Olympic and World silver medals by breaking his opponents' will to fight.

Wrestling heroes Dan Gable, Terry and Tom Brands and John Smith, to name a few, all have mastered the skills of breaking their opponents.

If you want to acquire the ability to break your opponent's will to fight, start practicing these 12 tactics in your every-day practice room. Remember, it starts with an attitude of relentless intensity and focus on staying in your partner's face constantly.

Continuing to wrestle in all positions and situations is important. Remember, scoring points is the ultimate breaker. The more you learn to develop this relaxed but intense wrestling style and focus, the more you will be able to use these tactics in your wrestling strategy and method of operation.

I have written in the past about the Grind Match and its benefits. The Grind Match is a one- to two-hour no-stop wrestling match that will greatly develop the tactics, skills and attitudes that are required when "breaking your opponent" – especially if you have identified these issues as an area to improve and perfect. This longer, usually lower-intensity wrestling exercise will really promote and allow for focus in this area.

Once you have felt what it is like to "break your opponent" in these one- to two-hour matches, then you can set the goal to break the next guy in less time, and so on, and so on, with the ultimate goal of being able to break your opponent in six minutes or less.

When you break your opponent's will to fight, you will see how much fun your wrestling will become. Once your opponent breaks, it's like taking candy from a baby! I wish you the best and "Make some babies cry!"

And, as always, "Expect to Win with Relentless Intensity!"

Going through Phases - The Yearly Training Cycle
(Specifically for the National Greco-Roman Team)

If you had been following the National Yearly Training Schedule from September through mid-January, you were in the Conditioning Phase of the schedule. This phase is sometimes referred to as the aerobic or endurance phase.

Your goal during this time was to develop cardiovascular and muscular endurance. Wrestling and running activity should have been longer in duration, slower repetitions and lower intensity level. Openness to new technical and tactical learning was the emphasis along with goal setting, self analysis and planning being the central focus. Gaining strength in the specific movements and muscles related to wrestling was important, along with the psychological training such as practicing 'performer' skills – like rehearsing tough acting and tough thinking skills, building solid self-talk habits and so forth.

Then in the Preparation Phase of the Yearly Training Cycle (mid-January thru mid-March) it is important to start developing explosive power and speed. Practice duration starts to decrease and activity intensity starts to increase. Training now starts to mirror the actual physical and psychological demands of wrestling competition. Pre-competitive routines, rituals, tough thinking and tough acting skills should be fully engaged.

Now, in the Competition (Peaking) Phase of the Yearly Training Cycle (mid-March thru April 23), the objective is to achieve maximum performance output in the context of competition. Power, strength and speed are peaked by reducing the volume of training stress. Training sessions are generally of high intensity but short duration. Again, mirroring the actual physical and psychological demands of the competition is important.

The days/week immediately preceding the U.S. Nationals should be less demanding and less stressful both physically and emotionally. Your goal is to enter the peaking phase well recovered, rested, eager, enthusiastic, physically healthy, motivated and confident. Competition goals and rituals are of great importance during this time.

The training focus of wrestlers during the competitive phase should be simply to maintain current fitness levels. Careful attention should be given to issues of diet, sleep, naps, fun, relaxation and recovery. Reviewing your past journal entries should help you determine what makes you peak. Dream about winning, prepare to have some fun in the battle. Be hungry for the fight. Enjoy your performance.

Smile. You're a Greco-Roman wrestler. There is NO tougher athlete!!!

Recovery: Key Element in Training

Wrestlers are constantly exposed to a variety of rigorous training stress. Wrestling, running, and weightlifting are the most common ways in which wrestlers tax their bodies. This is how one improves his physical, mental, and emotional conditioning. I think the well-known phrase "No pain, no gain!" really rings true.

When wrestlers drive themselves beyond their physiological limits, they fatigue their bodies. The more the fatigue, the more the negative training effects.... such as lower rate of recovery, less coordination and less potential of output. Fatiguing your body is essential to improving it.

But it also requires proper recovery (rest) to complete the development cycle. In other words, it takes both hard training and proper rest to improve one's conditioning in sport. This article will focus on identifying some recovery techniques wrestlers can use to help balance their training regimen.

Active recovery (active rest) helps in the rapid elimination of waste products (i.e., lactic acid) from your muscles, etc. Active recovery occurs with light to moderate aerobic activity. Examples of this would be continuous light jogging or easy swimming. Let's take jogging, for instance. There have been studies which show during the first 10 minutes of continuous light jogging, 62 percent of lactic acid is removed, an additional 26 percent of lactic acid is removed between 10 and 20 minutes of jogging. So it seems to make sense that maintaining an active recovery period of 10 to 20 minutes after strength training or intense wrestling would be advantageous.

Complete rest (passive rest) is probably one of the most common necessities which all athletes must adhere to. Most athletes of all sports require about 10 hours of sleep per day — usually about eight to nine hours at night and one to two hours in the form of naps. Of course, this can vary a bit depending on the individual. Usually, regular sleeping habits are also important, like going to bed no later than 11 p.m.

Massage, which is the manipulation of soft body tissue for recovery purposes, is another very effective way of enhancing the recovery process. The effects of massage include relief from muscle fatigue and reduction from excessive swelling. Proper massage, done by a certified specialist, also can stretch muscle adhesion. There have been many studies which show massaging the muscles helps the breakdown of waste products and their absorption into the circulatory system may be increased up to 2.5 times above resting levels. Massage in general helps increase blood circulation, which allows for greater interchange of substances between capillaries and tissue cells.

Heat therapy in the form of steam baths, saunas and heat packs can have a relaxing and rejuvenating effect on fatigued muscles. Although heat packs generally heat the skin, as opposed to the muscle, they can still be effective. Heat packs usually will increase the blood flow to a particular muscle area, which will increase the transference of waste products from the muscle. It is recommended to apply heat for at least 20 minutes so that it has time to reach the muscle. The problem is that sometimes in order to get the heat to the muscle the skin will get too hot.

Cold therapy such as ice, ice baths, ice whirlpools and cold packs can have a positive effect on helping fatigued muscles recover. Ten to 15 minutes immediately after an intense training session is the best time to apply ice. Rubbing ice on an excessively-strained muscle may help reduce swelling and treat any micro-tearing of the muscle which may have occurred.

Diet is very important in the recovery process. Eating well-balanced meals with the proper caloric intake is essential to replenishing one's body. Your energy intake should generally match your energy output. One way to judge this is if you are losing weight while on a rigorous training schedule, then you are probably not consuming enough calories. Excessive weight cutters beware.

Even if you consume a well-balanced diet, you should consider taking vitamins and mineral supplements. No matter how well-balanced your diet is, usually during training and competition your body will become deficient to some degree. During these periods of heavy training, supplements should be an important element.

It is also recommended by some dietary experts to eat four or five small meals a day as opposed to three large meals. Eating more small meals allows for better digestion and assimilation. No more than four or five hours should pass between daytime meals and no more than 12 hours between your last meal and breakfast.

Eating before a training session is not advised. Training on a full stomach can force the cardiovascular and respiratory systems to work harder. You should also allow at least 20 to 30 minutes to go by before you eat after a training session. During this time, wrestlers should consume only liquids which contain carbohydrates and mineral supplements.

Psychological recovery can greatly influence one's motivation and will power, thus affecting athletic performance. The more a wrestler can focus, the better he will react to intense training stress and the greater his work capacity will be. Lifestyle also affects one's recovery. Poor relationships – with spouses, girlfriends/boyfriends, siblings, parents, teammates and coaches – can lead to a negative impact on the recovery process. Relationship issues are a part of life, so it takes strong practice to separate certain normal-life problems from your wrestling training.

Relaxation techniques can greatly enhance the wrestler's ability to focus. If your mind is relaxed your body will be relaxed (and vice versa, for that matter). A good time to practice relaxing is just before you go to bed. Sometimes a hot shower or hot bath will help you to get to that relaxed state.

According to J.T. Kearney, former senior sports physiologist at the United States Olympic Committee (USOC), "The bottom line is... by increasing the level of blood circulation (with low intensity activity) you help eliminate muscle fatigue from the tissue. This helps muscles to rejuvenate back to a normal, productive, powerful state of being."

Hard Work Requires Hard Recovery

The one thing wrestlers and coaches know is that it takes a lot of hard work to become a strong wrestler. I don't think many people would dispute this theory. Wrestlers have the reputation of working harder than most any other athletes. The grueling wrestling practices, the running, the lifting, the calisthenics – all promote a great amount of physical, mental and emotional stress to one's being, which is essential to building a champion.

But to develop the ultimate toughness in a wrestler and to condition his mind and body which maximizes his "Ideal Competitive State," one must also consider the equally important issues of recovery.

Powerful peaks of training stress requires equally powerful valleys of training recovery. In other words, you must work hard but you must also recover equally as hard. Many wrestlers pay a lot of attention to the notion of training stress and working hard, no doubt. But sometimes they neglect the realization that they must give the same attention to training recovery.

What does recovery mean? At the most basic level, recovery means doing anything that causes energy to be recaptured. Your body expresses its recovery needs through feelings and emotions such as telling you "I feel hungry or tired." The fulfillment of these urges (eating or sleeping) is a form of recovery.

Just like with stress, there are three areas where recovery occurs — mental, physical and emotional. Recovery is where the growth and healing occurs in these areas.

Some common signs of mental recovery are mental relief or calmness, an increased feeling of creativity, fantasy or imagination. Some common signs of physical recovery are reduced feelings of hunger, thirst, sleepiness or tension. Some emotional signs of recovery might include increased feelings of joy, humor or happiness and a decreased feeling of anger, fear or frustration.

According to James E. Loehr, author of *The New Toughness Training for Sports,* there are five categories of how you can actually train the mechanism of recovery.

1. Sleep/Nap
2. Diet
3. Active and passive rest
4. Seizing recovery opportunities
5. Emotional catharsis

<u>Sleep/Nap:</u> Along with food and water intake, sleep is one of the most important recovery activities. Poor sleep habits can completely undermine the conditioning and toughening process. Both too much sleep (excessive recovery) and too little sleep (insuf-

ficient recovery) can cause problems.

Some general recommendations are to get between eight to ten hours of sleep per night; go to bed and get up within 30 minutes of your normal sleep times; attempt to be more of an early bird than a night owl; learn to take short naps (10 to 15 minutes) and wake up feeling completely refreshed and energized.

Keep a daily record of the quantity and quality of your sleep, especially during periods of high stress.

Diet: Consuming adequate amounts of water and nutritious food is another very important recovery activity. When nutrition and hydration needs are not met even the most fundamental recovery mechanism will tend to break down. This is an obvious issue for the wrestlers who tend to cut a lot of weight.

Some general rules are: Follow a consistent schedule of eating and drinking. This is a critical component of your overall training plan as an athlete. Always consume a nourishing breakfast. Eat more small meals (4-6), this will keep your blood sugar stable, giving you more energy over longer periods of time. Eat earlier rather than later in the evening. Eat a wide variety of foods, with a preference for natural, fresh foods (no preservatives, etc.).

Active and Passive Rest: Recovery from training stress can occur in both active and passive rest. Active rest is where there is physical movement involved. Passive rest is where there is no physical movement involved. Active rest is light physical activity that breaks the routine of the normal physical training regimen. Activities such as mall shopping, hiking, biking, golfing, tennis, basketball and swimming are all examples of active rest for a wrestler. Some examples of passive rest would include such things as watching TV, going to a movie, laughing, getting a massage, taking a whirlpool, reading or going for a relaxing drive.

All of these activities, if done specifically to enhance the recovery process, are forms of recovery training.

Seizing Recovery Opportunities: All sports have recovery opportunities within the event itself. Football players, for example, have the time in the huddle, timeouts, halftimes and when sitting on the bench. In wrestling, we have recovery opportunities when we go out of bounds, when an official calls for passivity and in between periods.

An important aspect of recovery training is working to improve your ability to extract the maximum values from recovery opportunities that exist during competitive matches. Training yourself to refocus on strategies or relaxing during these moments is performance enhancing.

Planning good use of your down time between matches or practices plays an important role in your recovery tactics, as well. How you spend your time and with whom can make a difference in how you manage periods of intense competitive stress. Having your cassette player and favorite music tapes with you or learning to sleep on planes or buses can make important contributions to you during these periods of time when you need to perform to your optimum capabilities.

VICTORY

Seize recovery wherever and whenever the opportunity exists. Good planning and preparation will only lead to enhanced performance and success.

<u>Emotional Catharsis:</u> The two most important ways of achieving emotional recovery after disappointments, failures or missed opportunities are to talk about it or write about it. Holding it inside does not allow you to fully recover and promotes future emotional stress. Here is where you need to listen to your true emotional needs. During competition you may block these emotions, but during the non-competitive times you must address these emotional issues which, again, is an act of recovery.

To enhance your overall "Ideal Competitive State" and success potential, include both training stress (hard work) and training recovery (hard rest) in your training plan. Realize that recovery is as equally vital to your performance as is tough training activity. Understand what recovery means (mentally, physically and emotionally) for you. Look for ways to maximize recovery opportunities both during competition and outside of competition. Remember, stress is the stimulus for growth. Recovery is where you actually grow.

How to Become a Fearless Warrior

A major component of competitive success deals with controlling fear. In wrestling, fear of failure, fear of looking bad, and fear of not meeting expectations all inhibit how a wrestler performs. Fear is a negative emotion that can be controlled (or eliminated) if identified and dealt with head-on.

Remember, when you are in your "ideal competitive state" you have feelings of energy, fun, confidence, courage, strength, relaxation and <u>fearlessness</u>. Your "ideal competitive state" is the state of being — physically, mentally and emotionally — which allows you to perform to the best of your abilities. It is a state of <u>being</u> when you feel your best and enjoy the battle. It is the state of being that all successful athletes should practice getting to upon command. Learning to control fear will help you reach your "Ideal Competitive State."

With that, we look to the U.S. Military for some tried and true exemplary training. The military is all about training young recruits to overcome fear, but not just fear of losing in sport. The military trains young men and women to overcome the fear of death in combat. If you choke in a wrestling match, you'll likely lose the bout. If you choke in a military battle, you'll likely lose your life.

It really is remarkable how the military can take a young recruit for two or three months and turn a scared, fearful kid into a fearless, courageous soldier. A soldier that, without hesitation, will step into battle, putting his/her life on the line. The military training throws light on many key aspects of the toughening process, some that can be applied to toughening young wrestlers who are stepping into battle putting their reputation on the line.

How does the military do it? How do they take a "fearful adolescent" and make him a "fearless warrior" in just a few short months? According to James E. Loehr, Ed.D, Author of *The New Toughness Training for Sports*, he says: The art of soldier-making (or, for us, athlete-making) goes as follows:

1. A strict code of acting and behaving under stress. This includes:
     • A disciplined way of responding to stress.
     • A precise way of walking – head and shoulders erect, chin up.
     • Quick and decisive response to commands – no hesitation tolerated.
2. No visible sign allowed of weakness or negative emotion of any kind in response to stress. The expression of negative emotion is simply not permitted. No matter how you feel – this is the way you act!
3. Regular exposure to high levels of mental, emotional and physical training stress to accelerate the toughening process. Obnoxious drill instructors – very tough individuals in the street sense of the word – provide all three kinds of stress.

4. Precise control and regulation of cycles of sleep, eating, drinking and rest. The regimen includes:
    - Up early and to bed early (lights out, no choice).
    - Mandatory meals including breakfast (no choice about timing, few choices about foods).
5. A rigorous physical fitness program. This essential component of the toughening process involves two elements:
    - Aerobic and anaerobic training.
    - Strength training.
6. An enforced schedule of trained recovery. This includes:
    - The regimen outlined in item 4 above.
    - Regularly scheduled rest and relaxation.
    - Enforced cycles of stress followed by enforced cycles of recovery.

These military training requirements seem to be essential when trying to create tough, fighting soldiers. The strict code of acting under stress, no visible signs of weakness or negative emotion, and exposure to mental, emotional and physical training all contribute to the development of fearless attitudes among these GI's.

Now, granted, not all aspects of military training apply to the sport of wrestling, but many elements of basic training provide valuable insights to the toughening process for athletes. Becoming a courageous fighter, and a fearless soldier in battle, is not only the key to battlefield success, but to success in competitive wrestling as well.

I encourage wrestlers to practice these strong discipline traits both on and off the mat.
1. Be on time for practice.
2. Listen to your coaches.
3. Do what is asked of you, especially when it is uncomfortable.
4. No matter what your coaches throw at you, be positive.
5. Establish a mind set so tough that nothing can bother you, you cannot be broken.
6. Get to bed on time, keeping good sleeping habits.
7. Push yourself to your physical and mental limits, then operate decisively and confidently while in that exhaustion zone.
8. Practice good acting skills, showing you are always ready and excited for the battle even when you might be feeling poorly that day.

During the tough times, practice looking like a soldier, never whining, never complaining, never negative, no matter how bad it gets. Fight your best to the bitter end. As long as there is a second on the clock, give it all you have and you will be the fearless warrior that will take you to the top.

Finally, live your wrestling career with passion!

Money In the Bank

Fall deposits yield high dividends for spring. What you deposit in your training "bank" now will multiply and allow for some hefty withdrawals come Nationals and World Team Trials in the spring and summer.

What the heck am I talking about?
Your spring/summer peak will greatly depend on your fall activity. To peak most effectively when it counts, you must establish an extensive conditioning base now.

What does this mean?
October through December should be three months of extensive training volume. We are currently in the "Conditioning Phase" of our yearly training cycle – the three training phases being (1) Conditioning, (2) Preparation and (3) Competition.

The main goals of the Conditioning Phase are:
   1. Develop aerobic cardiovascular endurance
   2. Develop anaerobic muscular power
   3. Develop new techniques and tactics
   4. Lower intensity workouts and longer duration of practice time

Running should be of the distance nature, four to six times per week/3-6 miles for 20-60 minutes. You may want to have one long run per week (6-10 miles).

Wrestling workouts should be longer in nature (approximately two hours) and lower in intensity. Long grind wrestling, situation wrestling, drilling favorite techniques and learning new techniques should be the emphasis.

Weightlifting should be more for power. Heavy weights, low reps, etc.

NOTE: You can always change up your workouts to avoid becoming stale or bored. Feel free to substitute short, sweet workouts every so often. For example: you could wrestle fast matches or run sprints to change the daily routine.

The volume you put in during this "Conditioning Phase" will build your base conditioning. Learning new technique and refining your favorite technique is crucial here.

Experiment! Experiment! Experiment!

Really look to expand your knowledge and style. Don't worry too much about feeling tired in this phase – you should feel tired. Longer workouts will tend to drain you both physically and mentally, but that is okay. When you start to shorten your practice time and start higher-intensity workouts is when you'll really feel fresh mentally and physically powerful.

So, put those dollars in the bank now! When the time comes for you to make a withdrawal, you'll have plenty of "bucks" to spend!

No Pain, No gain; Good or Bad?

It is the first week of wrestling practice, and every muscle in your body is sore and tired. You are right in the middle of a workout and you hurt everywhere. Your body is exhausted. You are hot, sweaty and cranky.

You are already sick and tired of your coach's demanding attitude. He is barking out orders, driving you and your teammates through relentless wrestling, running and exercise routines. It includes wrestling "goes," sit-ups, pushups and sprints, among other tasks. Your coach is determined to get your team in shape and you don't know if you can take another day of this.

This is an example of "over-training." Your body simply cannot adapt to the stress of the training your coach is putting you through. The volume of stress is greater than the capacity for recovery. Regardless of whether your coach is putting you through an unreasonable workout or you have under-trained in the preseason and come into the season out of shape, it doesn't matter — the fact is you are over-training and are at a higher risk of injury, shin splints, muscle pulls, groin pulls, calf pulls and cramping.

And then, suddenly, one of your teammates shouts out, "Come on guys, no pain, no gain!"

Now, we have all heard the phrase "No pain, no gain!" Every athlete must determine for his/her self whether this is a good philosophy or a harmful philosophy when considering the very important issues of "over-training and under-training."

This chapter will attempt to help you figure out *for yourself* what philosophy you should use in regard to your training and the "No pain, no gain!" theory.

First of all, I think we all know to increase one's toughness, conditioning and wrestling prowess it takes hard training. Stressing one's body, mind and soul is how you get stronger physically, mentally and emotionally. By stressing, I mean taxing your body with difficult physical tasks such as wrestling hard, running a certain distance or doing a strenuous weightlifting workout.

Stressing your mind might include changing the way you think when you feel tired or bored so as to feel energetic and excited. Stressing your emotions might include practicing feeling hungry for the battle when you really feel nervous. These are just a few ways you might apply stress in your daily training regimens to help make you tougher, better conditioned and a more skilled wrestler.

The big question is how much stress should be applied and for how long? What kind of balance do you use regarding these training issues?

Studies show that too much training (stress) for too long a period, with insufficient recovery, can lead to "over-training."

As already stated, when you get to a state of over-training, you are much more prone to injury or sickness. Your muscles feel sore and tired; you may have chronic fatigue. Emotionally, you may be bored, depressed, moody and unmotivated. Mentally, you may think more negatively, make more mental mistakes and have poor concentration. Instead of getting tougher and stronger, you actually start to get weaker when in this overtrained state.

On the other hand, under-training (or too little training stress) will create the same weakening effect as over-training. Let me explain why.

To keep yourself close to or at your "Ideal Competitive State" your body requires a certain amount of stress. For example, let's assume that to maintain your current level of fitness, you require 100 units of physical, mental and emotional stress per training session. The 100 units of stress is the amount you can take comfortably.

For you to achieve greater goals, thus moving you forward, it will require increasing your daily training stress to 120 units. But instead, you reduce your training stress to 80 units. After a period of time (say three weeks), your capacity to sustain stress will decline to 80. Now when it is time to perform or train back at 100 units, your body will react the same as it does when you over-train. Essentially, that is now what you are doing (over-training) because your current capacity to sustain stress is now at 80 units.

The idea is that to continually move forward and advance your toughness, you need to constantly be training close to the "over-training" mark. This is why it is so important for each athlete to listen to his/her body and know for yourself what is enough stress to move you forward, but not too much, too long, to push you over into the over-training mode.

There is a fine line between the real (destructive) pain and just pain (discomfort). That is why you have to figure out for yourself the "No pain, no gain" theory. In my mind, I define pain two ways:

(1) Good pain – discomfort pain which actually feels good because I know it is advancing my toughness, and

(2) Bad pain – real destructive pain which will lead to injury, lack of motivation, lack of enjoyment.

So when you talk "no pain, no gain," it really depends on how you define pain. The other thing we must realize is what might be pain to someone is discomfort to someone else. This is why all athletes must identify this for themselves.

For me, I like to always train on the border of over-training. Personally, I felt during my competitive days that I had a good handle on my body. I could read the signs pretty clearly, and if I did make a mistake, I didn't mind erring on the side of over-training because I figured I would achieve my goals quicker by doing this. I always knew if I went too far into the over-training mode, I could always take a break and recover.

Probably the most important thing wrestlers can learn for themselves is to know their body and how to read it. This allows the wrestlers to stay at the most productive level of training to advance their conditioning and skills.

Here is how I see it:

As an athlete, learning to distinguish what is good pain (enough stress) from bad pain (too much stress, too long a time period) is the key to keeping you on a fast pace to achieve your goals. The point is simple: no discomfort – no toughening; no pushing – no toughening; no personal confrontation – no toughening. To put it simply, without stress, you cannot achieve your goals.

I believe balancing your training stress is an ongoing issue and constant battle. You never totally figure it out. It is an ongoing process to which you must always pay attention. So determining the "no pain, no gain" theory and what it means specifically for you might very well be one of the greatest challenges you will have to meet if you want to achieve your full potential.

Chapter 6
Competition

The Art of Securing the Victory

How do you finish the last minute or seconds of a match when you are winning? What do you focus on? What is your strategy? Against a tough opponent when it is a close match and you are winning with one minute to go, how do you secure the victory? You must wrestle smart! But what does smart mean? Here is one strategy you might consider.

Obviously, there is no need to take a big risk. But the worst thing you could do is stall by slowing the match down, or holding your opponent tight. On the contrary, you should pick the pace up, sprint very fast but with short elbows. A lot of movement, sticking and moving, faking, circling, banging, pulling the head, pushing in and out, grunting, acting, light on your feet. Not giving any ground.

You may not have any intention to score again but the referee, the fans and your opponent must think otherwise. This is where being a good actor comes into play.

In the last minute (or so) you must smell the victory drawing near and totally dominate the pace and action. Momentum is the key here. You must create *your* momentum and not allow your opponent to gain his.

No static position. Short elbows, fast pace but protect from any throw. You must look and be aggressive but in your mind you are burning seconds off the clock. You should be very alert and quick to react. Stay close to your opponent but, again, no static position. Always move short and choppy. Stay one or two steps ahead of his movement. You must get the passivity call and either put him down or get right back in his face.

This will break him both mentally and physically. He is looking for that one last shot at scoring on you – but you never give him a second to get his wits together to set the move up. A lot of the time he will start to panic and make a desperation attack which will be sloppy, allowing you to capitalize on his bad attempt and score.

Being focused on this (or a similar) strategy will keep you mentally and physically strong…minimizing the chance for you to make a mistake.

This strategy requires confidence in your physical conditioning and technical pummeling skills. I encourage you to take time in practice to experiment with this tactic. Every U.S. wrestler should be totally confident that he/she can stop anyone in the world from scoring in the last minute by out-sprinting and moving the foe.

Why Wrestle in the Spring and Summer?

Spring is the time when most wrestling seasons start wrapping it up for the year and the wrestling room isn't consistently used until the following fall. Most wrestlers take this time off and wait until fall to resume their wrestling career.

Why? Many freestyle and Greco-Roman tournaments are held in the spring and summer months. These tournaments are great opportunities for young wrestlers to further develop their wrestling skills. In many of these tournaments participants may wrestle five to seven matches in a day. This many matches alone affords a wrestler much experience and a great opportunity to identify and improve one's skills.

Wrestling in these kinds of tournaments offers many benefits:
- Wrestling is wrestling. Wrestling freestyle or Greco will enhance an individual's folkstyle wrestling technique. Even though different techniques are involved and the rules differ slightly, the extra experience greatly improves one's skills.
- Wrestling through the year will keep you in wrestling shape.
- More attention to any activity allows you to get better at it. (i.e. if you play numerous chess games, eventually you'll get better at chess).
- Practicing your "competition skills" – competing one-on-one with another individual on a regular basis trains you to be less nervous in future matches.
- Practice dealing with the referees more.
- A wrestler can wrestle at whatever weight he/she is at (NO CUTTING WEIGHT). This allows the wrestler to focus on skills and the competition itself.
- Usually, there is no team pressure – you are there with a friend or two and the atmosphere is much more relaxed. You can focus on individual skills and experiment with different skills. This is a good time to learn and experiment.

Even though the rules are different, again, wrestling is wrestling. The skills necessary to be successful in freestyle and Greco-Roman are the same skills needed in folkstyle wrestling. The same physical conditioning components that it takes to be successful will be enhanced by wrestling in the spring and summer. The psychological aspects of wrestling are all the same and those areas will be developed also.

I remember one of my first Greco-Roman tournaments I went to as a 15-year-old. I wrestled six matches in one day and that intense (six matches) yet relaxed (just two buddies and me) atmosphere was one of the most important developmental experiences of my career. I went from being a mediocre 10th-grade wrestler to beating two high school state place-winners in this particular tournament. This tournament was the catalyst that ignited my hunger for the sport.

I encourage you to wrestle in spring and summer.

Are You Strong Enough To Handle Critics?

"It is not the critic who counts, not the man who points out how the strong man stumbles or where the doer of deeds could have done them better. The credit belongs to the man who is actually in the arena, whose face is marred by dust and sweat and blood, who strives valiantly, who errs and comes short again and again because there is no effort without error and shortcomings — who knows the great, who spends himself in a worthy cause, who at the best knows in the end the high achievement of triumph and who, at worst, if he fails while daring greatly, knows his place shall never be with those timid and cold souls who know neither victory nor defeat."

THEODORE ROOSEVELT
Twenty-Sixth President of The United States of America
(and wrestling enthusiast)

Finding Your Ideal Competitive State

Recently, I was asked by the U.S. Olympic Committee's Sport Psychology Department and Athlete Services Division to prepare a workshop on mental toughness. Mental toughness is a topic I write about often but can never fully express how important it is.

What is mental toughness? By definition, toughness is "to be strong and resilient; able to withstand great strain without tearing or breaking." Mental toughness to me is being able to reach your Ideal Competitive State (ICS) on command.

What exactly is your Ideal Competitive State? Your ICS is your personal state of being that allows an individual to perform to their greatest potential. It is a state of being where an individual feels most energized, most confident and most strong. It is a state where you are generating positive emotions that help you be most alert, instinctive, responsive and creative – when you have that positive fighting attitude and are enjoying the battle.

There are several emotions that can block your potential – fear, confusion, low energy, fatigue and helplessness. When you feel these negative emotions you should practice changing your mindset. This is when you must practice creating the positive emotions mentioned in the previous paragraph. There are every-day situations that can challenge your ICS: lack of sleep, which makes you sluggish and tired; referees that make bad calls; girlfriends/boyfriends that break up with you; pressure from school/work/family.

Toughness is being able to create these positive emotions upon command, thus enabling you to bring all your talent and skills to life at that moment, no matter what negative thing(s) might be affecting you.

An example of this for me was in the 1984 Olympics, the night before I wrestled Frank Andersson, a powerful, golden-haired athlete who enjoyed the status of a movie star in Sweden and who had claimed the World Championship in 1979, 1981 and 1982.

With his great strength and technique, his quickness and his superb sense of balance, Andersson had devastated his first three opponents in those Olympic Games. Each of Andersson's foes had served as a target for his most breathtaking and crowd-pleasing throw, the high arcing "back suplex." Andersson was flamboyant, a thrower who could literally hurl his foes out of contention. I was unspectacular, a grinding, physical fighter who pounded his opponents into exhaustion. Andersson was the international wrestling community's pick to win the Olympic title. I was considered a long shot.

Needless to say, I went to bed that night a bit nervous. I had won my previous two matches earlier in the day but in the morning I would face the biggest challenge of my entire career. Andersson had already been quoted in the L.A. Times as saying, "Since beating the Greek earlier today, now nothing stands in the way of my winning the gold medal."

VICTORY

So as I lie in bed, I focused my mind not on winning or losing but only on things I could surely control. You can't always control winning and losing but I knew I could control the pace and intensity of the fight. I wanted to make the match exciting for the American crowd. I visualized myself defending the "back suplex," Andersson's most powerful weapon. I saw myself stopping this spectacular throw over and over. Finally, I drifted off to sleep.

The next morning, Frank Andersson and I came together in the center of the mat and shook hands. Then the referee blew the whistle and the first period began. I came out sprinting, just as I had planned. And just as I had planned, I scored on Andersson almost immediately with my favorite throw, my slam headlock.

Fifteen seconds into the match, I swung my right arm through the air and slammed my shoulder across Frank Andersson's neck, hurling him down onto the mat. The blow came so fast and with such power that Andersson had no chance of stopping it. Having thrown him down, I was unable to hold him on the mat because he was so strong. Instantly, he was back on his feet. But I was leading, amazingly, 3-0. My quick score was certainly unexpected, and the crowd, which was 95 percent American, screamed furiously.

Moments later, I tried the headlock again. But this time, he stopped me and I slipped and fell to my belly. My botched throw not only earned Andersson a point from the referee, it gave him a chance to try the suplex as I fought for position down on the mat.

What followed then, I believe, was the turning point of the match. It all happened so fast. Frank Andersson got his hands underneath me and began to lift. The crowd was screaming. I remember thinking, "I've just got to fight!" For a second, my feet were off the ground, and then I adjusted and got my toes barely on the floor.

At this point, all my knowledge of technique went flying out the window. I just gritted my teeth and got as tough as I could. I was like a frenzied animal caught in the jaws of a trap. Survival was my only concern. And I was going to claw and writhe and do everything I could to survive.

I twisted and thrashed so violently that Andersson had to set me down. Then, deliberately, he lifted me again. And again he raised me slightly off my feet. This time I turned into him. I faced him. I didn't think to myself, "Oh, he's lifting me so I have to turn into him." I just did it. It wasn't necessarily a classic defense, but it was the only thing I could do at the time. I think it shocked him. And it worked. We both fell down on the mat.

Andersson, his arms still locked around me, lifted me a third time and tried to turn me in a different direction. I fought like a tiger and for a third time I rebuffed him. It was furious and frenzied. The whole episode lasted 45 seconds. The match itself was only one minute old.

The referee then blew his whistle to stop the action, and Andersson and I separated. I had survived. Perhaps I had done more than just survive. As I backed away from him, my head up, he remained on his knees for a moment, holding his back. Then he stole a few seconds so he could catch his breath. I don't know whether he had really hurt his back or whether he just needed a little rest. But I do know that lifting someone like that three times without success can take a lot out of you. I knew it must have taken something out of him. And it said a lot to me, too. I thought, "Yeah, I stopped him."

I went on to beat Frank Andersson that day by a score of 4-1, which the Los Angeles Times called one of the biggest upsets of the 1984 Olympic Games.

I had trained many years preparing for that moment. Being able to control my Ideal Competitive State at the time I needed it most was crucial for me to perform to my potential. This took a lot of practice throughout my career.

How do you practice and improve your ability to kick in to your Ideal Competitive State (ICS) upon command? First, you have to determine your own personal ICS. Think back on a great performance – how great it felt, how fun it was. These are the feelings you want to be able to recreate on command.

1. Next time you are feeling down or have low motivation before practice, take advantage of it. This is a great time to practice controlling your ICS. Become a great actor! (Anyone can act out how they really feel). Remember, your body helps your mind and vice versa.

2. Concentrate on your body language – smile, walk straight, head up, shoulders back, and look confident. Include a light skip to your step. If you force your body to act "alive and positive," it will tell your mind that you are "alive and positive." Same with your mind – think positive thoughts, think of all the good in your life (family, friends, life in sports). Thinking positive thoughts will help to get your body in a positive mode.

3. Perfect the mindset. No Complaining! Nothing can bother you! Nothing can break you, no matter what your coach throws at you, no matter what your opponent does. No matter what the situation, nothing can rattle you. And all because you're too tough, too resilient, too focused! Just like the dictionary definition of toughness, you are able to withstand great strain without tearing or breaking!

4. Put yourself in adverse practice situations and overcome! Imagine being behind on the scoreboard, the victim of a bad call or a cheating opponent. The more you can overcome, the better the training.

5. Toughness is learned, make no mistake about it! If you are not tough, it just means you need more practice. Just like learning or perfecting a technique or skill, toughness can be learned, refined and honed.

No matter how old or young, weak or strong, you can be tougher! Never believe you can't achieve because you are not talented enough, smart enough or weren't given the gifts to succeed. Your future is much more dependent on the decisions you make and what you do than on your genetic make up.

Believe me, the level of toughness you acquire through toughness training will be the most powerful FORCE in your athletic career, and in your life!

Chapter 7
Overcoming Adversity

From the Brink of Failure

Failure, I know now, can be a blessing. A mistake can be the greatest teacher. But failure can be a blessing and mistakes can work as a teacher only if they are followed by six simple but powerful words: What can I learn from this?

It was 1976 and I was in my freshman year at the University of Michigan. I remember it like it was yesterday. The year was a major turning point in my wrestling career and my life. Midway though the first semester I found myself failing a tough course entitled Physiology 101. The University of Michigan had strict academic requirements for athletes, and I knew that if I flunked this physiology course, my wrestling career would be in jeopardy.

If I couldn't make it at Michigan as a student, I certainly wasn't going to be able to fulfill my dreams as a wrestler. But to say I was in danger of flunking is putting it too mildly. We were nearly halfway though the term, and I had no idea what was going on. The text could have been written in Greek and I would not have understood it any less. I was not academically oriented in high school, and my poor study habits had finally caught up with me. I had earned a D minus on the first physiology test and an F on the second. Only two more exams remained. It was like being down on the mat, trapped in a suffocating headlock. It was a nightmare. I couldn't breathe.

For a few days, I was in a panic. I felt I was too far behind to catch up, but I was also willing to do anything I could to survive. So I started seeing a tutor, an athletic-looking graduate student at Michigan. Several other athletes, mostly football players, were in the tutor's class. I don't remember the tutor's name, but I'll never forget what he said.

"Steve," the tutor told me, "You're not going to be able to learn what's in these chapters by reading them once. And you're not going to be able to learn by reading them twice. You're going to have to read them three times."

When he said that, my heart sank. I can't read this stuff once, I said to myself. How am I going to read it three times? When I had tried to read the physiology book in the past, I would start reading and fall asleep. But this time I didn't have any choice. I wanted to stay in school too badly. I wanted my wrestling career too badly. All my dreams depended on my staying at Michigan. To survive I had to follow the tutor's plan.

Then the tutor gave me a second piece of advice.

"Go to the library and just stay there," he said. "The first time you read through the chapters, just read and don't try to figure everything out. Look at the diagrams, but if they don't make sense, keep going. The second time, start figuring out some of the words you don't know. Take a closer look at the diagrams. The third time through, look up everything you don't know and make sure you understand every diagram."

Just as the tutor advised, I went to the undergraduate library and sat down in a corner where no one would bother me. I had three chapters to read — one on the circulatory system, one on the reproductive system and one on the respiratory system. The heart does interest me, I said to myself. Maybe this won't be so bad.

Well, sure enough, the first time through the circulatory system chapter, I didn't understand a single thing. Just as I figured. But as soon as I finished the chapter, I went right back to the beginning and started to read it again. And you know what? All of a sudden, a few of the concepts became clear to me. A few of the diagrams made sense. I finished the chapter a second time and, excited and hopeful, I went immediately to the beginning. This time it was like osmosis. Everything made sense. Words I had never heard before had meaning for me.

I can't tell you how inspired I was. During the next lecture, which I attended with 300 other students, I sat in the auditorium and actually understood what the professor was saying. Sometimes I would understand concepts before he explained them.

I remember turning to a friend sitting next to me, a hockey player, and saying, "Dave! I know what he's talking about. I honestly do!" Dave, who was also struggling a bit in the course, didn't believe me. He probably thought the pressure was getting to me.

You may not believe it either when I say that on the third test I got an A and that my score was among the top five in the class. I scored 95 out of 100 points. And with three of my five mistakes, I erred because I had misread the question. In truth, I knew the answers to 98 of the questions.

What my professor thought, I had no idea. He probably thought I had cheated somehow. Shortly thereafter, I stopped working with the tutor. I received an A minus on the final, which brought my final grade for the class up to a B.

My main reactions to my stunning academic recovery were ecstasy, relief and pride. Going from F's to A's let me know deep in my heart that I could succeed at Michigan. I could graduate. I remember thinking that if I could succeed in physiology, I could succeed in anything. Finally, after 12 and a half years of schooling, I had learned the discipline necessary for academic success.

That success was represented not only by the grade on my report card and but also by the lasting appreciation I gained for the miracle of the human body. The systems of the body, the respiratory system, the circulatory system and the nervous system, work together in harmony as a complex machine. My physiology studies left me with a feeling of awe for the whole body, because so many sequences of events must occur for you to perform even the simplest task. Here I was, an athlete, and yet I had never understood or appreciated what was happening within my body.

My comeback from the brink of failure in the classroom also reinforced my belief that dreaming, goal setting, planning and learning from your mistakes apply to everything in life. Until my encounter with physiology, I had worried I might not be cut out for academic life at Michigan, that perhaps I hadn't been born smart enough to succeed. I had worried that no matter how hard I worked, I wasn't going to make it in the classroom because I wasn't special. But Physiology 101 taught me you don't have to be special to make it.

Not surprisingly, my improvement in the classroom was paralleled by marked improvement in the wrestling room. My renewed confidence in myself helped me to believe I really could achieve anything I set my mind to.

How to Refocus In Bad Situations

It was the 1977 Junior World Team final wrestle-offs in Murphreesburo, Tennessee, where I was competing for the spot at 82kg. The Junior World Championships were to be held in LasVegas, Nevada, later that month. I had beaten my previous opponents and was now in the final two-of-three wrestle-off with a tough kid by the name of Don Brown from Oregon.

Don Brown was a real cocky wrestler who had a great lateral drop. He threw almost everyone he wrestled with this powerful throw. Throughout our training camp prior to this final wrestle-off we had trained together a bit and I can say that there was no love lost between us. He was very vocal and loud, always talking smack. I was pretty quiet and reserved, not an angel by any means but mostly shy. This contrast in personalities made these wrestle-off matches very emotional for me. I wanted very much to whip him good.

The first match was a very close and competitive bout, with a lot of close scores and situations. I ended up winning the match by a score of 5-3. After the match I went over to the cafeteria to eat lunch and rest for my next match with him. When I was at lunch, Joe DeMeo, who was the head coach, came in and told me that he had decided that there were some controversial calls in the match and that they were not going to count it. They were going to have us wrestle it over.

This was devastating to me! I believed I had won this match fair and square and they were now cheating me. Needless to say, I was very depressed and down. I had been away from home for over a month training in this World Team Camp and I really felt alone. This was my first serious training camp where I was away from my home in the middle of the summer.

Approximately three hours later I had to wrestle the match over. This time, Don Brown caught me in his infamous lateral drop and pinned me in less than one minute. Now I was extremely down! I went over in a corner of the gym and cried my eyes out.

One hour later I wrestled the third match (officially our second match). This match started off terrible for me. Again, he caught me in his lateral drop, plus one or two other moves, and all of a sudden I found myself down 9-0.

Well, now I was ticked! No more feeling sorry for myself. I was done with that attitude. Now I was mad. Now I was thinking if I am going to lose, I am going to go down swinging! So I kicked into gear.

I turned up the burners and went to work. Long story short – I ended up coming back and beating Don in that match, 14-13. Now that felt *good!*

In our fourth match of the day, just 30 minutes later, I whipped him good by a score of 12-0.

What I learned that day was tremendously valuable to my wrestling career. I learned that no matter what happens you must let go of the disappointment or setback and refocus. I was feeling sorry for myself and I was upset, feeling cheated, up until that third match where I was down 9-0. Then I finally let go of the anxiety and refocused.

When trying to master the skill of *Emotional Power,* which means you can totally control your emotions, you must know what to do when you are distracted, upset, or in a bad situation. If there is one characteristic that separates the great athlete from his fellow man or woman, it is the ability to handle his own negative feelings successfully. In all of sport, setbacks will occur from time to time. Performances rarely go as planned. Murphy's Law inevitably occurs at times. Because of this you must be ready to deal with the problems that you encounter.

One of the best ways to deal with getting upset is to be prepared for it. Wrestlers need to refocus quickly after they have become distracted or experience adversity. They need to let go of the upsetting moment and refocus on the next moment or step.

In his book *The Achievement Zone,* author Shane Murphy, Ph.D., recommends using a four-point plan to refocus: React, Relax, Reflect, and Renew. In trying to summarize, Murphy states the following:

1. **React:** As we know, setbacks can cause emotional reactions. It is difficult not to get upset when something gets in your way of success. The first reaction when you make a mistake or the official makes a bad call is to get angry. You may want to allow for this reaction but the key is then to quickly let it go and refocus on your game plan and strategy. Do not allow for your negative emotion to take over.

    The best athletes will acknowledge that they are human and will make some mistakes from time to time. They don't try to shut their emotions down but they do get back on track quickly and learn from the situation. The good athletes know that this is part of the process of achievement.

2. **Relax:** When negative emotions occur, you need to calm down quickly. Many athletes practice relaxation methods to help them calm down after a situation happens that upsets them. A lot of them use deep, abdominal breathing. The key is to find what works for you and then practice it so that it becomes habit.

3. **Reflect:** By being able to calm down right away, this will allow you to think more clearly. Thinking clearly will help you to learn something from the situation and make good decisions on what to do next.

4. **Renew:** Once you have put all the negative feelings behind you and refocused on what you must do next, then you can refocus on the total goal at hand and renew your commitment to the outcome.

All great wrestlers encounter tough, grueling problems either in matches or in their training. Overcoming these adverse situations and being trained to refocus on the tasks at hand will help keep you on track at achieving success. As usual, this takes practice. Use every tough situation to practice these skills and you will advance rapidly.

Attaining Success is Difficult...
That's What Makes it Great

All of us wish that success came easily. No one likes difficulty; no one likes adversity. No one likes obstacles and setbacks. But it is the struggle for success that makes success so great. If success came easily, everyone would have it. The fact that success is difficult to attain is what makes it so special and rewarding.

All the above, I believe, is why wrestling is such a great sport. It is why, once you have wrestled, you feel a part of a special family. No matter if you wrestled for only one year or for 20 years, once you have wrestled you know what kind of sport wrestling is – and, more importantly, how difficult wrestling really is. District, state, national champion or not… just competing in the sport will give you a measure of success.

Few sports require all the skills and attributes that wrestling requires – tactical and mental conditioning, knowledge, physical conditioning, power, strength, agility, flexibility, eye-hand coordination, cardiovascular conditioning, strategic and tactical expertise, quickness and rhythm, to name just a few. Wrestling is truly one of the most difficult and grueling sports in the history of the world.

Hand-to-hand combat, no one to back you up if you make a mistake. One-on-one athletics, just you and your opponent, and when you lose it's tough!

Losing matches in wrestling is hard. Because of the one-on-one aspect of the sport, losing can become very personal. Not many wrestlers have had the good fortune to avoid losing from time to time. Cael Sanderson of Iowa State went undefeated his entire college career, winning four NCAA national championship titles. This is an amazing accomplishment. I can't even imagine how he did it or how he felt!

But the majority of wrestlers, even great ones, experience many losses along the path to success. It is with these losses that we gain valuable insight and knowledge. It is with these losses that we make adjustments and learn to change things that will help us to improve.

The process of overcoming these losses is what strengthens our mind and soul. Overcoming adversity is what makes us tough. Think about it – meeting resistance is exhausting. It tears us down, it wears us out. Compare it to lifting weights. In strength training we lift weights (resistance) so we can tear down our muscles. We get tired from lifting weights. And then with proper rest and nutrition, our bodies rebuild stronger than before. Then we lift more weights for more repetitions, tearing down our muscles again, and then again through proper diet and rest our muscles rebuild to an even stronger state.

Losses are just like those weights. They are heavy, they are difficult to handle, they are no fun. But by experiencing losses it allows for, and even promotes, the growth within sport that we desperately need to succeed. Without facing these losses head on and overcoming them it would be difficult to grow.

I recall in 1982, when I was 23 years old, I was training extremely hard and had been for a number of years, and yet I had never won a Senior National title. I remember discussing the fact with my girlfriend at the time, Leslie, who became my wife. I remember how frustrated I was and telling her. "I train my living butt off, and for what?"

The next day we were scheduled to leave Ann Arbor, Michigan, where we lived, and drive to Cincinnati, Ohio, so I could compete in the U.S. Greco-Roman Nationals. I remember suggesting to Leslie that we should just keep driving, right through Cincinnati, all the way to Florida and just take a vacation.

"I'm tired of busting my butt for nothing," I told her.

Fortunately, Leslie was thinking more rationally than I was so after I came to my senses and stopped feeling sorry for myself, I was back to my original plan of competing in Cincinnati.

Well, wouldn't you know it? The saying "It's always darkest before the dawn" really rang true. I went down to Cincinnati and won my first national Greco title by beating Mike Houck in the finals.

Losses, like weights, tear us down. But through proper evaluation and psychological and physical rejuvenation we get stronger. We overcome those losses and move forward in our quest for success.

From that victorious national championship day forward, I looked at losses differently. I realize now that I was afraid to lose. And when you are afraid of something you tend to hesitate or stay away from it. I made a conscious decision that I was going to run full-speed ahead. No more caution about failure or losing. I was going to give it my very best every time and, win or lose, I would learn from my experiences and I would be proud.

Don't Be Afraid of Adversity

When I was a senior at Hazel Park High School, I finally became good enough in the sport to win the wrestling state championship in Michigan. With that state title, I won a full scholarship to go to the best college in the entire nation, The University of Michigan (What? You don't all agree?), to get my education and wrestle.

You should have seen me... I thought I was one of the roughest, toughest guys around. "YEAH! *I'm* going to go the University of Michigan as a freshman. I am going to make the varsity team, no problem! I was state champ."

Well, the guy I had to beat to make the varsity team was Mark Johnson (now head coach at the University of Illinois). Mark was a senior, captain of the team and he had a different idea of what was going to happen when he and I wrestled, much different from my idea.

Mark Johnson and I wrestled almost every single day for the first four months of the season and never once, not one time, did I score a single point on him. He beat the living tar out of me every single day. You'd figure after about two months of him beating me up that he might feel sorry for me. You know, maybe let me score one lousy point on him. No way!

In the classroom, I was failing two classes, a history class and a physiology class, and I was going down for the third time, with big fat Fs all the way up through and including my mid-terms. There was no way I thought I could pass these courses. In fact, I'm sure my instructors had written me off already... saying, "We won't see him back."

I remember calling my mother on the phone, tears in my eyes, the whole shot. "Mom, I'm coming home (sniff, sniff). I'm failing these two classes and Mark Johnson keeps kicking my butt in the wrestling room." I mean, I was truly as low as I could be.

But what I learned from getting through all that mess is with me still today, and I hope will be with me the rest of my life. What I learned is that, "Yes, Steve Fraser can do anything he wants.... *if* he really wants it bad enough."

Now, the only solution I could think of was to get a tutor, which was tough for me to do. However, my options were limited, so I got a tutor. We started at square one and he basically taught me when to study, what to study, how to study properly – and I'll tell you what: I don't think I have ever had a comeback like this in the sport of wrestling. I went from complete failure in these two classes to As on my final exams. I mean, I was in total shock that I could make that dramatic of a comeback. Needless to say, my teachers were in shock also.

Back in the wrestling room (I will never forget this), I finally scored on Mark Johnson. I finally took him down. It was a Friday, December 15th, 3:36 in the afternoon, arm drag – took him down. Two-point takedown. I remember jumping up, "YEAH!" I was so excited. Now, he probably just slipped on some water or something that was on the mat, but my point here is not only is it easier for us to learn from our adversities but what we learn from them has a much greater impact and stays with us a lot longer than what we sometimes learn from our successes.

Obviously, it is no fun to fail, but failing can be good because it forces us to change, it forces us to re-evaluate and to stretch and grow. I am totally convinced that because I overcame those obstacles, those setbacks, I have achieved a much greater level of success than I would ever have been able to accomplish if I didn't have those experiences.

Throughout my life, I have found that the most successful people in the world make mistakes – they experience failure a lot. Tom Monaghan, founder and former owner of Domino's Pizza and the former owner of the Detroit Tigers baseball club, is a perfect example of someone who has made many mistakes. He started Domino's Pizza by opening his first store in 1960. Almost bankrupt numerous times, he turned the business around to $2.8 billion in annual sales. Monaghan is also an example of a man who has what I like to call "laser vision." He's focused, and concentrates on his goals so his goals happen. He has no college education, but he's got a focus and drive that is amazing.

Again, when it comes to making mistakes, when it comes to failing, I encourage all of us to look at these hurdles as positive things, as things that can help us get the true success that we may want further down the road. The more adversity we experience and overcome, the stronger we become. So, pray hard; pray that God will bless you with all the most grueling, agonizing and difficult problems He can find – and you'll have the opportunity to overcome those obstacles, thus allowing you to become stronger with each and every hurdle you jump.

Part Three:
Reflections

Advice From Champions

In 1996, I had the opportunity to attend the FILA Higher Wrestling School's Coaches Clinic/Conference held in Rome, Italy. Bruce Burnett, Dan Mello and I spent six full days of learning and sharing with some of the best wrestling minds in the world. A tremendous amount of insight and knowledge was exchanged by all.

Milan Ercegan, FILA President, kicked off the program by expressing the importance of keeping wrestling exciting for the fans.

"The future of Olympic wrestling will depend on how we can make it a dynamic, spectacular sport. A wrestler can only show his professional skills when he is properly prepared," said Ercegan. He talked about the "total wrestling" concept – how a wrestler must go all out for five minutes, must have the ability to execute many holds, be willing to take risks and be creative in the wrestling approach.

Numerous Olympic and World champions, as well as FILA experts, were on hand for technique demonstrations, as well as various other reports and lectures. Professor Harold Tunnemann, a highly-respected wrestling expert from the former East Germany state, shared the most up-to-date statistics and analysis on a plethora of important topics, including analysis of the Atlanta Olympics. Dr. Tunnemann does FILA research and analysis and was responsible for East Germany's rapid advancement in the 1980s and '90s. One very interesting report was explained with a major highlight I personally enjoyed. It stated that compared to the mean performance of the Olympic Cycle (1992-1995) the USA came out as one of the "Big Winners" of the Atlanta Olympic Tournament in Greco-Roman.

In the technique sessions for Greco we had a number of quality coaches go over their best stuff. This group included Guro Gurov, Bulgarian World champ; Misa Mamiachivili, Russian Olympic and World champ and head of the Russian Greco team; Ryszard Swierad, Polish World champ and coach of Poland's Olympic team; Vincenzo Maenza, Italian two-time Olympic champ and one-time silver medalist. Many techniques were demonstrated, analyzed and discussed.

In addition to the information being presented, I took this opportunity to personally interview a few of the clinicians and presenters, asking them a few basic questions. Here are their responses:

1. **What is the most important thing one must do to become a world-class wrestler?**

    Maenza: Get the right partner. That means going all over Europe, getting strong partners and different partners. He spent 10 months a year away from home. His trainer traveled with him, which is very important.

Tunneman: Tough training partners and tough training camps. Bringing your best wrestlers together is important because they learn from each other.
Mamiachivili: Many hours of very hard work with tough training partners.

2. **What advice would you give a senior athlete who is close to becoming world-class?**
   Maenza: Commit 100 percent; total commitment.
   Tunnemann: Train in the proper system.
   Mamiachivili: Work even harder.

3. **What's the biggest obstacle for a wrestler to overcome?**
   Maenza: Weight control.
   Tunneman: Identifying a system to track and evaluate one's progress and weaknesses.
   Mamiachivili: Skill development.

4. **What is the importance of weight training?**
   Maenza: Mostly work with partners; muscles of the back are most important. Not always heavy but more for endurance.
   Tunnemann: Important to do weightlifting and body-lifting.
   Mamiachivili: Very important.

5. **How important is running?**
   Maenza: He cycled a lot (outside). More cycling than running. (*Fraser's Note:* I get the feeling that overall, Europeans don't run as much as Americans. This is why we can out-condition them. Our intense training methods – which include wrestling hard and easy, weight lifting, drilling, body-lifting, running, cycling and cross-training – are our U.S. advantage.)

6. **What would you tell a senior athlete who has difficulty in attending national camps?**
   Maenza: If they cannot get to all camps, they must be very self-disciplined with their training.
   Mamiachivili: No problem in Russia.

7. **Identify general training differences between six months out, three months out, and one month out from peaking competition.**
   Maenza: One month before major competition, shorter practice, highest intensity.

8. How many kilograms did you lose?

Tunnemann: Olympic analysis shows average weight loss of Olympic champion was 3-5 kg.

Dan Gable once told me something that helped me through my careers both on and off the mat. I had asked him the question, "What does it take to be the best?" He replied that he "always tried to act naïve when it came to learning more about wrestling."

I took this to mean that you should always listen to what coaches and other wrestlers have to say – even less talented or less accomplished people. Digest the information; keep the valuable and disregard the rest. Always look for the valuable pieces of information that will help you improve. Continuous, relentless, obsessive hunger for wrestling knowledge will keep your career advancing forward. Be like a sponge and soak it all up!

Olympic Memories from 2000

The boys put it together when it counted. Winning three medals in the 2000 Sydney Olympic Games in Greco-Roman Wrestling and placing two other guys in the top six allowed our U.S. Greco squad to finish in third place as a team. In the unofficial team standings (there is no official team score kept in Olympic competition), Russia took first place scoring 41 points, Cuba was second with 39 points, and the USA finished third, with 37 points. For the U.S. Greco squad, this is arguably the best finish ever in World or Olympic competition.

Can we do better? Absolutely! We were so close to beating the Russians and winning the whole thing in Sydney. With just a hair more improvement and everyone wrestling up to their potential, we can consistently compete for the team title. We proved that by beating Russia's two best wrestlers (Koguouachvili at 97 kg and Karelin at 130 kg).

As many people realize, we have a great challenge in the U.S. with our Greco-Roman program. Because our U.S. wrestling system lends itself to developing collegiate/freestyle wrestlers, it is especially challenging to compete in Greco at the top world level. Keep in mind, Quincey Clark (our 85 kg Olympian) has only wrestled Greco for three years. Last year in the World Championships, Quincey beat this year's Olympic champion and bronze medalist.

Rulon Gardner did not even know what Greco-Roman wrestling was seven years ago. For our big-hearted, extremely-dedicated, tougher-than-nails Greco team to overcome this adversity and step up is truly an amazing accomplishment.

I hope our medals in Sydney, and Rulon Gardner's victory over the seemingly invincible Alexander Karelin, will inspire and motivate even more young wrestlers to realize the dream of becoming Olympic champions in Greco-Roman wrestling.

To see a wrestler like Rulon Gardner train the way he does — so intensely that his training partners try to avoid him in practice — makes me realize how tough our team is. To see people like Rulon wrestle in the Winter Classic when he is sick, knowing most wrestlers would just skip the event, makes me proud to be a part of it. To see Dan Chandler, U.S. Olympic head coach, and Rob Hermann, assistant Olympic coach (who, by the way, are volunteers), take so much time away from home and family for the cause of preparing our team leaves me humbled and proud.

Any success we had in Sydney was due to a huge team effort. Chandler executed the training plan throughout the year at all training camps leading up to the Games. Dan's leadership and knowledge of Greco-Roman wrestling is tremendous. Hermann played a big role in keeping our team focused and hungry for competition.

Jay Antonelli, Momir Petkovic, Pavel Katsen and Roman Wroclawski all contributed vastly to the preparation of our team. Ike Anderson, National Developmental

Coach, managed his responsibilities in Sydney superbly. Anatoly Petrosyan, Resident Coach, should get special thanks and praise for his year-long contribution in training our resident athletes, four of whom placed in the top six in Sydney. Rulon Gardner, 1st; Matt Lindland, 2nd; Jim Gruenwald, 6th; Kevin Bracken, 6th.

There are many coaches who could not travel to Sydney who deserve credit for our results. Beasey Hendrix, our mental skills coach, has spent numerous hours working intimately with most of our top guys. Joe DeMeo, Bob Anderson, Rich Estrella, Ivan Ivanov, Stephan Ivanov, Anatoly Nazarenko, and Andy Seras have all attended many National Team camps and worked hard at helping improve our team. These unsung coaching heroes all played a huge part in our team's accomplishments.

I feel proud to be associated with USA Wrestling, the wrestlers and the coaches involved. Jim Scherr, USA Wrestling's former Executive Director and now Chief Executive of the United States Olympic Committee, along with Rich Bender, Associate Executive Director, and Mitch Hull, National Teams Director, have all been great mentors and leaders for our programs.

The U.S. Olympic Committee deserves a lot of credit. The US Olympic Training Center in Colorado Springs, along with the many programs afforded us, is another big key to our development. The USOC has been very generous with the needed funding assistance, which allows us to establish and execute valuable programs for our elite guys.

"The Team, The Team, The ENTIRE Team" deserves all the credit! Thanks to the entire Greco Roman Family – our true team! We will continue to move forward in Greco-Roman wrestling. Maybe a bit slow, but always sure.

Here are some of my Sydney Olympic Highlights:

- Steve Mays (54kg) wrestling his heart out every match and setting an example of being a great champion.
- Jim Gruenwald (58kg) dominating Igor Petrenko of Belarus (fourth in the world) in one of his pool matches, grinding him down to complete exhaustion.
- Kevin Bracken (63kg) crushing Choi Sang Sun of Korea (world medalist) in the first round of the Olympics 12-5, starting our team off on a positive note. The Korean was so tired he could hardly stand up.
- Heath Sims (69kg) wrestled a very smart match beating Katsuhiko Nagata of Japan. Because of the pool system, Nagata went on to win the silver medal.
- Matt Lindland (76kg) buzzing through three of the toughest 76 kg wrestlers (UZB, GEO, UKR) in his weight class, soundly and decisively, on his way to the finals. Matt's iron-strong attitude was extremely remarkable and his silver medal victory a tremendous feat.
- Quincey Clark (85kg) giving his best in wrestling the defending World Champion, Mendez from Cuba. What a great competitor with incredible heart.
- Garrett Lowney (97kg) destroying five-time World Champion Gogoi Koguouachvili from Russia in overtime with the most spectacular throw of the entire Olympic Games, a high-arching back suplay. This shocked the entire Russian wrestling federation, as well as the rest of the wrestling world.
- Rulon Gardner (130 kg) beating the seemingly invincible Alexander Karelin (Russia) for the gold medal was obviously a highlight, but seeing the expres-

VICTORY

sion on Karelin's face, when he looked at the clock with 30 seconds to go in the match, was even a bigger highlight. He had a look of desperation that I never saw in Karelin before. Me jumping on Rulon's head (squeezing as hard as I could) immediately after his victory was another highlight for me.

Thanks to the team and our Greco Roman family for the memories!

America's Fighting Spirit is the Key

After arriving in Istanbul, Turkey, for the 48th annual European Greco-Roman Championships on May 10-13, I was greeted by my old friend and former teammate Abdurrahim Kuzu. Yes, Abdurrahim Kuzu. Does that name ring a bell with anyone? Abdurrahim Kuzu, who is of Turkish descent, came to the U.S. in 1970, eventually becoming a U.S. citizen shortly before the Los Angeles Olympics. Wrestling for the U.S., he became our first Greco World Cup Champion, in 1980.

In 1979, at the World Championships in San Diego, he won a silver medal for our country. Then, in 1984, at the Los Angeles Olympics, where Kuzu was wrestling for our U.S. team at 62 kg, tragedy struck! After his semifinal match against Canadian Doug Yates, who he defeated by a score of 3-0, the Canadian coach protested the match. Behind closed doors, FILA reviewed the match on video and rescored it. This time, they came up with a score of 3-3, with the Canadian winning the tiebreaker.

By this time, Kuzu was already back at the Olympic Village, where he had gone to sleep. I'm sure already dreaming about the possibility of winning the gold medal the next day. He was in the finals and guaranteed of winning a silver medal.

Now, with the reverse decision of the protested match, Kuzu was no longer in the finals. He was no longer going to wrestle for gold. Now he had to wrestle and win just to take the bronze medal. It was terrible. It was devastating! It was down right robbery!

I remember hearing the tragic news while I was in drug testing right after my semifinal bout. Ron Finley, our head Olympic coach, and I rode back to the Olympic Village together. When we arrived at the Village, we found Kuzu asleep. Coach Finley decided not to wake him. He figured it would be better to wait until morning to tell him.

Well, morning came and it was not pretty. Can you imagine how terrible that news would be to you? It was devastating! Kuzu was shattered. He could not believe it. Words could not describe how Kuzu felt. Still to this day, I too don't even like to think about that morning.

Kuzu ended up losing the match for the bronze medal and finished in fourth place at the Olympic Games. I know his heart was not there for that bout. And the Canadian? He wound up in fifth place. The winning of the protested match did not help him even move up a place.

Seventeen years later, I can still see the agony in Kuzu's eyes when he speaks about this. I just want to commend him. Kuzu was a positive influence on our American team back then. He broke new ground for our U.S. Greco guys. He helped remind us we can beat the Russians, etc., and he led the way in doing just that. He was/is a great fighter, one who all Americans can be proud of.

Kuzu is currently involved with the Turkish Wrestling Federation in the capacity of technical director. This is a new position for him. He has been in Turkey for more than

VICTORY

eight years now, where he owns and operates a successful restaurant.

Now for some comments on the European Championships:

The competition was great as usual. There is something about the European Championships which is special. You can see the prestige and importance of winning here. When a wrestler makes it to the finals, it is like he just made is to the World finals. It is definitely big time!

There were a lot of young teams competing this year. Some countries said their veterans will be in New York and other countries said this is their new young squad. Regardless, young or veteran, the competition was fierce.

The Turkish squad took advantage of the home crowd and won the tournament, beating the Russians by 10 points. Team Georgia ended up in third place followed closely by Poland and Bulgaria.

The Turkish crowd was unbelievable. They packed the arena with about 10,000 people. And if you have ever heard the Turks cheer for their team, you can imagine what it was like. The cheering, yelling, chanting, whistling, horn blowing, drum pounding and booing. It was completely deafening at times. I have never in my life been in such a loud, ear-shattering atmosphere. It was great! This is what wrestling is all about. Even the few unidentified flying objects which were hurled onto the mat when the Turks thought they were getting a bad call was kind of fun (not really). You can sure say one thing – the Turks are into their wrestling!

The European Championships are like a war. It looks like men are wrestling for their lives out there. You can see 120 percent effort. They are in it with all their hearts and souls, every inch of the way. They are truly in battle. And, you can see the ones who really enjoy it. Enjoy the fight. Enjoy the game. Enjoy the close match, the intensity, the crowd, everything! It is fun to watch.

Of course, that's where my heart is because I know that is where our team's American spirit plays so strong. This intense fight is right up our alley. It is our biggest strength. American wrestlers are the ultimate fighters.

Foreign coaches are constantly saying to me they wished their boys had our American fighting spirit. Don't get me wrong, we can still learn a lot from our foreign opponents. But one thing we are the best at is having that "fighting spirit." Since I've been in Istanbul at least 10 countries have asked me if their team can train with us this September in preparation for the Worlds.

So regardless if you are a youngster or one of my national team members reading this — now is the time to emphasize that great "fighting spirit" strength of ours. Focus on this in practice. Build on it, practice using it. I like to call it "using great technique with a street fighter's mentality."

That is how we can win. That is how we can beat all the world's competitors. That is how we will become the world's best some day.

2001 Greco-Roman World Championships

At the Greco-Roman World Championships of 2001, we fell a bit short of the goal, winning only three medals and placing third in the team race. But, we are moving forward. This third place finish was a first for our U.S. Greco squad. Never before in our Greco history have we placed in the top three in a World Championship. In 2000, we did place third in the Sydney Olympics, which was our best performance to date in Olympic competition.

Cuba won the tournament this year with 54 points. Our friends from Cuba wrestled extremely well, placing a man at every weight class and claiming four medals. Russia took second place with 38 points, and three medals. For Russia, this was the first time since 1950 that it did not win the World tournament. Needless to say, the Russians were not smiling too much.

We scored 33 points. Our boys wrestled like madmen. They did not let the September 11th tragedy get them down. The events of September 11th may have altered the date and place of the championship, but it did not deter our dedicated Greco team from adjusting its training plan/schedule appropriately to prepare for this event. This was not an easy thing to do. There was no complaining, no negativity, no hesitation from the guys regarding going to Patras, Greece, December 6-9 and it paid off in their performance.

Here is a short capsule on each of our guys.

Brandon Paulson was unbelievable in his performance. Winning the silver medal was truly remarkable. Each match was very intense. Brandon's focus and relentless intensity were tremendous. He won close match after close match. He stuck to his game plan and it proved to be successful. For Brandon, this was his third major World event. He won silver in the Junior Worlds and silver at the Atlanta Olympics and now a silver in the 2001 Greco World Championships. Three international world events and three world medals, not too shabby.

Jim Gruenwald is one great leader. He fell short of his goal of winning the gold medal by ending up in 10th place at 58 kg, but as usual, he wrestled his heart out. Not only did he represent our country honorably, but he helped us accomplish our third place team finish. His contribution to our squad as one of our veterans shines very brightly. His great attitude, positive thinking, hard work and friendly and fun attributes all helped to create a winning atmosphere throughout our training and preparation. This lent enormous positive energy to our team's performance. Jim is a wonderful leader of men and a great person.

Kevin Bracken placed seventh in one of the toughest weight classes in the world. He wrestled extremely well. Kevin is one of the most explosive, quick, technical wrestlers in the world. His dedication to improving his skills the past few years has been very obvious and impressive. He destroyed his first three opponents by a combined score of 30-2. Then in his fourth match against Israel (the eventual bronze medallist), Kevin was up 2-0 with 15 seconds to go in regulation when, off of Kevin's arm drag, the Israeli, hit a half-hearted, desperation throw and the official awarded a controversial point, making the score 2-1.

At the end of regulation, they went to the clinch where Kevin threw the Israeli and in a hair splitting exposure situation, Kevin exposed his own back before coming up on top to score himself. But the two-point exposure against him ended the match 3-2 in favor of the Israeli. It was truly one of the most heart-breaking losses I've ever experienced. Kevin is another great example of what it takes to be the best.

Marcel Cooper had a tough draw, facing the 1999 World Champion from Korea in his first match. Marcel went ahead of the Korean but lost a hard-fought, close match. He is very talented and very close to being able to beat them all worldwide. Marcel has a great attitude and with a little more work, he will beat them all.

Keith Sieracki ended up 11th with a 2-1 record. Keith has a European style of wrestling, where he is very strong on his feet and has a great lift from the mat. This was Keith's first World Championships and with more experience and focus in a couple of areas, he can be the best. He is a great person to have on the squad, a real team player.

Matt Lindland won his second consecutive silver medal in World/Olympic competition and he did it up a weight class at 85 kg. This accomplishment is truly remarkable for him, as well as our team. This is the first time in the history of U.S. Greco-Roman wrestling that we have won a medal in World/Olympic competition at this weight category. And we have had some great U.S. wrestlers at this weight.

Matt had a tough draw, beating Yugoslavia, Israel and Uzbekistan, and in his fourth match, in the semi-finals against former World Champion Menshikov of Russia, Matt truly outdid himself. With the Russian team title on the line, Matt went out and wrestled one of the best matches I've seen him wrestle. With 10 to 15 seconds in regulation and with a score of 2-2, Matt lifted the Russian champion with his patented Matt Lindland-back lift. It was a crushing, explosive throw, scoring four points and securing the tremendous victory.

In the finals, Matt wrestled against Vakhrangrdze of Georgia, where he had a heart breaking 2-1 loss. Matt is a fine example of what American wrestlers can do with hard work and determination. He is one tough, mean individual and has the mental attitude of a gladiator. Matt is one of the best competitors I've ever had the pleasure to work with as a coach.

Jason Loukides was the first alternate at 97 kg. for the U.S. when Garrett Lowney (our Sydney bronze medalist) of the University of Minnesota opted not to wrestle at the Worlds due to academic and college schedule issues. Jason represented our team admirably, considering that he was suffering from a pretty severe back ailment during the World event. He had a tough draw and lost both his pool matches. He is a tough kid with a great attitude.

Rulon Gardner is truly the heavyweight champion of the world! This man, and I mean man, is for real. Rulon had by far the most difficult draw of anybody in any weight class. He wrestled Israel, Ukraine, Russia, Bulgaria and Hungary. I would consider every one of those guys to be in the top five or six in the world. The highlight for me was the match Rulon had against Patrikeev, the new "Russian Machine" in the quarterfinals. Patrikeev is a spectacular-looking heavyweight who has beaten Rulon twice previously. At the 2000 Podoubny Tournament finals in Moscow, Rulon lost to Patrikeev when Rulon got caught in a throw and pinned. This Russian is extremely powerful.

So the stage was set. The Russians were going to get their revenge for Rulon upsetting their national hero, Alexander Karelin, at the Sydney Olympic Games. The atmosphere was electric. Everyone in the arena was anticipating this match. The President of FILA, Milan Ercegan, was in his traditional seat at the head table, front and center, much like Caesar in the days of the Roman Empire.

The match was tremendous, with both champions scraping and fighting for position. There were some close scores, but no points went up on the board. At the end of the first period, it was 0-0. The infamous clinch was called to begin the second period.

Rulon won the toss, which meant the onus was on him to score within the first minute. They clinched and at 30 seconds, the Russian circled around in a forceful manner and Rulon broke his grip as they went out of bounds. One point was awarded to the Russian and Rulon went down in parterre.

For the second time in the match, the Russian exploded with his powerful gut-wrench attempts one way and then the other. But Rulon fought back and did not go over. They went back to their feet where Rulon started to pick up the pace. He locked his arms around Patrikeev in a bodylock/clinch position. Rulon then bore down on Patrikeev, exploding into a bodylock throw.

The action drove them out of bounds where Rulon wound up on his back. The ref scored no points, but the chairman wanted to review the action on the video replay and they decided to give two points for the Russian, with Rulon down in parterre again. The call was very controversial. Again Rulon stopped his foe from turning him. They went back to their feet with Rulon behind 0-3 with about 1:30 left in the match.

Now Rulon went into his sprint mode, sticking and moving, trying to get something going. The Russian was visibly getting tired. Then suddenly with about one minute left on the clock, Rulon locked Patrikeev up with another body lock, where Patrikeev struggled to hip throw Rulon. But not this year. Rulon crushed down on the Russian like I've never seen before. It was like Rulon had made up his mind at that moment that he was not going to let this guy beat him.

In a slow motion type of action, Rulon sucked the Russian's body tight to his, lifted him off the ground and threw him to his back. With a great crash, the Russian's shoulders were glued to the mat, where Rulon was squeezing the tar out of him.

FALL!!! PIN!!! THAT WAS IT!!!!. It was over. The arena went crazy and Rulon.... well, he just got up, put his arms up in the air and smiled to the people. The tears are starting to roll from my eyes just thinking about it again.

In the semis, he body locked the tough Bulgarian, Moreyko, to win 3-0. In the finals, he avenged another loss to the gigantic Deak from Hungary, 2-0, to make Greco-Roman history again. The first double-gold winner ever for our U.S. program. The Rulon Gardner saga continues. Average boy from Afton, Wyoming, becomes a two-time World/Olympic gold medal winner.

VICTORY

Creating a good training and preparation atmosphere at camp is crucial in preparing a team for world competition. We always try to create a fun but intense training environment with a lot of positive vibes and flex so athletes can adjust to meet their specific needs. This year's world team staff did a remarkable job at doing this and much more.

Joe DeMeo was head coach and worked with the team throughout the year but was unable to attend the main event due to personal health issues. Andy Seras was the assistant coach who stepped up and did a remarkable job of working with the team. Shon Lewis, head Army coach, along with Momir Petkovic and Ike Anderson rounded out the coaching staff. This staff worked together superbly getting this team ready for battle.

Our medical staff included Dr. Bernie Feldman and Rod Rodriguez. These two gentlemen are true pros and gave our team great care.

Our training partners that went to France and Greece with us were outstanding, as well. They included Michael Santos, Dan Niebuhr, Brad Vering, Joe Warren, James Shillow, Dremiel Byers and Matt Lamb.

2002 Greco-Roman World Championships

The Senior Greco-Roman World Championships of 2002 were very competitive again this year, as usual. Russia won the competition by scoring 45 points and winning four medals (two gold, one silver and one bronze). Georgia just edged Cuba for second place, scoring 27 points and winning two medals. Cuba was third with 26 points and two medals. Our U.S. squad tied in points (22) with Bulgaria for fourth but Bulgaria had two medals to our one so we ended up in fifth place as a team.

The highlight for us was Dremiel Byers winning the gold medal at 120 kg. Yes... Dremiel Byers, following in Rulon Gardner's footsteps and becoming the 2002 heavyweight champion of the world! This unprecedented feat means the USA has won the 120 kg Olympic/World title for three consecutive years.

Another highlight was that the U.S. team had four wrestlers place in the top eight in the world. Besides Byers' gold medal, Brad Vering's rookie showing was fabulous. Brad ended up in fifth place. Brandon Paulson, who was our silver medalist in last year's World Championships, placed 8th along with Jim Gruenwald, who improved over his last year's placing.

We also had strong showings from TC Dantzler (11th place), Kevin Bracken (14th place), and Garrett Lowney (28th place).

Coaching for the U.S. team included head and assistant coaches Andy Seras and Shon Lewis, respectively. Dan Chandler, Jay Antonelli, Momir Petkovic, Anatoly Petroysan and Ike Anderson rounded out the rest of our coaching staff. Bernie Feldman and Jim Nielson were our medical staff and Jeff Levitetz was our team leader.

The tournament had 216 wrestlers representing 51 countries. Numerous World and Olympic champions were upset early and wound up placing way down in the standings. I think that showed the strength of the field this year.

Our U.S. team had its goals set on winning the team title, with a minimum of five medals. To some this goal may seem a bit high but as the National Coach I am convinced that we can achieve this feat. The U.S. Greco staff and wrestling team feel the same. We fell short of the mission this year but I was very happy with the performance and heart of this amazing group of guys. The wrestlers, coaching staff and the rest of the Greco family are 100 percent committed to achieving our mission of winning it all and becoming world champions.

We lost more matches than we wanted to but we must realize that losing is a part of a strong winning strategy. Winners know that losing should be a part of any plan. My military coaches tell me that in the military and in war there are always contingency plans in place, which are plans for times when things do not go the way we expect them to go. Being willing to risk losing allows us to try different things and learn from our mistakes. Being willing to face adversity head-on and overcome it is what will propel us to the top of the world field.

Our team taking fifth place is really a great accomplishment when you look at where we have come from. This makes it three years in a row that the US Greco team was close to the top (2000 Sydney Olympics – third place; 2001 Greece World Championships – third place) and in the hunt for the overall team title.

So, we are proud of our efforts and current accomplishments but definitely not satisfied – and won't be until we prove to the world that the USA Greco-Roman Wrestling team is the best on this planet!

Individual Summary of each World Team Member

55kg Brandon Paulson – Brandon is one of the great veteran leaders on our team. Both a World and Olympic silver medalist, Paulson came out strong in his pool, beating Huhtala (FIN) 4-0 and then crushing Oubrick (FRA) 11-0. Then in the quarterfinals he wrestled a great match against the Russian, Mamedaliiev, to a 3-1 loss. This match had numerous controversial calls, always seeming to go to the Russian. Paulson had the Russian gassed but Mamedaliiev held on to squeak out the victory. Mamedaliiev went on to win the gold.

60kg Jim Gruenwald – Jim wrestled really well, defeating Tufenk (TUR) in a very physical, tough, fast-paced scrambling match, 4-2. Gruenwald then beat Mulustin (KGZ) 4-0 to win his pool. In the quarterfinals he faced Nazarian of Bulgaria, a two-time Olympic gold medalist. Gruenwald went out really physical and got the passivity call against the Bulgarian but couldn't get the points. Later in the first period, Nazarian had his chance on top (in parterre) where he did his patented reverse lift on Gruenwald for six points then again for four, ending the match 10-0. Gruenwald is a great leader and team player. His positive attitude helps our entire team.

66kg Kevin Bracken – Kevin had a tough Czech wrestler (Jaros) in his first pool match. Bracken wrestled very well in beating the Czech, 8-5. Then he wrestled Mansourov (AZE) and lost a close match 4-1. Mansourov went on to win the silver medal. As usual, Bracken wrestled his heart out.

74kg TC Dantzler – In his debut appearance at the World Championships, TC wrestled extremely well, crushing his first two opponents, Iverson (NOR), 11-0 and Panagistou (GRE), with a pin. Dantzler executed many spectacular lifts and throws during both of these matches, then in his qualification round he wrestled Sasrykh (UKR) where he lost a tough 3-0 bout. Sasrykh ended up fourth.

84kg Brad Vering – The rookie of our team, Brad had an outstanding performance placing fifth – ahead of two-time Olympic Champion Yerlikaya (TUR). In his pool matches, Vering dominated Thomberg (EST) 4-0 and Minguggi (ITA), by pin. In his quarterfinal match he wrestled Abu El Faitah (Egypt), losing a hard-fought match where Vering battled to the very end. The score was 2-1 with about one minute left and Vering tried to escape. The Egyptian caught him with a throw and ended up winning 5-1. The Egyptian went on to win the bronze medal.

96kg Garrett Lowney – Garrett had the toughest draw of all, meeting the Russian, Bezruchkin who was the defending world champ, and Mollov (BUL), world medalist, in his pool. Lowney lost 7-0 to the Russian and 3-0 to the Bulgarian. The Bulgarian ended up winning the pool and going on to win the bronze medal.

120kg Dremiel Byers – The new 120kg weight class seems to suit Dremiel Byers just fine. The slim and trim Byers stole the show in Moscow, putting together five great matches en route to winning the gold medal. His first match was a spectacular display of athleticism and skill. Byers wrestled the Chinese, Song. In the first period Byers had two high, spectacular back suplays throwing the kid through the air like he was a lightweight. In the second period, Byers pinned him with a bodylock.

Byers' second match was against Debelka (BLR), who was a bronze medalist in the Sydney Olympics. Byers defeated the Belarussian in the clinch by pinning him, countering his bodylock attempt.

His third match was against Yuri Tevsheychyc (ISR). Byers was down 1-0 and again in the clinch in overtime, threw the Israeli to his back for the victory.

His fourth match was against the Greek, Koutsioumpas, who was a bronze medalist at the 2001 World Championships. Byers fell behind 1-0 before he lifted him for four points and a 4-1 final score.

In the finals, against three-time World silver medalist Deak Beardos of Hungary, the score was 0-0 when, again in the clinch, Byers threw Beardos to his back to score three points. He finished out the match with great intensity to win the world title, 3-0.

It was a tremendous feat of courage and skill for Byers to again claim the heavyweight title for the USA. In a spontaneous act of joy and happiness, Byers sprang out into a dance center-mat to the song "Tutti-Fruity" playing in the arena. The dance, which included a back flip and some of Byers' special groovin,' gained applause from the entire arena, which seemed to be celebrating with Byers. Here is the reaction from Dremiel himself:

"First, I thank God that everything worked out. I am more than happy with my performance. I'm also very grateful of the support that I have received from family, friends, coaches and teammates. This accomplishment is for all of us to share but it is our job now to perfect and repeat. Remember these three things: Train as hard as you can, train and live as close to a McDonald's as possible and, if for some reason in your finest hour you hear music, dance – and I mean really shake it! Then work it slow and if you can squeeze a back hand-spring in there, that would be sweet!"

A great deal of credit goes to Shon Lewis, head Army coach who helped Byers prepare for every match. Here was his reaction:

"Watching our 2002 World team members compete against the rest of the world was a sight to see – every team member came prepared and wrestled to win! Having made three World teams myself, I know there are several things that have to happen for you to medal. I really feel that our team is constantly striving to make it happen! Dremiel Byers ensured that the rest of the world took notice of our performance by winning the final match of the tournament and having our national anthem played to end the 47th World Championships!"

Gruenwald Defines Courage at 2003 Worlds

The 2003 Greco-Roman World Championships, held in Creteil, France, were a bit of a disappointment for our Greco-Roman athletes, coaches and fans. Our goal was to win the tournament with a minimum of four medals. We ended up tied for 12th place out of 73 countries, winning no medals. Jim Gruenwald, at 60kg, was our team's highest place-winner, ending up fourth.

The tournament, which was the first of three Olympic qualifiers, was very strong, as usual. The U.S. team qualified only three weight classes for the Olympics. Only three countries qualified more than three weights. Ukraine qualified five weights, Georgia and Germany qualified four, and Russia, along with the U.S. and a few other countries, qualified three weights. The rest of the world, including Cuba, qualified only two or less weight classes.

The Greco-Roman competition in the World Championships is very strong. There are at least 20 countries that on any given day could win the Worlds. Countries like Sweden, Cuba, Belarus, Ukraine, Turkey, Korea, Bulgaria and Hungary are all very tough with great teams. This year, Georgia won first place, Russia was second and Ukraine was third.

In regard to our overall performance in Creteil – as was previously stated, our Greco-Roman family was disappointed, to say the least. However, as national coach, I have to say that our team wrestled fairly well. Our overall squad was well prepared and fought hard every match. Our conditioning was excellent, and we were in every match we wrestled. We lost a few very close matches that, if we had won, would have moved our team right into the hunt for the top spots. Two more team points would have moved us into the top seven, instead of twelfth place.

You say, "Would've… Could've… Should've!" So do we! We know competition at this level is a game of inches. One point here, one point there, can make a huge difference in overall team performance. That's what makes the competition so great and rewarding; it takes the entire team of seven to contribute to the effort. When the team does that…there is no better feeling on earth.

At 55kg, Brandon Paulson, as usual, wrestled like a true warrior. After beating a world medalist in his first match, Brandon wrestled and lost to Rivas from Cuba (5-1). Rivas, a former World Champion, who many thought would win the worlds, ended up with the bronze medal.

At 66kg, Kevin Bracken, who was one of our most dangerous parterre wrestlers, lost a close one to the Korean, who is a former silver world medalist. Not making excuses, but Kevin and the Korean went to the clinch in overtime (score 2-1), where the Korean unlocked his hands twice before Kevin unlocked his. The video shows this very clearly and without a doubt. Even the Russian mat judge gave Kevin the point. However, after the chairperson reviewed the video, they gave the point and match to the Korean. I'm still not sure why.

<u>The lesson learned:</u> We have got to wrestle two or more points better than all of our opponents, so as to take it out of the officials' hands.

At 74kg, T.C. Dantzler was beaten in the first round by the German wrestler (3-1), who ended up with the silver medal. T.C. had one of the better draws and, had he beaten the German, he would have been in great position to make the finals. T.C., who is one of our most spectacular lifters, will really succeed when he learns to open up a bit more on his feet. Knowing T.C. Dantzler like I do, I believe he will do this.

At 84 kg, Brad Vering, who has been in the United States Olympic Training Center (USOTC) Resident Program for less than two years, finished in fifth place for his second year in a row. Brad overcame a very painful groin injury that really hampered his mobility and competed very well.

Brad was like a true American gladiator. Even with this serious injury, he wrestled fiercely. In the quarterfinals, he faced the Norwegian wrestler, who is one of the top 84kg wrestlers in the world. Brad battled back from a 2-0 deficit to tie the match 2-2 in overtime. Brad had the Norwegian dead tired, crushing him with intense pummeling. He then hit a "duck under" and was almost all the way behind him, when his groin injury pulled and Brad stumbled a bit. A tremendous scramble ensued…when both wrestlers came up neutral, the official signaled one point for the Norwegian for a correct attempted throw (correct call).

For me, as national coach, it was one of the most heart-breaking losses I have ever experienced. I'm not embarrassed to say that I had tears in my eyes for at least one hour after the match.

At 96kg, Justin Ruiz, who has been in our USOTC Resident Program for only two months, wrestled with great bravery and honor. Justin won his pool and was then beaten by a very tough and experienced Polish wrestler. Justin is a very hard worker and, with more experience, he will be a viable force in world competition.

At 120kg, Rulon Gardner made his first appearance in world competition since his snowmobile accident, where he lost one of his toes. Rulon wrestled well, winning his pool, and beating the former World medalist from Israel. Rulon met the Russian in the next round, where he lost a 3-0 match. The Russian went ahead early in the match, by "gut-wrenching" Rulon twice. Rulon came back strong, but the Russian was able to hold on to the 3-0 score and ultimately win the world title. Rulon ended up in tenth place.

I saved the 60kg weight class for last because I felt Jim Gruenwald's performance was the most heroic of the tournament. In the first round, Jim battled back from a 5-0 deficit to win the match with a 6-5 decision. This match was against the Armenian wrestler, who was a World Championship medalist.

It was superb demonstration of what happens when you "Never give up!" Jim slowly chipped away at the deficit while intensely breaking his opponent's will to fight. At the end, the Armenian was not only beaten by the score, but was also beaten to a pulp physically. He lay there on the mat in complete and total exhaustion.

VICTORY

Jimmy's second match in his pool was against a tough Hungarian that he had beaten before. Because of the good-mark system, we knew Jimmy had to score only one point in the match to secure the victory of his pool. Of course, he still wanted to win the match but for some reason, he wrestled a terrible match. He fell behind 4-0 and didn't score one point until there were only 30 seconds to go in the bout. It was disheartening, to say the least. Even though he won the pool, we were still upset.

Now here's a good example of re-grouping and re-focusing: Jim knew he couldn't wrestle that way and win the Worlds, so he analyzed his mental skills and his approach. He went out against the very strong Egyptian wrestler, crushing him 6-0, never leaving the Egyptian one moment to mount an attack.

Jimmy then faced Armen Nazarian of Bulgaria in the semi-finals. Nazarian is likely the best wrestler of all the weight classes combined. He is a spectacular "reverse lifter" who usually destroys most all of his opponents with his tremendous lifting and wrestling skills. He is a two-time Olympic champion and owns many World medals. Nazarian beat Jimmy last year at the Moscow World Championships by a score of 12-0 in about two minutes ("reverse lifted" Jim twice for six points apiece).

This year was going to be different. Jimmy began the match with the most intense pace and aggressiveness that you could ever imagine: It was a war. However, as we expected, Nazarian got the passivity call against Jim and got a chance to attempt his famous "reverse lift." Jimmy's defense was unbelievable! He stayed up in the parterre position (on hands and knees), which completely threw the Bulgarian off. Then, when Nazarian attempted his "reverse lift," Jimmy immediately stood up and reversed him.

The match continued at a fierce pace and, with about one minute left in the match, with a score of 1-1, Nazarian got his second chance on top. This was it for Jimmy: The moment of truth – make it or break it, do or die! The Bulgarian was tired, and looked like he was breaking; he did not want to go into overtime (trust me!).

So what happened next was one of the most intense struggles that I have ever seen. An intense struggle by both wrestlers – Nazarian fighting to lift Jim, and Jim fighting to defend. For twenty seconds or so (which can seem like a lifetime in wrestling), both warriors were inches away from winning the fierce battle for position. Nazarian, his hands locked in his reverse lift position, was pulling Jim up; Jim, his body stretched as far as it could possibly go and on his tippy-toes, was inches away from reversing Nazarian (as the author of this article, I must apologize as I do not have the writing skills to accurately describe the movements, actions, and emotions which were witnessed by thousands of screaming spectators at this pivotal point in the match; therefore, I will have to summarize).

All of a sudden, in desperation, Nazarian threw. Jimmy countered by arching his back in a way that caused a low amplitude throw. Jimmy, abnormally torquing his body so as not to expose his back, forced the maneuver to land himself on his upper left chest, where he took a tremendous impact. At that moment, Jimmy Gruenwald's shoulder came completely out of the socket, dislocating it.

Then came the scream of pain, and the match was abruptly stopped. Jimmy lay there in the packed arena in pure agony. The doctors, working frantically for several minutes, were not able to slide the shoulder back into place. Jimmy alternated between screams of pain and pleas to continue the match.

Finally, the stretcher arrived to carry Jim off the battlefield, but he refused. Jimmy stood up on his own, with his shoulder still dislocated and shook Nazarian's hand. It would be another twenty minutes before the doctors could re-position his shoulder.

My first thought was, "Why?" Why did this happen to Jim Gruenwald? Good things are supposed to happen to good people… and Jim Gruenwald is "good people." I think only his teammates, coaches and family can totally understand the courage and heroic effort that Jim displayed on this final day of the 2003 World Championships in Creteil, France.

Only the ones who see on a daily basis all the grueling training, total dedication, and extreme sacrifice Jim, and others like him, make when attempting to become the world's best can fully understand what "elite sport" is all about. It's not always about winning…. it's about the struggle to win that is so great.

Jim Gruenwald may have missed winning a World medal on this emotional day, but the memory of this battle with two-time Olympic champion Armen Nazarian will be one forever etched in my mind – one that I will personally draw from for many years to come. Jim Gruenwald is a true American, and a Greco-Roman wrestling hero!

U.S. Must Get Better at Parterre

Scouting at the European Championships is one of my favorite things to do as national coach for the U.S. Greco-Roman wrestling team. This year the event was held in Seinajoki, Finland where, as usual, the competition was tremendous. Russia won the tournament team title, followed by Bulgaria and Belarus.

This tournament is one of the most intense competitions in the world. The European wrestlers and coaches treat the event like we (Americans) treat the World Championships. There is a tremendous amount of prestige in winning or medaling in this fierce competition. The prestige and intensity of the event make it extremely fun and exciting to watch. Every year I see many spectacular battles.

There seemed to be as many new faces as veterans this year. One example of this is the new young champion at 74kg, Badri Khasaia from the Republic of Georgia. Khasaia trained with us in the U.S. (Colorado Springs) for one year in 2000.

After Khasaia's European Championship gold-medal victory he said to me, "I learned a great deal from my experience in Colorado Springs. Give my thanks to the coaches and wrestlers who helped me, like (national team members) Keith Sieracki, TC Dantzler, and Dan Neibuhr to name a few."

Each year, I learn so much from scouting and studying this tournament. Scouting our future foreign opponents obviously helps us in preparing to compete against them. Identifying their style and seeing the techniques they use allows us to develop our training strategy.

Studying how the FILA officials are scoring the various techniques and situations also helps us to get ready for the World Championships. I can see how the officials are executing the clinch, how they are scoring the various lifts, how they are calling the escape and many other related issues.

Being involved with the championships also allows me to make numerous contacts with FILA Bureau members, officials, athletes and coaches. Building good relationships with this group is good for our American team. I have been able to establish many joint training camps with the numerous national coaches from around the world. These training opportunities for our U.S. guys are very beneficial to the development and progress of our team.

All in all, the European Championships are a great event, one that I encourage you all to experience if you ever get the chance.

Now I would like to address one specific issue which I saw watching the competition. If you are either a wrestler or a coach who is preparing wrestlers to win at the world level (freestyle or Greco) please consider the following issue.

As a country, we must get better at parterre offense and defense!

If we are really serious about winning at the international level, we must focus more of our training and development on parterre. This is not new news! I know I harp about this every chance I get, but I truly believe this is the key to our future world success. The international wrestling game today is parterre.

We must spend the majority of our practice time in the parterre position. Now stop right here! Take a moment to think about how much time in your practice you really spend working in the parterre position. It is so easy to just wrestle on our feet. Stop it! We must start today by re-adjusting our training plans and goals.

Gaining the much needed parterre offensive and defensive skills and conditioning is the only way we will achieve our lofty World and Olympic dreams.

We have to face the facts. The majority of matches which I studied in Seinajoki, Finland, were determined in parterre. Gut wrenches, straight lifts, reverse lifts, straddle lifts, lift to guts, and front headlocks are where it is happening.

Most matches go like this: "Pummel, pummel, pummel" – then someone gets called for passivity and goes down in parterre. After the parterre sequence happens you go back to your feet and... "Pummel, pummel, pummel" then usually the other guy gets called for passivity and goes down in parterre. The matches are won and lost mostly in the parterre position. Great parterre offense and defense is crucial!

Don't get me wrong... there are takedowns being executed and scored. I am not suggesting we stop working on perfecting our takedown skills. What I am suggesting is we spend more quality time practicing the important skills of parterre offense and defense.

As a country, generally speaking, we are known for our tenacious attack on our feet. Great pummeling skills, great cardiovascular conditioning, great fight, great heart and determination are our forte. These attributes are what we seem to be known for internationally. Foreign coaches are constantly asking me for the secrets to our great physical conditioning advantages.

Usually, when we get beat it is because we got beat in parterre, either giving up too many points or not being able to score from there.

Dag nab it, we have to stop talking about it and start doing something about it!

At the Olympic Training Center in Colorado Springs, we are getting more serious about this issue. We recently executed a four-week parterre practice program we called P.D.O.B. This stands for Parterre Defense/Offense or Bust. The parterre-focused program had us spending approximately 70 to 80 percent of our practice time in parterre. We will continue to make parterre our main focus over the next few months in order to get ready for the World Championships.

I encourage all wrestlers and coaches to take a good look at their practice plans. Identify how much time you are spending in parterre. If you are not spending enough time there, re-adjust your plans. Realize that the best wrestlers in the world are winning the parterre game. In fact, the kids who are winning the Cadet and Junior Nationals are winning with parterre. Don't wait. Start today.

P.D.O.B. - Parterre Defense/Offense or Bust!

The Road To Athens

As I write this article the weeks, hours, days and minutes are drawing closer until it's SHOW TIME! With less than 20 days until opening ceremonies, the U.S. Greco-Roman wrestling team will join the other 550 athletes on the 2004 U.S. Olympic team to compete in the biggest sporting event in the world — the Olympic Games!

There's no looking back now. "The Road to Athens," is closing in.

On Aug. 13, the Olympic Games will return to its original birthplace where the first modern Olympic Games were held in 1896. These games are historic because they return to their origin and the place where democracy was born. However, the 2004 Games also have great significance for our sport.

Greco-Roman wrestling is one of the four original Olympic sports that were part of the ancient Olympic Games 2,500 years ago (776 BC). Our sport has the longest standing record in Olympic history and we share this remarkable spotlight with the sports of shot put, marathon and boxing. In other words, we're the real deal!

It goes without saying, it is our goal to win and win big in Athens, four medals to be specific. We qualified six of the seven weight classes, with Russia being the only country to qualify wrestlers in every weight class. As expected, the competition will be fierce and every dominant wrestling nation (Russian, Georgia, Cuba and Hungary) will be out to deny us a place on the podium. They all seek the same outcome: to win the unofficial overall team title and to walk away as the powerhouse country and undisputed leader in Greco-Roman wrestling.

The pressure is on. But we have the talent, experience, youth, hunger, thirst and drive to deliver the goods in Greece.

Heavyweight Rulon Gardner is heading to Athens to defend his gold medal from the 2000 Olympic Games in Sydney and to prove the "Miracle on the Mat" was no miracle. Just recently at the Pytlasinski International Tournament in Warsaw, Poland, Rulon beat the Russian Yuri Petrankeev, who is expected to be one of his biggest contenders and potential road blocks to winning gold again this summer.

Jim Gruenwald placed fourth in the Worlds in 2003 and has been knocking on the medal door for five years. He's due for a podium placement — a just reward for all his hard years of training.

Oscar Wood, one of this year's rookies on the Olympic team arrives on the scene in Athens by upsetting Kevin Bracken, who was the No. 1 wrestler in America at the 145.5-pound weight class for the past five years. Despite his lack of international experience, Oscar is a fearless warrior who will surprise the competition. Watch out!

This will be the third Olympic team for Dennis Hall, a world champion in 1995 and a silver medalist in 1996 at the Olympic Games in Atlanta. Dennis cut to a lower weight class this year to make the Olympic team and will be a strong force to be reckoned with on the mat in Greece.

As a 20-year-old in the 2000 Olympic Games in Sydney, Australia, Garrett Lowney reached the podium with a bronze medal. He came to the U.S. Olympic team this year after overcoming a severe neck operation. In the 211.5-pound weight class, he's looking to turn bronze to gold come Aug. 23.

Brad Vering, the other Olympic rookie on our team might be green to five-ring competition but has recent international experience that will prepare him for the world stage next month. He came in fifth in the last two World Championships. Competing in the 185-pound weight class, Brad brings hunger, enthusiasm and youth to our Greco-Roman U.S. Olympic team.

While this summary of athlete accolades, achievements and goals might seem simple, the journey and the "Road to Athens" for these individuals was anything but.

Training to go to the Olympics or any focused and committed goal for that matter — is a year-round commitment. It's a commitment of your time, a commitment of resources, and a commitment you make with the support of those around you — spouse, kids, family and friends. We're talking a 365-day-a-year training regimen. It is what separates the mediocre from the elite.

You know, most people don't realize the time and planning that goes into training for an Olympic Games. People just think the summer Olympic Games suddenly appear every four years. Bam! There they are again on NBC with 300 million people in the U.S. watching and cheering and lots of emotional and entertaining commercials featuring U.S. athletes.

Do you think those stories that NBC features on TV were created in a simple 30-60 days? Guess again. The two to five-minute stories you watch on TV are the result of camera crews following athletes like Rulon Gardner, Dremiel Byers, Dennis Hall and countless others for years and months before the Olympics even begin.

Training for Olympic athletes is every day. It's a daily exercise on the body and the mind. For many athletes, training begins the moment the previous Olympic Games end. It's the same with other summer sports and with the winter sports.

Right now, thousands of amateur athletes are training to compete in the 2008 Olympic Games in Bejiing, China, and the 2012 Games. And right now, while the rest of the world is waiting to see what transpires and what country, wrestlers and other athletes come out on top in Athens, the winter athletes in sports like speedskating, bobsled, skiing and hockey are laser focused on training for the 2006 Olympic Winter Games in Torino, Italy, in hopes of making the 2006 U.S. Olympic Team.

My point is the guys representing the 2004 U.S. Olympic Greco-Roman Team have made personal and professional sacrifices. These gentlemen have trained hours upon hours, days upon days, months upon months and years upon years to represent our country and prove to themselves and to the rest of the world that the U.S. Greco-Roman program is a true world contender and force on the international circuit.

They are sons, husbands and fathers and of course, Olympic wrestlers.

In another column I'll share with you the stories that led this 2004 U.S. Olympic

VICTORY

Team to where it is today. But for now, join me in congratulating them as they get ready to represent our country in one of the oldest and most historic Olympic sports, Greco-Roman wrestling.

Rulon Gardner:
The Making of an American Hero

My first meeting with Olympic and World Champion Rulon Gardner was in 1995 when I accepted the job as the National Coach of the U.S. Greco-Roman Wrestling Team. Little did I know at that point during our first meeting, and in the first years of training together what the future held.

Little did I realize that this 280-pound farmboy from Wyoming would become a hero in the sport of Greco-Roman wrestling, in the U.S. and around the globe. Little did I know at this initial meeting that with the help of the coaching staff at USA Wrestling and his teammates, Rulon would emerge as an Olympic gold medalist.

Nor did I know then that our meeting would turn into a nine-year relationship of not just the normal wrestling experiences of wins, losses, hardships and successes, but it also would involve great friendship, respect, understanding and lots of laughs and practical jokes along the way.

Prior to my arrival, Rulon was recruited from the University of Nebraska by then National Coach Mike Houck, a former World Champion himself. When Mike recruited Rulon, he had never even heard of Greco-Roman wrestling. However, Mike talked Rulon into wrestling Greco and right away Rulon achieved substantial success, placing in top tournaments.

In 1996, Rulon moved to Colorado Springs and joined the U.S. Olympic Training Center Resident Program. Not only did this demonstrate how serious Rulon was about pursing excellence but it also allowed me to work more closely with him. I was able to get to know who he really was, what he was made of and what he was capable of doing on the mat.

When I started working with Rulon full time, I began to see the real Rulon Gardner. I saw his inner drive, hard-work ethic, power, stamina and passion for the sport. I saw the ingredients of a champion.

Rulon's move to Colorado Springs put him into a regimented training environment that helped him to improve his skills and bring all his knowledge and intensity together into one training environment. Under the leadership and guidance of our coaching staff and with the competition from his peers, Rulon began to evolve.

Once he was a resident athlete, I started working with Rulon daily. I came to know his personality and what made him tick. I learned that he and I had a lot in common. We were both fiercely competitive, mentally tough and, while we were grown adults, we enjoyed friendly competitive wagers among friends. We both liked trying to one-up one another and we did this a lot.

One of the first "wagers" between us took place in Poland after the Pytlasinki

VICTORY

Tournament. It was a hot summer day in August and after an exhausting day of competition in a sweltering gymnasium, I challenged Rulon to carry our 97kg wrestler from the gym back to the hotel, which was approximately a mile a way. Dan Hicks was the wrestler he carried. If any part of Dan's body touched the ground, Rulon was the loser and I, of course, would be the winner. If he was successful in getting Dan back to the hotel and placing him in his room without ever letting Dan's body touch the ground, then I would eat my words. He'd be the winner and also $150 richer.

Needless to say, I didn't make the trip back to the hotel easy for the big guy. Let's just say that obstacles appeared along the path, the hotel elevator was stalled and the key to his room was missing. Hey, this was all just a test of toughness….not to mention that I wanted to make $150.

However, Rulon dodged the obstacles, overcame the "mysterious" elevator problems and after standing in the hallway for 25 minutes in a complete sweat, the key to the room was finally located and brought to his door. He was victorious.

The same way I challenged him off the mat with these fun-type activities was the same way we challenged and made things interesting for him and the other athletes in the practice room.

I remember a time when Rulon and I were doing a 90-minute grind match. After pounding me for nearly 20 minutes, I realized I needed help to give Rulon a workout (and to save my life)! From the mat, I saw our National Freestyle Coach, Kevin Jackson, and shouted over and asked for his help. Feeling sorry for me, Kevin jumped in and alternated with me every three minutes in wrestling Rulon for the remaining 70 minutes. Our goal was to try to break him and make him quit. Rulon never slowed down one bit. For the most part, he beat both of us up throughout the duration of the grind match. He was tough. He didn't like to lose.

Fun-like activities such as the Dan Hicks wager episode also created memorable moments between Rulon and me. It helped build a foundation between us. Having a solid foundation between an athlete and his/her coach is very important for success. An athlete needs to have faith and trust in his/her coach. Athletes need to know the coach cares about them not just in competition but also in life.

There are lots of ways to develop a relationship between an athlete and a coach. Coaches should listen to their athletes, share their own personal experiences and spend time getting to know them and what motivates them as individuals. In this scenario, fun wagers became a way for Rulon and me to connect. It was our way of developing the coach/athlete relationship. All coaches and athletes should find their own system or way of connecting.

FACING SETBACKS

Success was not an overnight thing for Rulon. Along his journey there where setbacks. For example, after training for two years to make the 1996 U.S. Olympic Team, he arrived a few minutes late to the U.S. Olympic Trials weigh-in. As a result, he was not allowed to compete in the Olympic Trials.

If he were to have competed, Rulon would have needed to beat Matt Ghaffari, who was the reigning national champion and World medalist. As one of Rulon's coaches at the Olympic Trials, I was very disappointed Rulon was not able to compete. However, that year Ghaffari was the guy to beat. Matt was also one of my athletes so I was equally proud to help coach him to his silver medal win during the 1996 Olympics in Atlanta. He lost the gold to the undefeated Russian of nine years, Alexander Karelin, by a score of 2-0 in overtime.

In 1997, Rulon made his first U.S. World Team. It was at the World Championships in Poland that Rulon wrestled Karelin for the first time. He wrestled a very tough match, defending against Karelin's trademark reverse lift. By twisting his body in a very unnatural way he countered Karelin's move, thus shielding himself against the high-scoring moves that Karelin typically scored with this spectacular technique. In doing so, Rulon had to endure his body being twisted in a very painful manner.

Karelin ended victorious in the match. Rulon placed fifth in the tournament. However, he showed signs that with continued proper training and preparation he could give the world's most decorated and feared wrestler a competitive match and could even quite possibly defeat him.

While his loss to Karelin may have been viewed as a defeat, it was really the turning point of setting him on the road to victory.

GAINING SELF-CONFIDENCE

Self-confidence is an important characteristic for a person to have in order to reach his or her full potential.

The other night I attended my 13-year-old daughter's play, "Alice in Wonderland." My daughter, Hannah, has been practicing and reciting her lines for weeks in our house. While I was proud and excited to see her so enthusiastic about acting, I was in awe of her ability to perform with such confidence. I couldn't help but wonder how she would actually perform in front of a live audience.

I have to admit I showed up the night of the play not really expecting a Broadway performance. After all, this was a play produced and performed by a bunch of middle-school kids. Boy, was I wrong.

Instead, I not only witnessed my daughter nail her character and bring loud outbursts of laughter from a packed house of parents, friends and teachers, but the entire play was non-stop entertainment. It was outstanding and I was entertained the entire time.

I couldn't believe my eyes. Here was my youngest daughter, in a lead role in a successful school play, belting out lines, singing tunes and doing so with so much pride, confidence and enthusiasm. And, she wasn't alone. There were lots of other kids in different characters that did the same. In fact, there are definitely some rising stars coming out of Eagleview Middle School. However, there were also kids that lacked confidence. While they managed to get through the play and perform, they were difficult to understand, hard to hear and not fully engaging.

Whether you're a young girl experimenting with acting or you're a rough and tough world-caliber wrestler striving for Olympic gold, you need self-confidence to be successful.

Two months before the 2000 Sydney Olympic Games, my U.S. Olympic Team and I were in Russia wrestling at the Poddubny Tournament. Alexander Karelin, nine-time World Champion, three-time Olympic Champion and the Russian superhero of international wrestling, was not competing in this tournament.

The Russian media, which obviously anticipated Karelin's fourth Olympic gold medal victory on the horizon in Sydney, was curious to hear the opinion of Rulon Gardner, the United States' number-one heavyweight. They asked him what he thought about a possible meeting and match between himself and Karelin at the upcoming Games.

I listened attentively to Rulon, as I was eager to hear his response. He was giving an enormous amount of respect to Karelin. He was being too respectful, in my opinion, and didn't give himself enough credit. As his coach, it made me uneasy to hear this lack of self-confidence coming from my athlete. I felt Rulon was selling himself short. I thought he could beat Karelin on any given day but he needed to believe this himself.

As soon as he was done with the interview I told Rulon to stop disrespecting himself. "You can beat him," I said. "You match up perfectly against him. You can beat him. Start believing you can beat this guy. If you don't do it, someone else will!"

These were my words to Rulon. He looked at me puzzled. He nodded his head to acknowledge, yes, and that he understood, but I could tell he wasn't fully grasping it nor believing that he could actually defeat this wrestling icon.

For the last few years I have been watching Karelin. I could see his weaknesses and I could see he was getting all the favors with the referees. I could see it was a matter of time before someone beat him and I thought, "Why not Rulon?"

Rulon had the exact style and tools to beat Karelin. Rulon's strengths were Karelin's weaknesses. Rulon's biggest strength was his cardiovascular condition. As Karelin got older, his cardiovascular was his biggest weakness. Another one of Rulon's strengths was his mental toughness. He wouldn't lie down for Karelin. In years past, I have seen so many heavyweights from around the world afraid of what Karelin might do to them. Like a puppy dog, they actually lay down, roll over on their backs and just cave-in to Karelin, in fear of what he might do to them.

Another strength of Rulon's is his physical power, which he needed to match Karelin's own power and strength. You would think after his experience in 1997 when Rulon gave Karelin a good match that he would have had more confidence that he could beat him. In hindsight, I think that match did provide him with the confidence he needed to keep progressing in this sport; however, for some reason at this given point, he sounded unsure about himself.

This slight lack of confidence and uncertainty is natural. Most people progress in peaks and valleys, taking four steps forward and then they hit a plateau or even take a step backwards before moving forward again. This is what happened to Rulon and it happens to most athletes. He was progressing and moving forward but then he was having doubts in the final stretch to Olympic gold.

I was nervous… we were two months away from the Olympics and it was no time for any of our athletes to be lacking self-confidence in their ability to win.

2000 SYDNEY OLYMPICS

Here we are, two months later…. and 45 minutes before the biggest match in Rulon Gardner's life. It's the match for the gold medal in the 2000 Olympic Games in Sydney, Australia. Up to this point, Rulon beat all his other competitors and was now up against

Alexander Karelin, the "Russian Bear."

In the audience, among the thousands of spectators, fans, coaches and athletes who were anticipating Karelin winning his fourth unprecedented gold medal, was Henry Kissinger, former Secretary of State, and Juan Antonio Samaranch, President of the International Olympic Committee.

Backstage as Karelin warmed up, Olympic coach, Dan Chandler and I noticed the look on Karelin's face. It was a look of concern and possibly even fear. In our opinion, even the world's greatest wrestler was facing some confidence issues of his own. We said, "Rulon, look at Karelin. He's nervous. He's scared. You can beat him. You have to go out there and confidently execute the plan and you will beat him."

We continued to discuss Rulon's strategy on how he would wrestle against Karelin. We decided to challenge Karelin by not over-defending Karelin's favorite and most spectacular throw, the reverse lift. We noticed throughout the Sydney Olympic Games that when Karelin attempted this famous lift, his opponents over-defended Karelin's attack. This allowed Karelin to execute his counter move, which resulted in him successfully pinning several of his Sydney opponents.

So our strategy was to challenge Karelin to lift Rulon with his favorite reverse lift. Rulon needed to defend this lift but not over-defend it. It worked. Karelin could not lift Rulon and it also took his counter move away.

The other strategic focus was for Rulon to get Karelin tired. He had to use his cardiovascular condition and his physical abilities to exhaust this great champion. It also worked.

Rulon wrestled the perfect match against Karelin. The first period was very physical and intense, with neither wrestler scoring a point. This was the start of Karelin becoming very tired. Because the first period ended zero to zero, international rules had both wrestlers going to the "clinch" position to start the second period.

After about 45 seconds of both wrestlers clinching, jockeying, fighting, scratching and clawing for the advantage in this position, Karelin unlocked his hands. This gave Rulon one point. During the remaining five minutes of wrestling, including an overtime period, Rulon successfully defended against Karelin's three attempts at his reverse lift.

From Rulon's corner with about 35 seconds to go in the match, I saw Karelin, the greatest wrestling champion in the world, glance over to the clock to see how much time was left. I saw a look on his face that I have never seen on him before. It was a look of total exhaustion, defeat and panic.

And then with five seconds to go, this great champion quit wrestling all together and as the final seconds clicked off the clock, Rulon, still in a cautious stance made history. Rulon Gardner stunned the world and became the story of the 2000 Olympic Games by defeating Alexander Karelin. He went from an average Wyoming farmboy to becoming an Olympic American hero.

As Rulon stood on the awards stand, as America's National Anthem played and the realization hit that this was the first time in 13 years that Alexander Karelin was not listening to his own Russian anthem, my thoughts focused on the importance of confidence.

Confidence plays a vital role on the road to success. However, I am not saying that everyone has to have the highest level of confidence at all times, because we all have moments of doubt about ourselves. What I am saying is that we need to understand the role confidence plays in our lives. In times of adversity or even during our daily routine, we need to continuously strive to believe in ourselves and to realize that confidence — real, true self-confidence – needs to come from within and is a crucial ingredient to being successful.

Learn to master your own self-confidence and recognize that moments of uncertainty are natural. However, never let these moments interfere with your ability to rise to the occasion. Continue to grow your own self-confidence and nothing will stop you from becoming the next Rulon Gardner, or a 13-year-old aspiring superstar actress.

Surround Yourself With Good People

Succeeding in life takes a lot of things. One thing that sticks out in my mind, when thinking about success, is having good friends, mentors and coaches to follow. If you surround yourself with great people… you will have the tendency to become great. If you surround yourself with mediocre people…. you will have the tendency to become mediocre. If you surround yourself with unmotivated people… you will have the tendency to be unmotivated.

If you want success in wrestling or life in general, then surround yourself with successful and motivated people. This is your responsibility. You usually can control who you associate with. So do it. Hang out with the people that you aspire to be like. Hang out with energetic, motivated and ambitious people and you will naturally push each other to the top.

I was fortunate that I had a great group of coaches throughout my career and life that helped me become the wrestler that I wanted to be. Some just happened my way but others I had to seek and search out. It was these great people that influenced my life in ways that propelled me forward.

• **Frank Stagg** was the coach of the wrestling team at Webb Junior High School in Hazel Park, Michigan. I was a bashful kid. He kept asking me to come out for the team because he'd seen me wrestle in gym class. I would always tell him "okay" but I would not show up. One day he put me in a sleeper hold in the hallway and said, "Fraser, I want to see you at practice tonight!" From that point on I loved the sport. I remember once telling Mr. Stagg, "Coach, I really like to sweat." And it was true; I really did like those sweaty hard practices.

• **Robert Morrill and Masaaki Hatta** were my coaches at Hazel Park High School. Mr. Morrill was a great role model for me. He was very knowledgeable and disciplined and during the actual high school season was my main coach. Masaaki Hatta was my off-season coach. Masaaki was a world silver medalist for Japan and the man who taught me Greco and freestyle. Masaaki was probably the most influential coach I ever had. He taught me so many things about wrestling I can't begin to write about them. I owe my overall wrestling success to this great man.

• **Bill Johanessen and Cal Jenkins** were my coaches for the first two years of my college career at the University of Michigan; and **Dale Bahr, Willie Gadson** and **Joe Wells** were the coaches my remaining years at Michigan. All of these great coaches played a big role in my development and career. Johanessen and Jenkins recruited me to U of M, where I became an All-American for the first time while receiving a wonderful education. Bahr, Gadson and Wells all helped me to improve my skills to the next level.

VICTORY

Joe Wells and I became very close and I will never forget the calming and confident words Joe shared with me just prior to the rubber match between Mike Houck and me in the 1984 final Olympic Trials.

I had beaten Mike in the first match and Mike had beaten me in the second match. It was getting very close to the final bout that would determine who made the Olympic team, and my attitude was still very down. I was feeling very sorry for myself when Joe came up to me and said, "Come on Steve... let that last match go. It is a new match. You can beat him, you just have to go out there and do it! Go out there and give it ALL you got, and then be proud!" Joe's words really helped me.

- **Mark Churella**, who was a three-time NCAA champion, was never my coach; however, he was my training partner while I was at Michigan. Mark taught me tenacity; Mark taught me techniques; Mark taught me wrestling at the toughest level. We trained together daily, taking my wrestling skills and conditioning to a whole new level.

- **Ron Findley** and **Pavel Katsen** coached me at the L.A. Olympic Games. Obviously, I owe these two guys a great deal. They were in my corner throughout the Games and guided me through all of the brutal matches that I encountered on my way to the gold-medal victory.

- **Dean Rockwell** is considered by many to be the "Father of Greco-Roman Wrestling" in the United States. Throughout Dean's entire wrestling career he was a promoter and supporter of Greco-Roman wrestling. When it wasn't that cool to be a Greco-Roman wrestler, Dean Rockwell was out there pushing as hard as he could trying to improve and promote this great upper-body sport.

Dean was Greco-Roman Olympic Coach for the USA in 1968. He was also the head of the Michigan Wrestling Club for many, many years where he led the charge for all aspiring Greeks (Greco-Roman wrestlers) that lived in or near the state of Michigan. This great man was not only a wrestling coach and avid Greco supporter all his life, but he was also a World War II hero, playing an extremely important and heroic role when our U.S. troops landed at Omaha Beach. For many years, I did not know of Dean's heroic efforts because he is such a modest and humble man.

Dean was an outstanding influence for many accomplished wrestlers – wrestlers such as John Matthews (fourth in Montreal Olympics), Tom Minkel (current head coach at Michigan State University), Steve Goss (national champion) and Rudy Williams (many-time national champion) and many, many others.

He impacted my career tremendously throughout the years. It began when he recruited me as a young, high school wrestler to wrestle for the Michigan Wrestling Club. He continued his mentorship during my entire wrestling career, including in Los Angeles in 1984 where he watched me win the Olympic gold medal.

A great coach, Dean always told it like he saw it. He did not pull too many punches. He had a gruff exterior that went perfectly with his very large frame. He was a big man who was very direct and to the point. However, he was also a very kind and caring man (and still is today at 93 years old).

Prior to the 1984 Olympic Games I had settled into the weight class of 98kg (198 pounds). I had been consistently wrestling both Olympic styles of freestyle and Greco-Roman for quit a few years. My goal, although very lofty, was to make both Olympic teams in L.A.

I remember in 1983, about a year prior to the L.A. Games, Dean called me on the phone and said, "Steve, I think you should be wrestling at 82kg instead of 98kg." Dean continued to say, "I think you may be too small for 98kg. Plus, Mark Johnson is at 98kg and is looking very strong."

Back in 1977, Mark Johnson was a teammate of mine at the University of Michigan where he used to beat the tar out of me daily in practice. During this time, he was a senior and I was a freshman. Then in 1980, Mark made the Olympic Team in Greco at 98kg. That year I ended up fourth in the Olympic trials at the same weight class.

Now, in 1983-84, Mark Johnson was making a comeback. And not just Dean, but everyone seemed to be talking about how Mark Johnson was still so darn tough! He was one of Dan Gable's assistant coaches at the University of Iowa, where the rumor was that he used to make soon-to-be Olympic champion Ed Banach cry every day in practice.

Well, Dean Rockwell's comments to me on this day really ticked me off, big time! Then Dean said, "Steve, I also think you should quit wrestling freestyle and just focus on Greco." Now I was really mad!

To this day, I don't know for sure if Dean said these things to motivate me and help me focus more or if he really meant what he suggested, but it worked. I was motivated! I really started focusing on what I had to do to beat Mark Johnson and Mike Houck (who was an even tougher opponent for me). I started working even harder at preparing myself to beat these two adversaries. Yes, I was staying up at 98kg and I was going to wrestle both freestyle and Greco to the end. However, now I was on an even stronger mission!

In regards to Mark Johnson, my thoughts were, "If Mark can take a couple years off and still come back and beat me, then shame on me!"

So, there I was in December 1983, running and visualizing on my early morning workouts in the dead of winter in sub-zero, snowy weather, where only a few stray dogs and I were out on the roads! I was visualizing! I was mapping out in my head how I would defeat Mark Johnson. As Mark would dig in with his patented powerful underhooks, I saw how I would slam headlock him right to his back!

And guess what? I wrestled Mark Johnson four times during the 1984 Olympic Trials process, headlocking him numerous times, for big points each time. I was victorious in all four of our meetings.

I did this visualization technique not only to beat Mark Johnson but to also defeat Mike Houck, who was actually a fiercer opponent for me that year. Obviously, I ended up defeating both Mark and Mike that year to make the Olympic team. Then in 1985, Houck went on to win the World title at 98kg for the United States.

Dean Rockwell helped me to get very serious and focused on my strategy and plan, which prompted me to use the mental skill of visualization. Dean helped me to devise my attack so that I could be victorious at overcoming my toughest competitors.

Dean Rockwell is a very smart man and coach. Greco-Roman wrestling and I owe this great icon tons of gratitude. As I write this article Dean is 93 years old and he is still ornery, still tough, still kind, still caring and still promoting Greco-Roman wrestling!

Surround yourself with great people and they will help you achieve your wildest dreams!

Fraser's 10 Basics of Successful Wrestling

Here is a checklist of wrestling to help you in your preparation.

1. TECHNIQUE
    - Take notes – always learn new techniques
    - Ask questions
    - Practice/drilling
    - Keep an open mind
    - Be naive
    - Never think you know it all
    - Expand your skills
    - Study what techniques the best wrestlers are scoring with
    - Review videotape
2. STRATEGY/TACTICS
    - Practice/develop offensive attack
    - Practice/develop defensive attack
    - Understand when to score
    - Practice edge-of-mat wrestling tactics
    - Practice end-of-period wrestling tactics
    - Practice overtime tactics
    - Use pummeling as a tactic
    - Understand pace strategy
    - Wrestle after whistle blows (two seconds)
    - Wrestle out of bounds to leave lasting positive impression
    - Scout your opponents
    - Focus on execution of techniques and strategy
3. IMAGE
    - Practice good mat demeanor
    - Understand how you look
        - To officials
        - In the zone
        - Regarding passivity
        - After whistle/out of bounds
    - Practice Acting 101
    - Act like a champion on and off the mat
    - Treat the referee like your friend
    - Do a little 'politicking'

4. CONDITIONING / PEAKING
   - Understand your yearly training schedule
     - Conditioning phase
     - Preparation phase
     - Competition phase
   - Understand and practice the 12 components of conditioning
     - Play wrestling
     - Sprint wrestling – pummel matches
     - Long-term wrestling – grind matches
     - Circuit wrestling practice
     - Drilling
     - Running
     - Exercise/calisthenics
     - Weightlifting
     - Cross training
     - Active Rest/Rest
     - Log/Journal entry and review
     - Specific warm-up routine

5. NUTRITION/DIET
   - Practice healthy eating
   - Understand high-octane gasoline
   - Eat fresh fruit/veggies
   - Use proper dieting to lose weight
   - Eat and be happy

6. MENTAL TOUGHNESS
   - Practice relaxing techniques
     - Good warm-up
     - Think about strategy/game plan
     - Think positive thoughts/rationalize
     - Heart and lungs open fully
     - Sprints or sprint wrestling
     - Sit and completely rest after opening heart and lungs
   - Overcome problems/adversity
   - Pit yourself against the toughest, most grueling problems and overcome them
   - Believe that anyone can be the best – why not!
   - Practice relentless intensity
   - Practice persistence
   - Train harder than anyone else
   - Learn to make it fun

7. ATTITUDE
   - Be positive vs. negative
   - Be a leader
   - Smile, life is too short
   - Enjoy the journey, have fun

VICTORY

- Practice a persistent, 'grit-your-teeth' mind-set
- Be confident, believe in yourself
- Be open minded to learning
- Be 100 percent committed

8. GOAL SETTING
   - Think big
   - Have goals written and posted
   - Have deadlines set
   - Have a plan of attack written in detail
   - Set daily, monthly, yearly goals
   - Be specific with goals
   - Use positive imagery
   - Do self-evaluation periodically

9. INJURY PREVENTION/REHABILITATION
   - Practice good warm-up routine
   - Train properly
   - Learn to listen to your body
   - Incorporate active rest
   - Use discipline in rehab
   - Get proper amount of sleep

10. HAVE FUN!
    - The best athletes in the world love what they are doing
    - Learn to enjoy the battle

Anatoly Petrosyan Shows True Courage

Anatoly Petrosyan is currently the head coach of the United States Olympic Resident Program Greco-Roman Wrestling Team. He has held this position with USA Wrestling for over 11 years.

He is of Armenian decent. He was brought up and trained in the former Soviet Union wrestling system. Before coming to the United States 14 years ago, he lived and coached wrestling in the country of Azerbaijan.

In 1989, Anatoly had to flee Baku, Azerbaijan, where he and his family were in grave danger due to political unrest. His life, and that of his wife, Julia, was in jeopardy. Two times in one afternoon people came to their door seeking to kill them. Luckily, they did not answer the door.

On the spur of the moment, Anatoly and Julia decided to sneak away that night, leaving all that they owned and cherished behind. This included two apartments, their beautiful summer home and all their personal belongings. Everything they owned was now gone!

They were well-off in Azerbaijan, enjoying the many luxuries of life. Anatoly had a nice job as a coach. They had a nice home with nice furniture. I remember Anatoly talking about the spectacular crystal chandelier hanging from one of his bedroom ceilings. They were very proud and happy.

Anatoly and Julia fled Azerbaijan and came to America to seek political asylum. They came here with nothing. At 49 years of age, Anatoly had to start all over in a country that he was not familiar with – in a country whose culture he did not understand, in a country that was very different then the one he had come from. Plus, he spoke very little English, if any.

In 1991, they landed in Phoenix, Arizona, where they began their new life. Soon Art Martori, who runs the Sunkist Kids Wrestling Club, heard about Anatoly. Art helped him by naming him a coach for the Sunkist Kids Wrestling Club. Then in 1994, Anatoly was hired by USA Wrestling as the head coach for the brand new Greco-Roman Wrestling Resident Program at the United States Olympic Training Center in Colorado Springs, Colorado. In 1996, Anatoly became a U.S. citizen.

Over the years I have written a lot about being tough. Talk about "tough"... Anatoly Petrosyan is as tough as they come. Just imagine how difficult it would be to overcome the things that he and his wife overcame. Imagine starting a whole new life from scratch, after you are almost 50 years old and have established yourself. This would be devastating, to say the least.

However, it is not surprising to me that this great man and coach could make this difficult transition. Anatoly Petrosyan is a wonderful man, with outstanding character and a caring heart. His friendly personality and superb coaching ability help make him stand out in a crowd.

As one of our Greco program's biggest assets, Anatoly has contributed a tremendous amount to our U.S. squad's success over the last 11 years. He was instrumental in developing and coaching Matt Ghaffari, one of our most decorated Greco-Roman wrestlers ever. Matt Ghaffari won four world and Olympic medals for the United States. This includes a silver medal in the 1996 Atlanta Olympic Games.

Matt Lindland was another one of Anatoly's students. Matt won two world and Olympic medals, including the silver medal in the 2000 Sydney Olympic Games.

Then there was Rulon Gardner; almost everyone knows his accomplishments.

Anatoly has a very unique coaching style. He is very consistent with his approach to coaching. He is very direct. He is quick to say what he thinks even if it is not the popular thing to say. He is very technical and understands the strategic nuances of the game.

He has come to learn what makes the American athlete tick. And this can be a very difficult thing for some foreign coaches to learn and understand. Our American culture is very different from a lot of other cultures, which can make this issue a challenging one.

I remember one practice when one of our resident athletes said to Anatoly that he could not practice on this particular day due to a breakout of mat funk (impetigo or herpes) on his face. In front of the whole team, Anatoly said something like, "Herpes… what is this herpes? This is nothing. This is normal stuff." Then Anatoly proceeded to rub his own face on the infected wrestler's face. "See, this is nothing! Let's start practice," Anatoly said.

Two days later when Anatoly came to practice with a full breakout of funk on his own face, he then admitted, "Okay, if you have the funk you can miss practice that day." To this day the team still has a good laugh about this incident.

There is another incident that stands out in my mind. It took place in a practice where we were scheduled to do a "grind match," which is a two-hour, non-stop wrestling match. Rulon Gardner was in a spunky mood, as he often was; when he challenged me to go the grind match with him. He said, "Fraser, You and I… let's go today." My quick response to Rulon was, "I'll go with you and I'll kick your butt, big guy!"

Rulon then replied, "I'll bet you $50 bucks that I can score 60 points on you in one hour." Now, this ticked me off a bit. He challenged me in front of the entire team and people were now egging me on saying, "Come on coach, you gonna take that?"

I may be a bit older but I still am competitive, and my competitive juices started to flow. I paused for a moment and then barked out; "Let's make it $200, chubby!"

Now, Rulon stopped to think for a moment. You have to know something about Rulon Gardner… when it comes to money, he is very cautious. He does not like to lose it. However, he loves to win it. Then he said, "You're on!"

Of course, I had NO intention on really going with him on this particular day. I was just giving him some smack talk. However, I looked over at him as he was warming up and I noticed that he was really serious. I could tell he was in his more determined competitive mind set as he kind of glared at me from a distance.

So I immediately walked over to Anatoly, who was in charge of the practice, and I said, "Toly… whatever you do today, DON'T let Rulon and I wrestle. When you see us about to start wrestling, stop us and tell Rulon that you want him to go with someone bigger. Do not, I repeat, do not allow for us to wrestle, please!"

Anatoly agreed not to allow us to wrestle. He did not hear the bet we had made, but that was irrelevant in my mind.

When it was time to start the grind match I was on the mat facing off with Rulon acting like I was anxious to start wrestling. Rulon, of course, was licking his chops. He was ready and anxious to put a huge whipping on me. Then, just as planned, Anatoly stepped in between us and said, "Rulon…I don't want you to go with Steve Fraser. I want you to go with someone bigger today."

Rulon then said, "No Toly, I want to go with Fraser today!" Toly again said "No!" Rulon said, "Coach Fraser wants to go with me, please let us go." Toly again said "No."

By this time I started to back away stating, "Hey, Anatoly is the boss here; maybe we will go some other time." As I continued to walk away Rulon was getting enraged. He started pleading with Anatoly, "Please, coach, please let us go today. I will give you $50!" Anatoly hesitated for a moment but then said, "No." Rulon said, "Come on coach, I will give you $100, please just let us wrestle!"

All of a sudden, Anatoly said, "Okay! $100. You can wrestle Steve Fraser."

I immediately went to Anatoly and whispered, "Toly, why? Why did you allow this? I thought I told you NOT to let us wrestle!" Anatoly whispered back to me, "Don't worry! I will split the $100 with you and give you $50."

Twenty-eight minutes and 60 points later, Rulon was $100 richer, Anatoly was putting $50 in his pocket and I was licking my wounds!

Anatoly Petrosyan has been a huge reason for the Greco-Roman wrestling success that we have experienced over the years and he still continues to produce champions for the United States of America. Thanks to his inner strength in overcoming his struggles in Azerbaijan, Azerbaijan's loss is the USA's gain.

Thanks Anatoly, thanks for all you have done – except for the aforementioned Rulon incident.

Momir Petkovic Leads by Example

Momir Petkovic is the Assistant Resident Coach and Assistant National Coach for the U.S. Greco-Roman Wrestling Team. He has been in this position for about four years. Momir is originally from the former Yugoslavia, where he won five world medals for his homeland. These honors include an Olympic gold medal from the 1976 Montreal Olympic Games.

I first heard that Momir P was living in the United States back in 1998 when Dan Chandler, three-time Olympic team member and current coach of the Minnesota Storm, mentioned it to me. Dan told me that Momir was living and working in the New Jersey area. I had been the National Greco-Roman coach for a couple of years and was not aware of this.

I contacted Momir soon after finding this out and before long Momir was volunteering as one of our Greco coaches. He had been in the USA for around 13 years and had never been involved with the U.S. National Greco team or program. I was shocked. How did we allow this great champion, who had won five world-class medals, to live in the United States and not be involved in our program in some way?

In 2001, a position became available and USA Wrestling hired Momir to his current spot. He has been a great addition to our Greco-Roman staff. His knowledge of the sport, along with his superb coaching tactics and abilities, has made a huge impact on our U.S. squad.

Momir Petkovic brings many great things to our U.S. program. One thing that stands out is his competitive nature. He is a great example of what it takes to compete at the top world level. At 51 years old, Momir still bleeds competitive spirit and drive. It shows not only in his coaching intensity, but also in the way he still caries himself.

I remember two years ago Momir and I made a gentleman's bet to make our old fighting weights. Yes, we were going to weigh-in at our former competition weight classes. It was right after Christmas. Why were we doing this? Just for the heck of it, mostly. Momir and I had made numerous challenges to each other over the years. We were always trying to push each other in this way. Plus we wanted to correct some of the holiday cheer that we had just experienced.

So, for the Dave Schultz Cup, which was scheduled to take place in early February, we were going to have to weigh in, him at 82kg. and me at 90kg. This meant that we were both going to have to lose about 15 to 20 pounds. Needless to say, this was not an easy task for either of us.

Two weeks before the Dave Schultz Cup weigh-in, Momir hurt his back pretty seriously. He was in terrible pain and was not able to work out at all. In fact, he was on crutches and was having a lot of trouble even walking.

One week before the weigh-in, I was at the Concord Cup in Concord, California.

The Concord Cup was an annual international wrestling tournament which brought in many foreign teams from around the world. I was within five or six pounds of making weight on this day when in between wrestling sessions I walked outside of the arena to see the tournament hosts cooking steaks and brats on a huge open grill. They were throwing a barbeque for all of the competitors.

The smell in the air was ravishing. The aroma was so enticing to my senses that I could hardly stand it. I thought, hmm… this food is unbelievable. My mouth was watering and my mind was focused on the wonderful odor. And boy, was I hungry!

Then it hit me: "Momir is really hurting and I have not been a very good friend to him. I should have let him off the hook regarding our bet because how can I expect him to make his old fighting weight when he is on crutches. Shame on me! He is really hurting."

I immediately called him on his cell phone, catching him back in Colorado Springs, lying in bed still in great agony. I said "Momir, hey… I have not been very thoughtful. Listen, since you are laid up and really in a bad way, let's just postpone our weigh-in. No need for you to try and make your scratch weight when you are like this."

Momir immediately barked back at me and said, "No way! I will make it! Don't you worry about me. You just make sure that YOU make it!"

"Dang!" I hung up the phone, walked right past the grill, where everyone was eating, and continued to cut my weight. "Hmmm…Momir!" I thought to myself, "That is why he became Olympic champion."

I think this is a good example of a competitive man – someone who when he says he is going to do something, he does it! No excuses and no complaining!

This is the attitude we try and establish in our practice room at the U.S. Olympic Training Center, in Colorado Springs. We try and establish a "no excuses… no complaining" attitude among our national team members. We feel that having this type of attitude is what it takes to be the best in the world.

Take "excuses," for example; excuses are worthless. They do not help us get closer to our goals; they only allow us to have a reason for not attaining our goals. We all can usually find many excuses for why we did not accomplish something if we look hard enough, but why?

"Complaining" is another thing we try to discourage at the USOTC. Complaining usually gets us nowhere. Complaining can become a bad habit. Once we start complaining about things, we may start complaining about everything. Pretty soon we stop taking our careers into our own hands and we start blaming everyone else for our struggles.

In my experience, I have noticed that the world's best wrestlers, when they are on their way to the top, usually have this "no excuses, no complaining" type attitude. They are so focused on doing all the right things that they don't waste their time thinking about excuses or thinking about things to complain about. They have laser vision and it is like nothing can stand in their way.

However, some of these great champions, once they reach the top, start to forget this. They start to expect breaks from officials. They start to get a little complacent. They start to forget that it was this "no excuses, no complaining" mentality that got them to the top. Staying at the top is as tough as getting to the top. And one must realize that they must continue to practice the same tough-thinking principles that got them to the top in the first place.

Momir Petkovic has helped to establish a tough wrestler's attitude in our practice room, an attitude that will help our athletes overcome tough situations, both on and off the mat. He has led our team by example and continues to push all of us (including me) in ways that help us grow and move forward. He is a true wrestling hero and an inspiration to all who know him.

Oh, and by the way - we both made weight at the Dave Schultz Cup that following week!

About the Author

Steve Fraser joined USA Wrestling, the sport's national governing body, as the National Greco-Roman Coach in October of 1995. He serves as a full-time professional coach, working with the national Greco-Roman wrestling program and helping develop Greco-Roman coaches and programs in the United States. He has coached at three Olympics and at elite-level events all around the world. In 2000, he guided the Greco-Roman team to its best Olympic performance ever, including Rulon Gardner's colossal upset of Russian superstar Alexander Karelin.

He also works closely with the U.S. Olympic Committee Greco-Roman resident athlete program in Colorado Springs. Fraser has created a number of new programs to assist in the development of age-group wrestlers and coaches in Greco-Roman.

In 1984 in Los Angeles, Fraser became the first U.S. wrestler to ever win an Olympic gold medal in Greco-Roman wrestling. He won five matches on his way to the title at 198 pounds. He also won a gold medal at the 1983 Pan-American Games. A member of the 1979 and 1982 U.S. World Teams, Fraser captured national titles in Greco-Roman in 1981 and 1983, and was national freestyle champion in 1984.

Fraser was inducted into the National Wrestling Hall of Fame in 1994. He was named USA Wrestling Athlete of the Year in 1984, and was a finalist for the James E. Sullivan Award that year. He has been inducted into the Michigan Wrestling Hall of Fame and the Michigan Amateur Sports Hall of Fame.

A two-time NCAA All-American at the University of Michigan, Fraser received a bachelor's degree in physical education in 1980. He was a Michigan state high school champion for Hazel Park High School.

After retiring from competition, Fraser was an assistant coach at the University of Michigan from 1980-87, and at Eastern Michigan University from 1987-1993. He also coached with the Michigan Wrestling Club for 10 years, working with their elite wrestlers in both freestyle and Greco-Roman.

Fraser came to USA Wrestling after serving with Domino's Pizza for 10 years. His final position with the company was the Senior Operations Director for the Flagship Academy for Domino's Pizza, Inc., where he directed 65 stores, including Domino's most elite corporate stores.

A well-known public speaker and clinician, Fraser lives in Colorado Springs and has three children – Kellen, Kerrin and Hannah.

US Camps Presents...

Steve Fraser's
Michigan Wrestling Camps
Adrian, MI

"BAD BOYS" INTENSIVE
"TEAM COMPETITION"
"CHAMPION TECHNIQUE"
"KIDZ" CAMP

FREE Wrestling Articles, Tips & Communication!
Sign up by sending an email to steve@stevefraser.com requesting to receive the latest in wrestling news and communication.

**For additional camps, information, & dates
visit www.stevefraser.com or
www.uscamps.net
or contact us by phone at 719-531-6540.**